Power of Sisterhood

Women Religious Tell the Story of the Apostolic Visitation

Edited by
Margaret Cain McCarthy and
Mary Ann Zollmann

University Press of America,® Inc.
Lanham • Boulder • New York • Toronto • Plymouth, UK

Copyright © 2014 by University Press of America,® Inc.
4501 Forbes Boulevard, Suite 200, Lanham, Maryland 20706
UPA Aquisitions Department (301) 459-3366

10 Thornbury Road, Plymouth PL6 7PP, United Kingdom

Library of Congress Control Number: 2014943024
ISBN: 978-0-7618-6430-1 (paperback : alk. paper)—ISBN: 978-0-7618-6431-8 (electronic)

Cover illustration: Watercolor painting: *Visitation*
Barbara Cerny, BVM
Copyright 2014, Sisters of Charity, BVM

This book is dedicated to the women religious
who were serving in congregational leadership
during the Apostolic Visitation.
Your witness to integrity,
your unwavering courage,
your commitment to collaboration,
and your spirit of contemplation
not only formed your response to the Apostolic Visitation
but also shaped the unfolding of religious life into the future.
Holding a moment in time gracefully,
you changed us forever.
Thank you.

Contents

Prologue

Framing the Apostolic Visitation as a Story

Mary Ann Zollmann

On December 22, 2008, the Vatican Congregation for Institutes of Consecrated Life and Societies of Apostolic Life announced a process, canonically
known as an Apostolic Visitation, to look into the quality of life of women in
U.S. apostolic communities of Catholic sisters. During the past five years the
event, with its multi-layered implications for U.S. religious life, religious life
around the world, and for the Catholic Church in the U.S. and internationally,
has captured the attention of the media. It is an understatement to say that
there is a veritable plethora of written and oral information about the event.

Even as the complex dynamics of the Apostolic Visitation were being
reported in the public venue, women religious were aware of the desire to
capture its meanings from the inside out, from the heart of our own life
experience. Bonded together by that common desire, some women religious
serving as leaders in their communities came together in 2010 and formed a
group known simply as the Grassroots Group. This self-initiated group included Marcia Allen, CSJ; Pat Bergen, CSJ; Rosemary Brennan, CSJ; Susan
Hames, CSJ; Lynn Jarrell, OSU; Nancy Reynolds, SP; Jean Wincek, CSJ;
and Mary Ann Zollmann, BVM. In order to capture the experience of the
Visitation from as many perspectives as possible, the group decided to develop a survey designed to gather information from the leadership of U.S. wom-
en's institutes about their experience. Because the validity of the data to be
gathered was of utmost importance to the Grassroots Group, the group engaged the services of Margaret Cain McCarthy, PhD to assist in the design of
the Apostolic Visitation Survey and the interpretation of its data. The Grassroots Group invited member institutes of the Leadership Conference of
Women Religious (LCWR) and the Council of Major Superiors of Women

Religious (CMSWR), through their respective leadership, to participate in the survey. Citing the fact that the Apostolic Visitation had not yet come to a conclusion, the leadership of CMSWR chose not to participate. In the spring of 2011 the survey was sent to 328 major superiors who are members of LCWR. One hundred forty-three accepted the invitation and responded to the survey.[1]

Reading, analyzing, and reflecting on the results, the Grassroots Group responsible for the creation of the survey became convinced that the content needed to be shaped and preserved in a more accessible narrative form; hence this book. Flowing from the process described above, the pronoun "we" as used throughout the text represents each chapter author's engagement with the women religious whose insights are documented in the survey. From the beginning we want to state clearly that this book does not include the voices of women religious who are members of CMSWR. Honest about that limitation, we humbly present the experiences recorded here as a significant part of one moment in the ongoing life of many religious communities in the church.

As we introduce this book, *Power of Sisterhood: Women Religious Tell the Story of the Apostolic Visitation,* we acknowledge with gratitude the contributions of the media through articles in journals and newspapers as well as reporting via television, public radio, and electronic communications. We honor the essays and books written by women religious and lay persons highlighting the event and its implications as it has unfolded. These contributions have been invaluable in raising public awareness and in calling us as women religious to ongoing reflection on the wider meaning of what was, and still is, occurring in us. The perspectives offered in these arenas, both religious and secular, deepen our consciousness that something much larger than a confined focus on religious life is happening in us and through us.

Having affirmed the value of all that has been and continues to be communicated, we believe that this book holds a unique and irreplaceable position in the ongoing corpus of information about the Apostolic Visitation. The following chapters render an account of the event as experienced by women religious. The narrative emerges, not from secondary reporting, but from its primal place: the embodied flesh and blood of those of us who have actually undergone the event; who have held its requirements day in and day out in an asceticism of wisdom, grace, and fidelity; and who still stand in it and before it open to its ongoing revelatory power.

The text is written in language formed by our participation in the long tradition of religious life. Its referents are rooted in scripture and in the experiences of the founders of our congregations. There are specifics particular to church structure, processes, and canons. There are multi-layered and multi-faceted descriptions of the dynamics of community, mission, and ministry that define the essence of our lives. And there are places where, true to our lives themselves, the words ooze out suggesting the surplus of mystery and grace at the very heart and soul of who are. This is the language that shapes the unique lifeform that is religious life and, immersed in the realities these words carry, we women religious speak them with ease and familiarity. It is our hope that the distinctiveness of the language we use to tell our story will not obscure but rather make transparent, disclose, and release the truth of who we are.

Moreover, we recount the experience in the only way that it can be carried in all its originality and freshness: the medium of story. Compelled to tell about an event that, at the very least has made a difference in our lives and, at most, has been utterly transformative, we find ourselves relying on the only genre adequate to its utterance: "Let us tell a story."

Stories take us beyond the constriction of mental logic, beyond the surface texture of a few dominant feelings into the rich, multi-layered complex place of the spirit. Only the story with its easy unselfconscious flow, porous edges, and openings between word and line is sufficiently spacious to contain what is say-able and simultaneously to suggest the unsaid still seeking necessary articulation. Even as a story carries the contour, texture, and detail of an event, one senses that there is ever so much more in, around, and beyond the spoken or written word. There is always the sense of remainder, excess, overflow. In a story each period serves not as an ending but signals a new thought, another feeling struggling for liberation. Though often composed as having a beginning, middle, and end, stories arise out of the fullness of life already lived and toss us beyond its last articulated word into a future where the story continues. Narrative creates a hospitable place of welcome for the precious stuff of our humanity: inconsistencies, diversity, perspectives in tension, revelations discovered in its telling, and stirrings on the horizon of mystery beyond verbalization. Story is the official language of the soul.

Laying bare the soul in giving voice to a story is accordingly an act of immense risk and immeasurable courage. Revealing ourselves to ourselves and to the reader, we are unshielded from the vulnerability such revelation entails. As the spoken word moves in us, we see more clearly who we are, claim who we are with enhanced conviction and commitment, and listen more keenly to who we are called to be. As the story does its revelatory work we open ourselves to being changed by what we see afresh. The story holds us to a fierce honesty in its telling and its living. In the end, we can do nothing less than be faithful to what it speaks and go, no matter what the cost, where the en-courage-ment of the story directs.

Aware that we never get it whole and complete, we tell the same story in different ways turning it to the light of speech in a ceaseless attempt to garner the fullness of its meaning. The word runs after, without ever truly seizing the mystery it is describing. Indeed, there is something of the infinite, the breath of God's word, in every story. Sometimes our clear awareness of being gripped by the sacred at work in the ordinariness of our experience reduces us to silence, a silence out of which authentic words previously beyond our reach find their form.

The irresistible imperative to proclaim our story is the divine in us crying out to be heard. In the process of giving language to our experience we come face to face with a sacred Mystery active in our life. Doing what prophets do, making the workings of God visible to ourselves and others, our speech is a genuinely prophetic act. Bearing witness, with transparency and integrity, to a slice of life as we have known it and felt it, we release its meaning and influence into our world, church, and universe. The truest action we can take is that of telling our story.

Yet, the power of the story transcends the words of the teller; the one who speaks forth a story does so counting on its active reception by a listener. Story-telling sets up a relationship of mutuality; it assumes, creates, and re-creates community. We make our personal stories public relying on the conviction that, though each story is unique, it is also communal, emerging as it does from that deeply human place where we are all bound to one another in real and yet inexplicable communion.

In this narrative that we, the tellers, and you, the readers, now take up together, we women religious open up a place of deep ache and immeasurable grace. The Apostolic Visitation broke open the very heart of who we are, placing under question and scrutiny life-long whole-hearted commitment to God and to God's people. This is the story of our response to a critical moment in the much longer and larger story of religious life. We write the story to chronicle its unfolding and to trace its more elusive movements of grace. We write the story so those of us who experienced it will remember the women we have become in this process and derive from our remembering the strength to live forward with uncompromised integrity. We write the story for those laity who have asked and will ask: What was the experience like for you? We write the story for those women religious who will come after us, who will wonder about an event in time that changed us forever and, who, for their understanding and interpretation, will seek a credible story-teller.

And, beyond a particular event at a particular time in the life of U.S. women religious, we write this story for all of you who know the ache of having your own heart placed in question and who yearn to trace and track consequent moments of surprising grace. So, we trust that you, the reader, will identify with some aspects of our story, thereby deriving strength for greeting similar events in your own lives. Even more, we harbor the hope that the release of our story will evoke you, the readers, to bring your stories to speech, letting them circulate liberally in all their richness and diversity; that each of us individually and all of us together will be transformed by the power of honest sharing stretching beyond any illusion at easy accord; and that the solidarity generated will lead us together to a place of goodness and beauty we can only imagine at the outset of our telling.

It is within this rich context of the power of story that we Catholic sisters offer the content of this book. We enter into this story with gratitude for all who have in any way contributed to shaping it, with certitude that the story needs to be told, with freedom to let this story land where it will, with willingness to open ourselves to live in deeper fidelity through its telling, and with trust that Holy Mystery will, through our humble and honest words, do God's necessary work in us and among us for the good of all.

In the text that follows each author brings one facet of the Apostolic Visitation to the light of speech such that a chapter becomes a story itself, a shorter story within the overarching narrative that is our experience of the Visitation. For that reason, the writers rely on similar common data to ground their narrative, letting that data come to life in new and fresh ways as guided by the focus of their particular chapter.

In a spirit of anticipation and expectation, we now enter the narrative *Power of Sisterhood: Women Religious Tell the Story of the Apostolic Visitation.*

NOTE

1. Margaret Cain McCarthy, "Apostolic Visitation Survey Analysis: The Apostolic Visitation as Experienced by Women Religious in the United States" (report, October 15, 2011).

Chapter One

What Is an Apostolic Visitation?

Mary Ann Zollmann

ACKNOWLEDGING A COMMUNITY OF AUTHORS

As we begin our story of the Apostolic Visitation of women religious in the United States, we want to provide the reader with a context for the narrative that unfolds in the following chapters. To describe an apostolic visitation as accurately as possible in its specificity and particularity, we need to locate it within the larger context of visitations in general. Accordingly, in this chapter, we will highlight the origins of visitations in the early church, trace the historical development of diocesan visitations and visitations of religious by identifying significant turning points, illuminate the unique nature of an apostolic visitation, and conclude with a reflection on the experience of an apostolic visitation as informed by Vatican II consciousness.

Responding to the question, "What is an apostolic visitation?" is to tell a story in itself, the story of how the canonical processes of the church are intertwined with theology and ecclesiology, history, culture, and socio-political systems. Engaging in such an exploration requires the competency of canonists who have researched the evolution of church law through the centuries and who understand from experience the value and challenge of its interpretation and application. Accordingly, from the outset, the author acknowledges with appreciation her significant reliance on the work of John P. Beal, the Legal Resource Center for Religious Institutes (RCRI), Dan Ward, OSB, and the canonists who contributed to the *Code of Canon Law, A Text and Commentary*, most notably John A. Alesandro, Thomas J. Green, Sharon Holland, IHM, and Jordan F. Hite, TOR. These voices permeate the text as, weaving their insights with her theological and spiritual perspective and her experience of religious life, the author creates an integrated context for the Apostolic Visitation of women religious in the U.S.[1]

1

ORIGINS OF THE INSTITUTE OF VISITATION
IN THE EARLY CHURCH

Visitations have had a long history in the church existing in some form since the time of the early Christians. Reading the Acts of the Apostles and the letters of Paul, we witness the leadership of the original community, either in person or through their representatives, constantly on the move visiting the various "churches" in Corinth and Ephesus, Thessalonica and Colossae, Philippi and Galatia.

Paul's letters commissioning Timothy to visit the people of Ephesus and Titus to visit the people of Crete communicate tone and content for these visits. To Timothy, Paul writes:

> I urge you to remain in Ephesus so that you may instruct in love that comes from a pure heart, a good conscience, and sincere faith . . . so that the people may know how one ought to behave in the household of God. . . . Set the believers an example in speech and conduct, in love, in faith. . . . Proclaim the message; convince, rebuke, and encourage, with the utmost patience in teaching. . . . Do the work of an evangelist; carry out your ministry fully (1 Tim. 1:5, 3:14, 4:12; 2 Tim. 2: 4:2, 5). [2]

And to Titus,

> Teach what is consistent with sound doctrine. . . . Exhort and reprove with all authority. . . . Show yourself in all respects a model of good works, and in your teaching show integrity, gravity, and sound speech that cannot be censured. . . . Remind the people to speak evil of no one, to be gentle, to show every courtesy to everyone . . . to devote themselves to good works in order to meet urgent needs (Titus 2:1, 7-8, 15; 3:14).

As visitors among the people, Timothy and Titus are to preach the gospel, teach sound doctrine, correct errors, be zealous for good works and, in so doing, build up the community. They are to engage the visit in a spirit of genuine "administration," ministering to the people with firmness and credibility derived from their own integrity in the faith.

Although there is primacy of authority vested in Peter and Paul and those commissioned by them to visit the people, there is a flow of mutual influence between those in the local churches and the recognized center of the church in Jerusalem. A significant example of this mutuality of influence is what happens when Peter sends Paul and Barnabas to the people of Antioch as narrated in the Acts of the Apostles, Chapter 15. Their visit occurs in the midst of tension between Jews and Gentiles regarding requirements for admission of Gentiles to the community that had formed around Moses and the new community forming around Jesus. While in Antioch, Paul and Barnabas experience firsthand the faith of the Gentiles as well as the rigorous objections of some in the Jewish community insisting upon circumcision as essential to membership. In the midst of debate and dissension, "Paul and Barnabas and some of the others were appointed to go up to Jerusalem to discuss this question with the apostles and the elders. So they were sent on their way by the church" (15:2). Accordingly, Paul and Barnabas, now commissioned by the local church in Antioch, return to Jerusalem to give testimony about what they had learned in their visit to Antioch; "they reported the conversion of the Gentiles . . . and all that God had done with them" (15: 3, 4).

In response to the report of Paul and Barnabas, the apostles and elders meet in council to consider the matter. After much debate, Peter addresses the assembly:

> God, who knows the human heart, testified to the Gentiles by giving them the Holy Spirit, just as God did to us; and in cleansing their hearts by faith God has made no distinction between them and us. Now therefore why are you putting God to the test by placing on the neck of the disciples a yoke that neither our ancestors nor we have been able to bear? On the contrary, we believe that we will be saved through the grace of the Lord Jesus, just as they will (15:10-11).

Following the testimony of Peter, Paul and Barnabas speak to the assembly of all "the signs and wonders that God had done through them among the Gentiles" (15:19).

> Then the apostles and elders, with the consent of the whole church, decided to choose men from among their members and to send them to Antioch with Paul and Barnabas with the following letter: "The brothers, both the apostles and elders, to the believers of Gentile origin in Antioch and Syria and Celicia, greetings. Since we have heard that certain persons, who have gone out from us, though with no instructions from us, have said things to disturb you and have unsettled your minds, we have decided unanimously to choose representatives and send them to you, along with our beloved Barnabas and Paul. . . . It has seemed good to the Holy Spirit and to us to impose on you no further burden than the essentials" (15:22-28).

With that Paul and Barnabas and the selected representatives return to Antioch where they gather the congregation together and deliver the letter. "When its members heard it, they rejoiced at the exhortation" (15:30-31). After some time, the representatives are sent back in peace to Jerusalem. Paul and Barnabas remain for a while and then after some days Paul says to Barnabas, "Come, let us return and visit the believers in every city where we proclaimed the word of the Lord and see how they are doing" (15:33-36).

Reflecting on the content of the epistles and the narrative from Acts 15, we can cull out the dynamics of these early visits. Their primary purpose was to create and sustain a relational bond of love and faith between the center of the emerging church in Jerusalem, its locus of primary authority in the persons of Peter and Paul, and the people in the local churches. These visitations, firm and pastoral, exhortational and relational, were at the service of building up the community of faith and clarifying the meaning of fidelity to Jesus' way of life. It is clear from the narrative in the Acts of the Apostles that what it meant to adhere to the faith of Jesus was constantly being refined as the community extended beyond the Jews to include the Gentiles. Visitations and the dialogical relationships that characterized them were essential to the ongoing organic processes of shaping the identity of the emerging community. The church in Jerusalem sent visitors to the local communities; the visitors returned with reports from the local church that challenged some of the understandings at the official center. Those at the center called a council to discern through further, more widely based consultation, the direction of the Holy Spirit. Attentive to their own wisdom, while taking seriously the experience of the people of Antioch, those in Jerusalem arrived at a decision that made it possible to hold on to the essentials of the faith while embracing a new teaching and extending the boundaries of inclusivity.

The expansion of the church, as early as the time of Paul, necessitates more formal vehicles for maintaining the connection between the people in the faith communities and the center of the church in Jerusalem and eventually in Rome. Bishops are appointed by the head of the church as permanent residents among the people to oversee the life of the local church. Invested with the authority of the head of the growing church, these bishops became the representatives of the official church in the local faith community. We hear of such Pauline appointments in Paul's letter to Titus:

> I left you behind in Crete so that you should put in order what remained to be done, and should appoint elders in every town, as I directed you: someone who is blameless. . . . For a bishop, as God's steward, must be blameless; he must not be arrogant or quick-tempered or violent or greedy for gain; but he must be hospitable, a lover of goodness, prudent, upright, devout. He must have a firm grasp of the word that is trustworthy in accordance with the teaching, so that he may be able to preach with sound doctrine (1:5-9).

In the embryonic church structure, bishops are God's stewards who manage the affairs of the particular local church under their jurisdiction as would a servant in a large household. They are appointed for the ministry of assuring fidelity among the faithful through personal example, preaching, pastoral exhortation, and correction. Close to the beginnings of the church, these bishops carried a fresh mindfulness of the spirit of Paul and the experiences recorded in the Acts of the Apostles. Pastoral orientation, insistence on fidelity to the way of Jesus, dialogical communication between ecclesial centers and the people through regular visits and councils became the model for these diocesan bishops in their canonical visitations to the churches.

THE DEVELOPMENT OF THE INSTITUTION OF VISITATION
FROM THE EARLY CHURCH TO VATICAN II

With the passage of time and geographical and spiritual distance from the founding community the original forms of visitation shifted in and out of prominence and practice even as new forms emerged. Due to ongoing church expansion, resulting complexity in its organization, the influence of civil and societal structures of governance, and perceived needs to assure unity in the understanding and practice of faith, the institution of visitation kept undergoing adaptations, assimilations, and mutations. Through all its metamorphoses the institute of visitation has remained a part of ecclesial life in dioceses and in religious institutes. Although there are differences in how visitations in dioceses and religious institutes have unfolded, they share significant points of intersection. Accordingly, it is beneficial to trace the historical evolution of both simultaneously letting their processes be mutually illuminative. [3]

During the first 500 years of church history, known as the patristic period, visitations of the local churches and the newly forming monasteries were identified as the bishop's responsibility. In the early years of that period local churches were structured somewhat loosely around charismatic and authoritative bishops proximate to the people. When the Edict of Constantine (321) freed the church to evolve openly, the diocesan church and the orders of monks and mendicants expanded rapidly in numbers and geographical extent. Episcopal visits became sporadic and their procedures irregular. Recognizing the need for widely applicable norms to foster church unity in a time of exponential growth and diversity in membership, the Council of Nicaea (325) addressed issues of identity, coordination, and regulation. As one of the efforts to assure greater cohesion, diocesan visitation by the bishop was revived; included among its purposes were inquiry into the ministry of clerics, the instruction of catechumens, and exhortation of the faithful. In the domain of religious life, abbots, aware of the importance of regular discipline, reform, and renewal to the ongoing viability of monastic life, visited their communities to promote communion and to assure observance of the monastic rule of life. By the 4th century this practice of visitation had become part of the monastic structure itself.

In the Carolingian period that followed (750–887) the literal fusion of church and state and the consequent intertwining of ecclesial reform and political reform placed the revitalization of spiritual life at the service of socio-political life. Spiritual fidelity and civil responsibility were inextricably linked such that laxity in either area was deemed to weaken the strength of both church and state. In this environment, where the power of the body politic was dependent upon the moral character of the Christian faithful, ecclesial processes took on a rigorous judicial character mirroring the courts of judgment in civil society. Diocesan visitations assumed the prevailing political format of assemblies around the prince. Visitation by the bishop became a parochial synodal event that was investigative, judicial, and penal. All the faithful and clergy gathered, witnesses were called forth to testify under oath to the moral, civil, and ecclesial fidelity of the community and, where breaches were identified, the bishop had the power to inflict sanctions.

In response to this Carolingian Reform, characterized by ecclesial identification with the political empire and consequent entanglement of the secular and ecclesial, the next period was marked by the move to separate the church from secular control. Beginning with the papacy of Gregory VII and extending through Pope Innocent III and the Fourth Lateran Council (1213), the church acted to extricate itself from secular control through reinforcement of is unique rules and independent norms. Identified broadly as the Gregorian Reform this period was primarily directed toward strengthening the sovereignty of the church and accordingly the authority of the papacy. This effort to establish clear lines of authority vested in Rome affected not just the political reality of the times but, even more significantly, internal ecclesial structures including the institute of visitations in dioceses and religious communities. The effects of this time in church history endure today.

To promote significant universal church reform the entire ecclesial governance system was institutionalized in a hierarchical structure with the pope as its head. This centralization of reform in the power and authority of the papacy brought into prominence the particular form of canonical visitation known as an apostolic visitation.

> What distinguished an apostolic visitation from the more familiar form of canonical visitations was not the manner of proceeding but the authority in virtue of which the visitation was carried out. The apostolic visitation was an exercise of the primatial authority of the pope himself; other visitations were exercises of inferior levels of jurisdiction. [4]

One of the means used by Gregory VII to promulgate reform was the annual Roman synod. The synod became the forum for drafting reform decrees, binding not just for the Roman church but for the universal church, correcting abuses, and judging the non-compliant. Because some bishops resisted those reforms, it became necessary to assure their implementation by empowering legates or delegates to visit the churches in the name of the pope, to assess their alignment with the decrees, and then report back to the pope; hence, the emergence of the apostolic visitation. Although earlier popes had used the service of legates, Gregory VII institutionalized this service by making these papal representatives central to papal governance.

> From the time of Gregory VII on, legates of various kinds were central figures in papal efforts to project their authority over the universal church. Apostolic

visitations by legates were important ways by which the popes gained information about the condition of the church outside of Rome, insured that their decrees were implemented in local churches and exercised their authority for the good of the church.[5]

While in the diocese, the authority of the legate, as an extension of papal authority, superseded that of the local bishop. Modeled on the Roman synod, legates often convoked local synods to present and enact the decrees of reform, to judge violations, and to decide non-major judicial cases.

This process undermined the authority of the local prelate and over time that of the synod itself. As the power of papal delegates and the synods over which they presided became more established, the authority of the local prelate diminished. Additionally, the subsequent move from an accusatorial to an inquisitorial form of visitation in the latter part of the 12th century further divorced authority from the synod. In the accusatorial model the synod informed and then directed the action of the bishop. In contrast, the inquisitorial model separated the visitation from synodal processes and empowered the superior independently to pursue suspicions or rumors of wrongdoing even in the absence of formal accusations. Mere public complaint about some offense was sufficient basis for the initiation of an inquisition and the dispatch of a legate who could determine the manner of proceeding, evaluate the validity of the accusation, and issue decrees. The inquisitorial character of the visitation allowed the emergence of a variety of special visitations to complement the traditional, periodic general visitation.[6]

An additional critical ramification of this shift was the loss of judicial rights of the accused that had been protected through the public processes of the synod. With the introduction of an inquisitorial visitation, an ecclesiastical superior could undertake an investigation of an individual or a community based solely on the perception that the common good of the faith community was in jeopardy. These inquisitions were often conducted in secret and deprived those accused of the right to know the identity of their accusers, to hear the rationale for the charge, and to refute the accusations in the presence of their accusers. Moreover, the mere fact that the pope had found it necessary to send a legate to investigate could be construed as confirmation of some wrongdoing. Simply said, the apostolic visitation became the way to assure the primacy of papal authority and enforce cohesion throughout the universal church in the implementation of reform.

The movement toward strengthening the unification of the church through the papacy also affected processes for the canonical visitation of religious communities. In the 11th century religious communities became exempt from the canonical visitation of the bishop and were placed more directly under the auspices of Rome. Accordingly, the Fourth Lateran Council (1213) decreed that the canonical visitation and ongoing reform of religious communities occur through their provincial chapters, a process not unlike that of the synod in the larger church. An often cited example illustrative of this process is that implemented by the Benedictine Order of Cluny.[7] At each general chapter two visitors were selected to visit all of the houses in the province during the coming year. They inquired about fidelity to the monastic rule of life and had the power to introduce corrections when called for. Upon completion of the visit they made a report to a committee of the general chapter. This committee determined the necessary actions in response to the report and issued decrees based on the findings. These were then read aloud at the next general chapter, which included the priors of the respective communities, who swore by oath to implement them in their houses. Additionally, as was true in the diocesan model, so it was for religious communities now directly under the auspices of the papacy: the papacy had the authority to initiate a special canonical inquisitorial investigation of a religious community at any time for the sake of the common good whether in the presence or absence of formal accusations.

Due to the investiture in the legate of the authority of the papacy, an authority that superseded that of the bishop, regular canonical visits of bishops in their dioceses lapsed during the Middle Ages. As a consequence, the faithful were rarely convened to engage in matters of faith, to lend their experience to the growth and sustenance of the faith, and to actively participate in the assessment of the community's fidelity to the faith. This disengagement of the people from the official church resulted in a loss of vitality in the local ecclesial communities.

Recognizing the effects of the lack of connection with the faithful and the necessity of reform throughout the whole church, the Council of Trent (1545–1563) restored the bishop's annual visitation as a way for reform to permeate the entire community of the faithful. The council underscored the importance of the visit as the primary means for the bishop to be personally aware of the spiritual health of the faithful under his jurisdiction and to assure the local church's fidelity to the faith. As stated in the council documents, the purpose of the visit was

> to secure sound and orthodox doctrine by the eradication of heresies, to maintain good morals and to correct by admonitions and exhortation such as were evil, to animate the people to religion, peace and innocence, and to initiate whatever else might be prompted by the prudence of the visitor for the benefit of the faithful as time, place and opportunity would allow.[8]

The Council of Trent limited the power of the legates by decreeing that they could no longer come into a diocese and conduct an inquisition apart from the jurisdiction of the local bishop.

This diminishment of the power of legates occurred through two simultaneous processes: the restoration of the appropriate jurisdiction of local bishops and additional enhancement of the authority of Rome with the formation of the Roman Curia. Whereas legates had previously been directly connected to the pope, their visits initiated by the pope and personally reviewed by him, the insertion of the dicasteries or congregations of the Roman Curia added an intermediate layer of authority between the papacy and delegates. The appropriate dicastery initiated an apostolic visitation, appointed visitors, instructed them in the purpose for their visitation, and received their findings and recommendations. Ordinarily the report of the visitor was secret and it was the responsibility of the particular dicastery to decide how to act on the report. At the time of the origination of the Roman Curia the office responsible for visitations of dioceses and bishops as well as religious communities was the Congregation on Consultations of Bishops and Regulars.

An additional post-Tridentine initiative reconnecting the people with their bishop and the bishop directly with Rome occurred in 1585 when Pope Sixtus V issued the constitution *Romanus Pontifex* formalizing a vehicle of relationship between the bishop and his local church and the Holy See. A new bishop took an oath to visit Rome at established intervals for a personal meeting with the pope and a presentation on the spiritual vitality of his diocese to the congregation of the curia to which the bishop was accountable. This *ad limina* visit was an opportunity for the responsible congregation or dicastery in the Roman Curia to inquire about the diocese and to address any perceived problems. The report presented was called the quinquennial report and, over time, the Roman congregations themselves provided formularies for these reports. In essence the *ad limina* visit and the quinquennial report became the equivalent of the ordinary visitation of dioceses.

As was true for diocesan visitations, so for religious houses, the practice of canonical visitation lapsed during the height of the Middle Ages. Accordingly, just as the Council of Trent emphasized the need for diocesan reform and correspondingly the revival of diocesan canonical visitation, similarly concern for religious discipline resulted in a council decree binding abbots and other major superiors to visit their monasteries frequently for the purpose of their ongoing reformation. Moreover, just as the Roman congregations provided formularies for the reports of the bishops, likewise major monasteries of orders were to be visited according to constitutions prepared by the Apostolic See for each order. In the course of the visitations, the visitor questioned the superior and others in leadership as well as members of the community and was available to meet with any members who wished. Ordinarily the result took the form of directives for internal implementation.

Having traced the twists and turns of canonical visitations up to post-Trent, it is not surprising that between the Council of Trent and the promulgation of the first Code of Canon Law (1917), canonists attempted some clarification and systematization of the historical visitation corpus. Visitations were classified as general or special. General visitations are ordinary visitations built into the structures of diocesan life or life in a religious community. They are undertaken by the local bishop or the religious superior as the formal periodic way to assess the fidelity of the local church to the Christian faith or the fidelity of the religious community to its life and mission. A special visitation is distinguished by the fact that it is initiated by the ecclesiastical superior outside of the regular visitation processes as an extraordinary response to an accusation. Visitations may be paternal or judicial in approach. A paternal visitation is an investigation conducted for the purpose of paternal, non-penal correction. It occurs outside the realm of formal judicial processes which, on their part, are public, directed toward judging the truth of a situation or an accused individual, and inflicting punishment if necessary. An additional distinction arising in the process of this classification is that of an administrative non-penal visitation conducted for the purpose of promoting the common good.[9]

The formal classification of a type of visitation defined as non-penal administrative is a significant development. It validates visitations evoked solely by the rationale that they are being conducted for the common good; furthermore, such visitations are divorced from any kind of judicial procedures and safeguards. In these administrative visitations there are no public juridical norms to insure fair treatment of the accused and to promote accurate fact-finding. As observed by John Beal:

> By the time of the Pio-Benedictine Code (1917) the traditional forms of apostolic visitations had survived but the complementary procedural safeguards had virtually disappeared. Apostolic visitors were limited by their mandates but possessed all the powers necessary and opportune for the carrying out of their mission, including the power to levy sanctions against those who impeded the course of their visitations. However, no public procedural norms governed the apostolic visitor's conduct of the investigation.[10]

Moreover, because these administrative apostolic visits were conducted to promote the common good, they were confidential undertakings in order to prevent scandal that would further disturb the common good.

Ordinarily apostolic visitations are administrative in nature because their purpose is to assist the ecclesiastical superior in understanding the situation of the local church or religious community in order to promote the common good. Furthermore, not intended to lay the foundation for a penal trial, administrative visitations carry a paternal tone and so seem, on the surface, to be positive, pastoral, even familial in approach. However, the absence of judicial safeguards, the secrecy and lack of transparency, and the nebulous unspecified nature of an investigation conducted for the sake of the common good have profound implications for the subjects of such a visitation. The post-Tridentine pre-1917 Code of Canon Law classification of visitations with its provision for a non-penal administrative visitation lays the foundation for the dynamics operative in the apostolic visitation of women religious in the U.S. that is the subject of this book.

THE INFLUENCE OF VATICAN II ON ECCLESIAL PROCESSES

This history now brings us to Vatican II and its release of a renewed theology and corresponding ecclesiology into church structures and the laws which govern them. The formulation of the law which follows the council is intricately linked to and evolves from the spirit of the council. At the 1965 plenary session inaugurating the work of the Commission for the Revision of the Code of Canon Law Paul VI stressed the close relationship of the revision to the council in these words: "Now, however, with changing conditions—for life seems to evolve more rapidly—canon law must be prudently reformed; specifically, it must be accommodated to a new way of thinking proper to the Second Ecumenical Council of the Vatican, in which pastoral care and new needs of the people of God are met."[11]

Almost twenty years later in his introduction to the actual promulgation of the 1983 Revised Code of Canon Law, Pope John Paul II emphasizes that foundational to this new spirit is the process of collegiality. He notes that collegiality is not only the content of the new Code of Canon Law, but that the law itself was created collegially with input and involvement of bishops and experts from around the world in the fields of theology, history, and canon law. In his own words,

> If we consider the nature of the work which preceded the promulgation of the code and also the manner in which it was carried out, especially during the pontificates of Paul VI and John Paul I, and from then until the present day, it must be clearly pointed out that this work was brought to completion in an outstandingly collegial spirit. This applies not only in regard to the material drafting of the work, but also to the very substance of the laws enacted. This note of collegiality eminently characterizes and distinguishes the process of developing the present code; it corresponds perfectly with the teaching and character of the Second Vatican Council.[12]

In order to assure harmony between the revised law and conciliar documents, principles were approved by the synod of bishops to guide the revision. The application of these principles directed the translation of the pastoral decisions of the council into the juridical content of the canons. Among the guiding principles pertinent to our exploration of a context for canonical visitations are the following:

- Pastoral care should be the hallmark of the code. Laws should be marked by a spirit of charity, temperance, humaneness, and moderation. The code should be reluctant to impose ecclesiastical penalties unless the matter is of grave importance and such norms are necessary for the public good and church discipline.
- The principle of subsidiarity should be more broadly and completely applied to church legislation in order to strengthen the bond between those exercising authority and those subject to authority.
- The pope and the diocesan bishops are totally empowered to fulfill their responsibilities for the service of their respective communities. The use of power in the church should not become arbitrary. The rights of all the Christian faithful should be acknowledged and protected. While individual Christians fulfill various roles in the church, all possess the same fundamental rights by reason of the radical equality arising from their personal human dignity and their common baptism. Rights and duties should be clarified by the canons of the code. [13]

The words of John Paul II in his introduction to the code and the principles that guide the code present a vision of church defined as the people of God in an organic relationship between the members and the head of the church, bound together through baptism with distinct gifts and functions to be used collegially for building up the church. It is this vision that inspires the 1983 Revised Code of Canon Law as it translates the ecclesiological doctrine of the Second Vatican Council into canonical terms.

With Vatican II as our context, we pose the question at the heart of the matter for the content of this chapter and for interpreting the experience narrated in this book. What does this new way of thinking, this new understanding of theology and ecclesiology, mean when translated into the 1983 Revised Code of Canon Law regarding canonical visitations in general and the specific kind of visitation that is the apostolic visitation? If the reader is so inclined and merely picks up the 1983 code selecting a few canons in isolation, it can appear that the new norms simply echo the provisions of 1917. Yet, as noted by John A. Alesandro in the *General Introduction* to the 1983 Code of Canon Law:

> Even when texts of the 1917 code are retained verbatim or in slightly amended form, they may not be interpreted in precisely the same way in which they were sixty years ago. Now they must be re-examined, related to the other canons, placed in context, and studied in the light of the council. In short, they must be subject to an interpretation based on a renewed ecclesiology. [14]

At first glance the canons on episcopal visitations (396–400) seem to be a mere repetition of the 1917 provisions. They affirm the responsibility of the bishop to visit his diocese at least once every five years in person; describe the scope of the diocesan visitation with the exemption of pontifical religious institutes; restate the paternal and diligent approach to conducting the visitation; and emphasize the importance of the quinquennial reports and the *ad limina* visit. However, when we place these canons in the context of other canons in a mutually illuminative approach, we see significant shifts integral to a post Vatican II consciousness.

One such example is the retrieved emphasis on the local church, the diocese, as the life-giving source for the vitality of the church: "Particular churches in which and from which exists the one and unique Catholic Church are first of all dioceses" (Canon 368). As noted by Thomas J. Green,

> This partly theological canon reflects the shift in conciliar ecclesiology from a church understood in almost exclusively universalist terms (1917 code) to the vision of a variety of communities in vital relationship with one another. . . . The church is universal only insofar as it is particularized in the different cultures of the world. The self-realization of the church requires an exchange between the gospel and the life, traditions, and customs of the people to whom it is preached. [15]

One process for attending to the experience of those in the particular church and then releasing that experience into the larger church is identified in canons on the diocesan synod (460–467). New to the revised code, canon 460 states that "a diocesan synod is a group of selected priests and other Christian faithful of a particular church which offers assistance to the diocesan bishop for the good of the entire diocesan community." Historically, the synod had been an exclusively clerical institute. Expressive of the theology and ecclesiology of Vatican II the 1983 code commits to the inclusion of "other Christian faithful" in the composition of the synod. As John Alesandro notes,

> This revision represents the law's commitment to utilize the gifts of the entire Christian community. While the bishop is the legislator, other members of his particular church perform the critical tasks of guiding and facilitating his legislative action. . . . The synod is intended to bring the diocesan bishop together with many responsible clerics, religious, and lay persons in order to hear open discussion and ponder the acts of governance which will prove most beneficial to the diocese. [16]

A subsequent canon (467) speaks to the requirement that the bishop share the information from the synod with the conference of bishops. Furthermore, one can expect a report from the synod to be part of the bishop's canonical *ad limina* visit to Rome. These processes, now codified, revitalize the flow of communication between and among the people, the bishops, and the Holy See. Canonically, they locate the assessment, renewal, reform, and accountability central to the purposes of a canonical visitation in the mutuality of relationship.

As evidenced in the following examples, the spirit of Vatican II catalyzed an emphasis on the pastoral nature of ecclesial leadership and so recast the purpose and procedure of the bishop's visitation. Paul VI, in his allocution on the occasion of the opening of the pastoral visitation of the Diocese of Rome in 1967, describes the event as "an act of the apostolate . . . , not a bureaucratic inquiry, not a juridic formality but a life giving event."[17] This intentionality is also reflected in the description of the purpose of visitation in the 1973 *Directory on the Pastoral Ministry of Bishops:* "The principal reason for the visitation of parishes is that the bishop may meet together with persons, namely, the clergy, religious, and laity. Everything done in the visitation should tend in this direction."[18]

Having considered some of the shifts the new mentality of Vatican II effected in the episcopate and diocese, we turn now to its influence on relationships between the church universal and religious communities. Key to this exploration is the fact that, on October 28, 1965, almost 20 years prior to the 1983 revision of canon law, Pope Paul VI promulgated *Perfectae Caritatis, the Decree on the Appropriate Renewal of Religious Life* (PC). The decree is grounded in the foundational principle that religious life finds its meaning and vitality in the faithful following of Christ according to the particular charism of the institute and encourages religious institutes to claim their particular identity with renewed vigor, commitment, and joy.

In keeping with this conviction and the spirit it engenders, the decree calls for the appropriate renewal of religious life through "a continuous return to the sources of all Christian life and to the original inspiration behind a given community." Moving forward these efforts toward renewal, communities are to be guided by the supreme law of following Christ of the gospel; preserve the spirit of their founders and their unique traditional heritage; claim and foster according to their own individual character the objectives of the church; promote an awareness of contemporary human conditions and needs of the church; and be sourced and re-sourced in an interior renewal of spirit (PC 2).[19] Affirming that renewal originates within the religious community itself and not with the Holy See and emphasizing the value and necessity of unity in diversity, this decree gives expression to Vatican II principles of collegiality and subsidiarity and the organic communion created by varied gifts.

These principles and their application to religious life as outlined in *Perfectae Caritatis* permeate the 1983 Revised Code of Canon Law and its underlying significant shifts from the 1917 code. In his reflection on the section of the code pertaining to institutes of consecrated life, Alesandro writes:

The most important developments in this field are the more expansive implementation of the principle of subsidiarity, the relegation of many decisions to the proper law of the institute, and the encouragement of institutes to be distinctive in their manner of following the gospel. This approach contrasts starkly with that of the 1917 code which was meticulously detailed in its norms for religious and thereby encouraged not the uniqueness of individual institutes but their uniformity. . . . This code relies principally on the renewal of the constitutions and statutes of the individual institutes, in accord with universal law, to shape the future of religious institutes. [20]

There are underlying theological premises pervading the canons on institutes of consecrated life that become particularly pertinent to our exploration of canonical visitations in general and apostolic visitations in particular. The first is the primacy of the Holy Spirit in the birth and sustenance of consecrated life. It is through the agency of the Spirit acting in the founder that an institute comes into being and through the extension of that same Spirit in the members that an institute continues and evolves. Canon 573, the first canon addressing consecrated life, testifies to the originating initiative of the Spirit:

Life consecrated by the profession of the evangelical counsels is a stable form of living by which the faithful, following Christ more closely under the action of the Holy Spirit, are totally dedicated to God. . . . Consecrated faithful who profess the evangelical counsels according to the proper laws of institutes freely assume this form of living in institutes of consecrated life canonically erected by competent church authority.

Consecrated religious life is, therefore, a generation of the Spirit rising up in freedom and grace from within the Christian faithful who then seek recognition of their Spirit-inspired charism by official church authority. As Sharon Holland, IHM observes,

Within the experience of each foundation, the fundamental charism has been received and has evolved; constitutions and statutes based upon that lived charism have been presented to the church for approval, rather than the church's first having developed norms by which the institutes must organize. . . . Consecrated life grew up within the church, not as part of the structure but as a gift of the Spirit within that structure. This gives institutes a certain freedom and autonomy within the church. [21]

As developed in the revised Code of Canon Law, the activity of the Spirit has a primacy of location in the institute, its constitutions, and proper law. The canons, therefore, codify some of the processes by which institutes evaluate and maintain accountability for living their life and mission in fidelity to the inspiration of the Spirit: ongoing study and reflection on the founder and the institute's heritage; writing constitutions and proper law according to this spiritual patrimony (canon 578); and assessing fidelity to the constitutions through the general chapter as described in canon 631:

> The general chapter, which holds supreme authority in the institute according to the norm of the constitutions, is to be so formed that, representing the entire institute, it should be a true sign of its unity in love. Its foremost duty is this: to protect the patrimony of the institute and promote suitable renewal in accord with this patrimony, to elect the supreme moderator, to treat major business matters and to publish norms which all are bound to obey.

In addition to the collegial model of a canonical chapter, superiors are designated by the proper law of each institute to visit the houses and members entrusted to them (canon 628). These ordinary canonical visitations provide a vehicle for mutual exchange of ideas and experience as leadership and members offer observations on the institute, its communal life and its mission, raise questions and concerns, and so attend to the stirrings of the Spirit in them and among them. Through these canonical processes of chapter and visitation, the assessment of an institute's life and mission and the corollary work of reform and renewal rest originally with the institute itself.

At the same time, the institute exists within the church. So while the law recognizes that institutes have a proper autonomy especially regarding its internal life, the law also reflects the reality that institutes are, as part of the church, subject to ecclesiastical authority. To that end canon 576 specifies that "it belongs to the competent authority of the church to interpret the evangelical counsels, to regulate their practice by laws, to constitute therefrom stable forms of living by canonical approbation, and, for the most part to take care that the institutes grow and flourish according to the spirit of the founders and wholesome traditions." In her commentary on this canon, Sharon Holland points to the inherent creative tension between the authoritative role of the official church and the authoritative role of the institute:

> The responsibility to maintain this form of life means that the church has the duty to point out to an institute when its way of life seems to have drifted outside the gospel or its own particular charism. This is to be accomplished by church authority without blocking the growth and development of the charism of the institute from within. This in no way diminishes the primary responsibility of the members of an institute for their own fidelity. [22]

Ordinarily the relationship of an institute to the authority of the church occurs through the dicastery in the Roman Curia formed by Pope Sixtus in 1586 as one of the intermediate ecclesial authorities directly responsible to the papacy. Enduring under many names and with some shifts in role and function according to the times, it received its current name in 1988 when Pope John Paul II identified the office as the Congregation for Institutes of

Consecrated Life and Societies of Apostolic Life (CICLSAL). In the spirit of Vatican II, the 1983 canons define some specific means to assure the mutual flow of communication between religious institutes and CICLSAL. One such vehicle is described in canon 592:

> In order that the communion of institutes within the Apostolic See can be better fostered each supreme moderator is to send a brief report on the status and life of the institute to the Apostolic See in a manner and at a time determined by the latter. The moderators of every institute are to promote knowledge of the documents of the Holy See which affect members entrusted to them and be concerned about their observance of them.

In terms of reporting to CICLSAL many institutes have the practice of sending these reports after a general chapter. This process connects the collegial actions of the institute's supreme internal governing body and the spirit inherent in those actions directly with the authority of the church.

An additional formal way of realizing communion consistent with the spirit of Vatican II is through canonically erected conferences or councils of major superiors, such as the International Union of Superiors General (UISG), the Leadership Conference of Women Religious (LCWR), and the Council of Major Superiors of Women Religious (CMSWR). As prescribed in canons 708 and 709, these conferences and councils, whose membership is voluntary, are established to promote greater collaboration among the institutes themselves and more direct contact with the Holy See.

These processes, now codified, formally structure the flow of communication among members of religious institutes, between the members and major superiors, and between institutes and Rome. Canonically they locate the assessment, renewal, reform, and accountability central to the purposes of a canonical visitation in the mutuality of relationship.

A REFLECTION ON THE APOSTOLIC VISITATION OF WOMEN RELIGIOUS IN THE SPIRIT OF VATICAN II

Keeping in mind the spirit of Vatican II and its effect on the 1983 Revised Code of Canon Law in its application to accountability in both episcopal structures and in the structures of religious institutes, we can cull out some guiding dynamics.

First and primarily, the entire faith community inclusive of the Holy See, bishops, major superiors, and the entire people of God is bound together by a single common desire: fidelity to the gospel of Jesus. The whole aim of the Christian life is to live in the image of Jesus' love for God and for others. The laws are intended to be in service to living in the spirit of love or charity. In the words of John Paul II, spoken upon the occasion of the promulgation of the new code:

> It appears sufficiently clear that the code is in no way intended as a substitute for faith, grace, charisms, and especially charity in the life of the church and of the faithful. On the contrary, its purpose is rather to create such an order in the ecclesial society that, while assigning the primacy to love, grace and charisms, it at the same time renders their organic development easier in the life of both the ecclesial society and the individual persons who belong to it. [23]

Secondly, the new code emphasizes that the organic development of love, grace, and charisms does not originate with the Holy See but rather among the faithful within their particular churches in the case of the diocese and within the religious institute in the case of those living the vowed life. Something fresh, vital, integral to renewal emerges from the faith community as the local church experientially and practically lives gospel love. Something fresh, vital, integral to renewal emerges from the religious institute as, retrieving the spirit of its founder, the religious community experientially and practically lives gospel love.

Thirdly, the code makes provision for significant interactive dialogue at the local level directed toward sharing the experience of faith, communally assessing fidelity to the way of Jesus, and discerning the call of the Spirit in the signs of the times. In the diocese this occurs through consultative processes with the bishops through diocesan synods, councils, other advisory structures and through the bishop's ordinary and regular canonical visitation of the churches in his diocese. In religious institutes this occurs through the congregational chapters and the visitation by the major superior or her delegate.

Fourthly, the code addresses necessary vehicles for the release of the experience of the faithful into the Holy See. The move from the faithful in the local church or diocese occurs as the bishop brings the experience of his diocese to the United States Council of Catholic Bishops (USCCB) as appropriate and to his regular canonical *ad limina* visit to Rome, meeting there with the pope and/or with the Vatican Congregation for Bishops. The move from religious institutes to the Holy See occurs through regular reports sent from the major superior, usually following a chapter, to CICLSAL. Although, as indicated earlier, not all religious institutes hold membership in the Leadership Conference of Women Religious (LCWR) or the Council of Major Superiors of Women Religious (CMSWR), the regular visits of the leadership of this conference and council to CICLSAL provide some indication to the Holy See about how the Spirit is working in the life and mission of U.S. religious institutes.

Running like a mantra through this reflection on canonical visitations in light of Vatican II is the clear recognition that the council's applied principles codified in 1983 canon law locate the assessment, renewal, reform, and accountability characteristic of a canonical visitation in the mutuality of relationship. In the words of John Paul II, "This mutual communication between the center of the church and the periphery does not enlarge the scope of anyone's authority but promotes *communion* in the highest degree, in the manner of a living body that is constituted and activated precisely by the interplay of its members."[24]

However, if one attends carefully and critically to the flow of communication as specified in the code, there is no clear provision for how the Holy See dialogues in a relationally immediate way with the faithful in the local churches. It happens through the mediation of the bishop who, no matter how pastoral and perceptive, cannot speak with the living voice of the laity. Similarly, for religious, the flow of communication to the Holy See occurs through periodic reports from individual institutes; the response from the Holy See happens ordinarily in a written message of gratitude for the regular congregational report with some exhortations about ongoing fidelity. Communication to and from Rome also occurs through the mediation of the leadership of LCWR or CMSWR who, no matter how attentive and engaged with individual congregations, cannot speak to the variegated spiritual texture of charismatic life in religious institutes.

The omission of direct personal immediate dialogically engaged communications between the ordinary faithful and Rome in the code and in corresponding canonical processes is significant to the initiation of the Apostolic Visitation of U.S. women religious by Rome and in understanding the manner of its reception by many women religious. It seems to violate the processes of collegiality, communion, and the mutual flow of communication at the heart of Vatican II ecclesiology and of ecclesial canonical processes generated from that renewed ecclesiology. The gap leaves the extraordinary administrative apostolic visitation as a rightful way for Rome to respond to perceived irregularities in the teaching and practice of the faith.

For many women religious, steeped in the theology of Vatican II, the initiation and implementation of a special non-penal administrative apostolic visitation as currently understood by the Congregation for the Doctrine of the Faith (and as essentially unchanged since its post-Trent, pre-1917 code classification), comes as a radical rupture in the ecclesial spirit of Vatican II and is experienced, therefore, as a surprising, shocking, and hurtful violation of right relationship. Defined by the Congregation for the Doctrine of the Faith the apostolic visitation is "an exceptional initiative of the Holy See which involves sending a Visitor or Visitors to evaluate an ecclesiastical institute such as a seminary, diocese or religious institute. Apostolic visitations are intended to assist the institute in question to improve the way in which it carries out its functions in the life of the church."[25]

A canonical reflection on visitations prepared by the Resource Center for Religious Institutes further elaborates on the apostolic visitation and echoes understandings of this special extraordinary visitation as we have seen it described and implemented throughout the history traced in this chapter:

> An apostolic visitation is administrative in nature. It is used by the pope or a Roman dicastery to gather information in order to remedy a situation that is problematic. . . . An apostolic visitation is not merely a "friendly visit." While it may be framed within the context of a pastoral or paternal visit, and thus not penal or judicial in nature, it is being conducted because of a perceived need to correct or amend. [26]

The information from the Resource Center for Religious Institutes goes on to confirm what we have learned from our review of the apostolic visitation's history in the church. It can arise from complaints remaining anonymous to the subjects of the visitation, may be executed by the ecclesiastical superior who perceives a need to act on behalf of the common good, and often lacks transparency in the real reasons for its origination and in the secrecy of its reports.

Accordingly, the processes of the apostolic visitation seem to be in tension with one of Pope John Paul II's hopes for the new code when he states as one of its purposes: to assure "that the mutual relations of the faithful may be regulated according to justice based on charity, with the rights of individuals guaranteed and well-defined."[27] Reflecting on the apostolic visitation in the context of Vatican II seems to affirm that there is, indeed, something missing as current ecclesial structures and procedures strain to be true to its spirit. In the salutary words of Jordan F. Hite, TOR:

> It should be recognized that no law is perfect. Some of the important questions are not answered by the revised law, if indeed those questions are capable of legal resolution. The law is always open ended in the sense that experience will show what lies ahead for its proper understanding and development. With this in mind the imperfections that remain form the agenda for the coming years in the ongoing response of institutes and societies to the Spirit of God.[28]

In the meantime we women religious live faithfully, that is to say, consciously, creatively, and courageously, in the gap. It seems right and good that we imagine ourselves in that original council assembly in Jerusalem with Peter and Paul, Barnabas, Timothy and Titus as, in the intensity of dialogue and the power of discernment, they attend to the experience of the people of Antioch and their yearnings for change born of their experience. In that space, we voice the questions of our time. Putting on the new mentality of Vatican II, is an apostolic visitation a faithful and, therefore, effective way to assure reform and renewal in the church? With the strengthening of the role and gifts of the particular churches and individual religious institutes in building up the Body of Christ, how does the whole church discern together whether incidents of difference are in fact deviations in need of correction or the work of the Spirit acting for the growth and goodness of the church?

In the following pages we women religious, contemporary kin to the faithful of Antioch, bring our experience to the whole church. We offer our voices, humbly and generously, breath and word of the Spirit stirring in us, as in our time the church discerns what it is that "seems good to the Holy Spirit and to us" (Acts 15:28).

NOTES

1. John P. Beal, JCD, canon lawyer and professor at the Catholic University of America, is the author of an excellent study of the institute of visitations, "The Apostolic Visitation of a Diocese: A Canonico-Historical Investigation," *The Jurist* 49 (1989): 347–398. The writer of this chapter relied on his study to shape the framework and content for her presentation of the history of visitations between the time of the early church and Vatican II.

The Resource Center for Religious Institutes (RCRI) is an organization created to serve the needs of women and men religious. It offers resources in a variety of areas integral to religious life, including canon law. Dan Ward, OSB, directed the center until his retirement in 2013.

To understand the historical development of canon law, particularly the influence of the Council of Trent on the 1917 code and Vatican Council II on the 1983 revised code, the author studied the commentaries of particular canonists. These commentaries are found in *The Code of Canon Law: A Text and Commentary*, ed. James A. Coriden, Thomas J. Green, and Donald E. Heintschel (New York: Paulist Press, 1985).

2. All scripture citations in this chapter are taken from *The New Oxford Annotated Bible*, ed. Bruce M. Metzger and Roland Murphy (New York: Oxford University Press, 1991).

3. The section that follows takes the reader from the early church up to Vatican II. In order to address shifts in the practice of canonical visitations, it is essential to place their development within a larger context: the ecclesiology that emerges as church history unfolds within an ever-dynamic socio-political environment. In order to integrate, in broad strokes, the mutuality of historical and ecclesial influences that shaped evolving forms of canonical visitations, the author weaves together the research of John Beal, "The Apostolic Visitation of a Diocese," John Alesandro's synopsis of the development of church history in "General Introduction," in *The Code of Canon Law: A Text and Commentary,* and the author's study of ecclesiology.

4. Beal, "The Apostolic Visitation of Diocese," 376.

5. ibid., 370.

6. For a discussion of the difference between an accusatorial model and an inquisitorial model and the effects of the inquisitorial model on the institute of visitations, see Beal, "The Apostolic Visitation of a Diocese," 352–354, 375–376.

7. Beal describes this visitation practice of the order of Cluny in a footnote elaborating on his presentation of one form of canonical visitations in religious communities, Beal, "The Apostolic Visitation of a Diocese," 362.

8. Council of Trent, sess. 24, *de reformation*, c. 3, cited in Beal, "The Apostolic Visitation of a Diocese," 355.

9. For a discussion of the classification of visitations, see Beal, "The Apostolic Visitation of a Diocese," 356–358.

10. ibid., 393–394.

11. Paul VI, plenary session inaugurating the work of the Commission for the Revision of the Code of Canon Law, *Communicationes* 1 (1969) Vatican City, cited in John A. Alesandro, "General Introduction," in *The Code of Canon Law: A Text and Commentary*, ed. James A.

Coriden, Thomas J. Green, and Donald E. Heintschel (New York/Mahwah, NJ: Paulist Press, 1985), 5.

12. John Paul II, *Apostolic Constitution Sacrae Disciplinae Leges,* January 25, 1983, in *The Code of Canon Law: A Text and Commentary*, ed. James A. Coriden, Thomas J. Green, and Donald E. Heintschel (New York/Mahwah, NJ: Paulist Press, 1985), xxiv.

13. Alesandro summarizes these principles in "General Introduction," in *The Code of Canon Law: A Text and Commentary*, ed. Coriden, Green, and Heintschel, 6.

14. ibid., 10.

15. Thomas J. Green, "Particular Churches and Their Groupings; Title I: Particular Churches and the Authority Established in Them," in *The Code of Canon Law: A Text and Commentary*, ed. James A. Coriden, Thomas J. Green, and Donald E. Heintschel (New York/ Mahwah, NJ: Paulist Press, 1985), 315.

16. John A. Alesandro, "The Internal Ordering of Particular Churches," in *The Code of Canon Law: A Text and Commentary*, ed. James A. Coriden, Thomas J. Green, and Donald E. Heintschel (New York/Mahwah, NJ: Paulist Press, 1985), 378.

17. Paul VI, allocution on the occasion of the opening of the pastoral visitation of the Diocese of Rome, April 9, 1967, in Beal, 359–360.

18. Sacred Congregation for Bishops, "Directory on the Pastoral Ministry of Bishops," May 31, 1973 (Ottawa: Canadian Catholic Conference, 1974), 86, cited in Beal, 360.

19. Paul VI, *Perfectae Caritatis, Decree on the Appropriate Renewal of Religious Life*, in *The Documents of Vatican* II, ed. Walter A. Abbott, SJ (Piscataway, NJ: America Press, 1966), 466–482.

20. Alesandro, "General Introduction," in *The Code of Canon Law: A Text and Commentary,* eds. Coriden, Green, and Heintschel, 16.

21. Sharon L. Holland, IHM, "Section I: Institutes of Consecrated Life; Title I: Norms Common to All Institutes of Consecrated Life," in *The Code of Canon Law: A Text and Commentary*, ed. James A. Coriden, Thomas J. Green, and Donald E. Heintschel (New York/ Mahwah, NJ: Paulist Press, 1985), 455.

22. ibid., 456.

23. John Paul II, "Apostolic Constitution *Sacrae Disciplinae Leges*," in *The Code of Canon Law: A Text and Commentary*, ed. Coriden, Green, and Heintschel, xxv.

24. John Paul II, "Apostolic Constitution *Pastor Bonus*," June 28, 1988, cited in Beal, 394.

25. This definition is found on line in the glossary of terms of the Congregation for the Doctrine of the Faith, http://www.vatican.va/resources/resources_glossary-terms_en.html.

26. Resource Center for Religious Institutes, "The Apostolic Visitation of Women Religious in the United States: a Canonical Reflection," March 9, 2009.

27. John Paul, II, "Apostolic Constitution Sacrae Disciplinae Leges," in The Code of Canon Law: A Text and Commentary, ed. Coriden, Green, and Heintschel, (xxv).

28. Jordan F. Hite, TOR, "Institutes of Consecrated Life and Societies of Apostolic Life," in *The Code of Canon Law: A Text and Commentary*, ed. James A. Coriden, Thomas J. Green, and Donald E. Heintschel (New York/Mahwah, NJ: Paulist Press, 1985), 452.

Chapter Two

Situating the Apostolic Visitation in Historical and Theological Context

Patricia Walter

THE APOSTOLIC VISITATION

On January 30, 2009, Cardinal Rodé, prefect of the Congregation for Institutes of Consecrated Life and Societies of Apostolic Life (CICLSAL), sent a letter to the Leadership Conference of Women Religious (LCWR) and the Council of Major Superiors of Women Religious (CMSWR) announcing an Apostolic Visitation of apostolic women's institutes in the United States. This announcement astounded most women religious, who were not aware of any problems widespread and grave enough to warrant an apostolic visitation across a whole nation.

The stated purpose for this Apostolic Visitation was to examine the quality of their life and to encourage vocations. Although these two concerns could easily apply to men religious, whose numbers have also declined and who might also have benefited from such pastoral concern, no institutes of men religious were included. Furthermore, no similar investigation has been initiated of all women religious in any other country, although some of those sisters are members of the same international religious congregations as the American sisters and, therefore, share the same constitutions as well as the same self-understanding and practices. In addition, the decline in vocations has been far more longstanding and drastic in European congregations, yet CICLSAL has not extended pastoral concern to these congregations through national apostolic visitations. So it seems that there are factors unique to the United States institutes or provinces of apostolic women religious that prompted such an extraordinary action.

It has become clear that the roots of this investigation reach back to the years following Vatican II and that the Apostolic Visitation is intimately connected with the contentious process of receiving the Second Vatican Council. It seems apparent, too, that the tensions which contributed to the Apostolic Visitation and which the Apostolic Visitation in turn has heightened are not unprecedented. At least from the Middle Ages onward, there have been documented controversies over what genuine religious life is and what the role of non-monastic religious life in the church and in the world is or ought to be.

This examination of the roots of the Visitation, then, briefly identifies key points or themes in conciliar and post-conciliar theologies of religious life as well as the significance of the mandate to religious to renew their lives. It then looks at subsequent developments as part of the process of the reception of Vatican Council II by the whole church.

PRE-CONCILIAR CONTEXT OF AMERICAN WOMEN RELIGIOUS

In the decades before the convening of the Second Vatican Council, women religious in the United States undertook some steps which would have significant impact on their readiness for, and reception of, conciliar teachings. In 1957, in his encyclical *Fidei Donum,* Pope Pius XII had issued a challenge to dioceses and religious institutes to promote and support evangelization in missionary territories. Many congregations of American women religious responded generously to this call to share financial and human resources with poorer countries, particularly in Africa and Latin America. [1]

In the decades before Vatican II, the Catholic Church in the United States was flourishing. The parochial school system, unparalleled in any other country, was filled beyond capacity with children, some of whom are now referred to as the "Baby Boomers." Classes were taught in schools, storefronts, mobile classrooms, and school and rectory basements to respond to the need. Although extraordinary numbers of young women entered religious life during World War II and the following twenty years, there was a constant demand for more teaching sisters. The network of Catholic hospitals continued to expand, responding to the needs of a growing Catholic population and their neighbors. The G.I. Bill enabled thousands of young Catholic men to get college educations, which in turn increased their desire for better education for their children.

Meanwhile, in 1950, Pope Pius XII convened the First General Congress of the States of Perfection. Among other matters, he asked women's institutes to examine and simplify the rituals which had developed over decades or even centuries. In 1952, he urged superiors to streamline and modernize the habits worn by their sisters, particularly when the habits were unhygienic or demanded great expenditure of time and energy to maintain. In 1958, he asked congregations to examine their practices and customs to see whether they encouraged isolation from the world. Professional and cultural development was also urged.

At the same time in the United States, the continual upgrading of government standards for teacher certification meant that women religious had greater need for education and professionalization themselves. In order to educate their sisters as well as other young Catholic women, many congregations founded colleges during the twentieth century. All of these factors meant that a growing number of sisters obtained not only their bachelor's degrees, but also master's and doctorates.

In 1954, the Sister Formation Movement was formed. This organization worked to ensure that sisters received an excellent formation and acquired their undergraduate degrees before beginning to teach. The Sister Formation Movement was a vehicle for intercommunity awareness and exchange on topics related to religious life.[2] Two years later, the Vatican asked the superiors of apostolic women religious in the United States to form a conference, which was named the Conference of Major Superiors of Women (CMSW). The conference assisted members in attending to both the spiritual and apostolic dimensions of religious life and promoted cooperation and communication internally as well as with other ecclesial bodies.

In summary, then, both civil and ecclesiastical factors had been slowly moving women religious in the United States to begin simplifying and adapting their lives to contemporary conditions and to look beyond diocesan and national boundaries to identify needs in the developing world at the same time that they were becoming the most educated group of women in the church. This background prepared them for the work of Vatican II.

VATICAN COUNCIL II ON RELIGIOUS LIFE

The initial drafts of the Vatican Council Preparatory Commission on the church contained an ecclesiology which viewed the church as an institution devoted to the salvation of souls, a society with clearly defined states and ranks. Within the church, religious life was honored as the "state of perfection" undertaken by those called to and capable of obeying the counsels of Christ as well as the commandments. There was a focus on individual perfection attained by total consecration to God and through a life of penance, separation from the world, and the threefold renunciation of the vows. This was the theology of religious life that was enshrined in the constitutions of most religious institutes.

As the council unfolded, *Lumen Gentium* (LG), *Dogmatic Constitution on the Church* promulgated by Pope Paul VI on November 21, 1964, deliberately refused to give a formal definition of religious life or to use the term "state of perfection."[3] Rather, it placed the chapter on religious life (Chapter 6) after the chapter on the universal call to holiness. Chapter 5 states that "all the faithful of Christ of whatever rank or status are called to the fullness of Christian life and to the perfection of charity" (LG 40). The link between the two chapters lies in Christ's gift of the counsels. Religious life is "constituted by the profession of the evangelical counsels." Religious profession intensifies baptismal consecration to God's service. In this way, religious can grow in charity. This charity unites religious to "the church and her mystery in a special way" and calls religious to promote the reign of Christ (LG 44).

The title of the 1965 conciliar decree on religious life, *Perfectae Caritatis* (PC), *Decree on the Adaptation and Renewal of the Religious Life*, has a double significance.[4] First, it is, notably, the only document which incorporates the conciliar focus on *aggiornamento,* renewal and adaptation in light of the signs of the times, into its title. Second, it repeats the phrase in *Lumen Gentium*—"the perfection of charity"—to which all the faithful are called and to which religious commit themselves more intensely through profession (PC 1f; 5a). Religious life is not a state of perfection in this document either. *Perfectae Caritatis* presents religious life as a richly variegated historical phenomenon which emerges throughout the centuries in response to the promptings of the Spirit. The *sequela Christi*, the following of Christ, is "the fundamental norm of the religious life" and the "supreme law" for all religious communities (PC 2a).

The basic contours for renewal are limned in chapters 2 to 4 of *Perfectae Caritatis.* Renewal entails: "a continuous return to the sources of all Christian life and to the original inspiration behind a given community and an adjustment of the community to the changed conditions of the times" (PC 2). Religious institutes are to be the agents of renewal (PC 4) "under the influence of the Holy Spirit and the guidance of the church" (PC 2). The text then identifies five principles for this task. First, "the fundamental norm of the religious life is a following of Christ as proposed by the gospel"; this is the "supreme law" for all religious communities (PC 2a). The next principle identifies a second set of sources and criteria: "the spirit of the founders" along with the specific purposes and solid traditions that comprise the heritage of institutes. This cluster of sources is the root of rich and beneficial diversity in the church (PC 2b). The third principle urges religious to share in "scriptural, liturgical, doctrinal, pastoral, ecumenical, missionary, and social" activities of the church consonant with their particular characteristics (PC 2c). Fourth, in order to be more effective in their ministries, religious institutes are to do social analysis and identify the needs of the church (PC 2d). Finally, external adaptations must be preceded by interior renewal.

In section 3, *Perfectae Caritatis* states that the whole of religious life is to be adapted, according to "the physical and psychological conditions of today's religious" and, according to "the needs of the apostolate, the requirements of a given culture, the social and economic circumstances." Section 4 asserts that "effective renewal and adaptation demands the cooperation of all the members of an institute." In other words, the members are co-responsible within the normal structures of institutes. Without in any way diminishing the authority of superiors, *Perfectae Caritatis* notes the key role of general chapters in setting directions and calls superiors to consult members on decisions affecting their institutes' futures.

RECEPTION OF VATICAN II COUNCIL

Phase One: Study of the Documents

It would be difficult to overstate the importance of Vatican II in the lives of American women religious. In many congregations, although certainly not all, the documents were read, discussed, prayed with, taught and, where possible, implemented as they were promulgated. Congregations sent sisters to lectures, workshops, and courses on conciliar theology; they also sponsored such events themselves. The theological principles that effectively shaped these women's worldview were: the church as Trinitarian communion; the mission of the church in and to the world; the centrality of baptism; the call of all to holiness; collegiality; the Bible as the living Word of God; and the Eucharist as the "source and summit of Christian life" (LG 11), involving the "full, conscious and active participation" of all (*Sacrosanctum Concilium* 14).[5] The specific conciliar teaching on religious life flowed from many of these principles; conversely, these principles informed the women's understanding of the teaching on religious life.

Phase Two: Implementation and its Contexts

The Charge

In 1966, Pope Paul VI issued *Ecclesiae Sanctae* (ES), *Implementing Four Council Decrees,* which initiated the second phase of the process of reception of the council—the shift from studying the conciliar texts to experimentation based on their principles.[6] *Ecclesiae Sanctae* stressed the importance of spiritual renewal and made the institutes the primary agents of their own renewal and adaptation, particularly through their general chapters. Every institute was to convoke a special chapter of renewal within two or three years. Every member was to be involved in preparing for this chapter and to have some part in the selection of delegates to the chapter. These chapters had the authority to change the institutes' regulations on an experimental basis and were assured that prudent experimentation which involved matters of canon law would be favorably received by competent ecclesiastical authority—either the local bishop for diocesan congregations or the Vatican Sacred Congregation of Religious for congregations of papal right.[7] Heads of institutes with the consent of their general councils could also change the particular law of their institutes and approve experimentation within the guidelines established by the general chapters. This extraordinary time of experimentation could extend until the second ordinary general chapter following the chapter of renewal, a period of time which might extend over two decades, depending on the frequency of general chapters within religious institutes. For religious accustomed to lives regulated even in minutiae, this was an amazing charge.

In preparation for such an extraordinary period, *Ecclesiae Sanctae* counseled religious to study Scripture, the conciliar texts, and the theology of religious life. It also urged them to "strive for a genuine knowledge of their original spirit, so that faithfully preserving this spirit in determining adaptations, their religious life may thus be purified of alien elements and freed from those which are obsolete" (ES I, 16.3); this was to be done for "the good of the church." The norm for obsolescence was "those elements . . . which do not constitute the nature and purpose of the institute and which, having lost their meaning and power, are no longer a real help to religious life" (ES II, 17). Yet there must also be care to maintain the witness expected of religious life.

The Context: Church Teaching

There were many significant events in both church and in society that shaped these two phases of reception in institutes of American women religious. First, within the church, there were several post-conciliar documents which also influenced the theologies of religious life developing within congregations and ultimately embedded in their constitutions. *Evangelica Testificatio*, promulgated by Pope Paul VI in 1971, following *Lumen Gentium,* has a thoroughly Trinitarian ecclesiology and stresses the diversity and mutuality of vocations within the church.[8] The document distinguishes between the church and the reign of God. The church serves the reign of God and religious life is a total commitment to the promotion of this reign. Religious life should serve as a reminder to all members of the church of their own vocations as Christians. For the first time, religious life is called a charism.[9]

This theology of religious life and the vows was fully consonant with another document which was highly influential in many congregations, *Justice in the World* (1971 Synod of Bishops).[10] Many religious took to heart the statement "Action on behalf of justice and participation in the transformation of the world fully appear to us as a constitutive dimension of the preaching of the gospel, or, in other words, of the church's mission for the redemption of the human race and its liberation from every oppressive situation" (6). They wholeheartedly agreed that "Christian love of neighbor and justice cannot be separated" (34). *Mutuae Relationes* (Mutual Relations) was issued jointly by the Sacred Congregation for Religious and for Secular Institutes (SCRIS) and by the Sacred Congregation for Bishops in 1978, in response to tensions between religious and bishops in various parts of the world. It continued the description of religious life as a charism, a gift of the Spirit. Drawing parallels between the episcopal ministry and that of religious superiors, *Mutuae Relationes* noted that fidelity to the founding charism is the first responsibility of superiors. The Spirit is the source of diversity, innovation, and originality within religious life; this may at times be problematic, so discernment is often required.[11]

Religious and Human Promotion (RHP) promulgated in 1980 by SCRIS, states that religious "are called to give singular witness to this prophetic dimension" of identifying and reading the signs of the times through the lens of the gospel.[12] Furthermore, "the prophetic nature of religious life requires that religious 'embody the church in her desire to give herself completely to the radical demands of the beatitudes' [*Evangelii Nuntiandi,* 33–34]" (RHP 4). Religious do this with a focus on communion, as "experts in communion" (RHP 24). *Religious and Human Promotion* (13) identifies four criteria for discernment: "Fidelity to humanity and to our times; fidelity to Christ and the gospel; fidelity to the church and to its mission in the world; fidelity to religious life and to the charism of one's own institute."

Another factor within the church which affected many American women religious' understanding of themselves, religious life and mission was the gradual development of liturgical roles and various ministries in which they served (e.g., director of religious education, director of adult faith formation, member of a pastoral team, parish administrator). Women religious had the education and credibility to develop and fill these roles and, in doing so, to blaze the trail for other women and men.

The Context: Society

The 1960s and 1970s were marked by significant cultural shifts in the United States. Among these were the movement of Catholics into the mainstream of society, due in no small part to the education many veterans received through the G. I. Bill; the struggle for civil rights and the unionization of farmworkers; feminism; the Vietnam War and the peace movement; the integration of schools and subsequent White flight from cities or areas of cities; the closing of Catholic schools due to population shifts and the ensuing loss of convents, for in the United States, unlike most other countries, most women religious served in parochial or diocesan schools and lived in convents connected with the schools. These events and shifts were part of the "signs of the times" that women religious contemplated and in the midst of which they responded to the conciliar call to renewal.

The Context: Within Congregations

The experience within religious congregations of this second phase of the reception of the conciliar call to renewal was extremely challenging, and often conflictual. Women religious were not highly skilled in talking with one another in a group at any level of depth. In addition to their socialization as women to avoid conflict and anger, they were formed in religious life to speak politely, to obey, and to value docility and humility. In most communities, conversation had been limited to one hour of recreation each day and, on very special occasions, to conversation at meals. Furthermore, there was deference not only to superiors but to those senior in religious life. Sisters were seated in chapel and at table according to their dates of profession. Yet the significant increase in the number of women entering from 1940 onward meant that there was a large population of younger sisters.

In his study of paradigm shifts, Thomas Kuhn concludes that those who are most invested in a particular paradigm—those with the longest experience in it, and those considered authorities within it—are the least likely to see its drawbacks and the least desirous of change. Conversely, those least invested in a particular understanding and practice (here, least invested in a particular understanding and practice of religious life, not religious life itself) tend to see the inconsistencies and lacunae in that paradigm and are thus often more willing to seek new models which better address these problems. [13] Added to that mix was the fact that every congregation had some combination of innovators, early adopters, early majority, late majority, and laggards, and the creative tensions, chaos, and conflict waited in the wings for their cues. [14] There were heated discussions about whether particular changes were a return to the intention of the founder, whether they were legitimate adaptation to the needs of the time, or whether they were simply an abandonment of religious life in favor of uncritical adaptation to cultural mores. For women who had followed the same schedule, worn the same garb, and, for the most part, engaged in the same ministry, the questions linked to experimentation—about what, to what extent, how—were magnified. Into this volatile mix were, unfortunately, too often added toxins of self-righteousness, judgments, and lack of charity. The process of renewal, even on the part of those committed to it, was painful.

These were some of the internal challenges and resistances presented by renewal. There were also a number of factors which assisted *aggiornamento*. First, American women religious grew up in a participative democracy. Second, the leadership of many congregations had heeded calls from previous popes and from SCRIS for renewal and had taken some steps in that direction. They had also insured that many or all of their sisters were educated theologically and ministerially. Third, the common study of conciliar and post-conciliar documents in many congregations provided a common framework for discussion and decisions. Fourth, many sisters experienced significant dissonance between their ministerial life where they exercised personal initiative and professional responsibility and their community life where they were dependent on superiors for permissions and regulation of minutiae. Furthermore, some sisters felt as though they were replaceable parts of a machine; due to the need for teachers, women were assigned to classrooms and grade levels whether or not they were capable of teaching, or teaching well, at that level. Fifth, the range between innovators and "laggards" was usually found in every age group in congregations, which helped to diffuse the potential for conflicts based simply on age. Sixth, as women religious, particularly in congregations founded before the nineteenth century, studied the spirit of their founder, their charism and history, they often discovered models of communities in mission as well as theologies and practices of authority and governance that differed significantly from those found in Roman theology and embedded in canon law. As their historical consciousness developed, many communities and individuals became aware that the way religious life in general, and their charism in particular, was being understood and lived at the time was not the way it had always been understood and practiced. So some groups discovered that their semi-cloistered status had been imposed on them, in direct contradiction to the reasons they were founded. In obeying the conciliar imperative, many congregations engaged in a process best described not as innovation or "revolution" but rather as a radical (in the sense of "rooted") transformation, a return to, or recovery of the original charism and the way that charism shaped spirit, purpose, ministry, relationships, and structures. Seventh, many congregations had sisters who had been or were in mission in other countries or in places of extreme poverty in the United States. They often brought a sense of urgency and a conviction that renewal was necessary in order to respond more freely and fully to people in need. The final factor is linked with this. Many religious desired to be more involved in the church and in the world, whether in parish renewal or the charismatic movement, or in work on behalf of justice and peace.

There were myriad other influences on this stage of reception. For numerous reasons—the doctrine of the call of all to holiness, the expansion of women's roles in church and society, the desire for even greater freedom (or security), the fast or slow pace of renewal, the greater acceptability of leaving religious life—a growing number of women religious left, formed new communities, or transferred from one congregation to another. There was a sense of loss and grieving as sisters bade farewell to friends and community members.

Context: The Wider Church

Within the Catholic Church in the United States, ecclesial reform occurred at an uneven pace, usually depending on the commitment of local bishops and pastors to the process of renewal. Some in the church accepted reforms wholeheartedly while others were highly critical and still others simply baffled. Unfortunately, all too often the laity did not receive good pastoral preparation, education, and formation in the reasons for, and theology underlying, the changes. And far too frequently charity was strangled and dialogue muted by judgments and self-righteousness all around. Not only were there tensions within religious congregations, there were also tensions within parishes, dioceses, and between religious congregations. Religious congregations were often praised or condemned, hired or fired, based on their pace and degree of change, usually signified by their manner of dress.

Externally, there was a wide variety of reactions from laypeople, priests, and bishops. In 1968, for example, Cardinal McIntyre told the Sisters of the Immaculate Heart of Mary that they could not teach in the Los Angeles archdiocesan schools unless they continued to wear habits and, among other things, to follow their previous *horarium* with its prescribed times for meals and going to bed.[15] Although this was a *cause célèbre*, it was not an isolated incident. The broader ecclesial community had strong responses to the degree and pace of renewal among religious—the symbol of which was the habit.

Religious institutes varied in the pace and degree of renewal. One reason for this was simply the difference in the dates of their chapters of renewal and in the length of time between their general chapters. Cultural and ethnic differences also impacted the speed and shape of renewal. Religious institutes whose members were from cultures with very defined expectations of women in general and women religious in particular, or which had less experience of participative democracy and placed less value on rights and freedom, received the directives on renewal and inculturation within those frameworks. American provinces of international institutes also tended to change less extensively and more slowly, as they negotiated the complex issues of unity, diversity, culture, and subsidiarity within the institute. It was also the case that in some congregations and provinces the place and extent of renewal depended on the degree to which major superiors actually did follow the directives to insure their sisters' education in theology and other fields and also to involve all members in the process of studying conciliar texts and their own history and charism, discussing these, and being involved in pre-chapter preparation.

In 1971, when the Conference of Major Superiors of Women (CMSW) met to update its bylaws and decided to change its name to the Leadership Conference of Women Religious (LCWR), a split developed which has significantly impacted the church in the United States in general and women religious in particular. A group of superiors objected to the name change and to LCWR policies. They formed a group called *Consortium Perfectae Caritatis*. From the time of its inception, the consortium repeatedly attempted to gain canonical recognition as a conference separate from, and equal to, LCWR. In 1974, the Institute on Religious Life was formed. With membership drawn from religious, laity, priests, and bishops, this group worked closely with members of the consortium. Both groups were critical of the direction most women religious in the United States had taken in renewal. Influential members of the institute frequently brought those concerns to the attention of Vatican officials.

Phase Three: Codification and Controversy

The third phase in the reception of Vatican II, at least from the perspective of religious life, began in the early 1980s. During this decade, most institutes finished writing their constitutions and engaged in the process of getting them approved. The period of extraordinary experimentation was over. In 1983, the Code of Canon Law was promulgated. Although the code clearly reflected the teachings of *Lumen Gentium* and *Perfectae Caritatis* on religious life, nonetheless, it did not incorporate some of the more promising developments in the theology of religious life in subsequent teaching, to a great extent because all references to charism were struck from the 1982 draft. With this decision, a key category for understanding both church and religious life disappeared. Furthermore, in the code, religious life became a subset of consecrated life. Although many of the official documents linked consecration and mission, subsequent developments sometimes places them in opposition.

Also in 1983, Pope John Paul II issued *Redemptionis Donum* (Gift of Redemption), a reflection on religious life in the context of the mystery of redemption.[16] Paragraph 7 states: "Hence, the church thinks of you, above all, as persons who are 'consecrated': *consecrated to God in Christ Jesus* as His exclusive possession. This consecration determines your place in the vast community of the church, the people of God" (RD 7). For Pope John Paul II, then, the primary key to religious life is consecration, a spousal and redemptive response to Christ's love. The vows have redemptive significance as "the most radical means for transforming in the human heart this relationship with the world" (RD 9).

A third critical ecclesiastical event for American women religious was the formation of the Pontifical Commission on Religious Life, chaired by Archbishop John Quinn of San Francisco, with Archbishop Thomas Kelly, OP, of Louisville and Bishop Raymond Lessard of Savanna as members.[17] This group became known as the "Quinn Commission." According to Pope John

Paul II's letter to the United States bishops in which he announced this commission, the commission was to facilitate the bishops in giving "special pastoral service to the religious in their dioceses" and to study the decline in vocations.[18] In tandem with this study, the Sacred Congregation for the Religious and for Secular Institutes issued a summary of church teaching and legislation on religious life, called "Essential Elements in the Church's Teaching on Religious Life as Applied to Institutes Dedicated to Works of the Apostolate." The essential elements identified in the text are: consecration by public vows; community; mission; prayer; asceticism; public witness; and an intimate connection with the broader church. The document also discussed formation and government.[19]

This papal initiative generated anxiety on the part of religious and some confusion on the part of bishops regarding the specific nature of their "special pastoral service." The commission obtained the support of the episcopal conference and the two conferences of religious—the Leadership Conference of Women Religious (LCWR) and the Conference of Major Superiors of Men (CMSM). Grounding its approach in the dialogical principles laid out by Pope Paul VI in the encyclical *Ecclesiam Suam* (Paths of the Church), the commission adopted a three-step process of listening, dialogue, and evaluation.[20] Each bishop held listening sessions with the religious in the local church. This step was quite successful. Bishops came to a better understanding of the religious and their experience of renewal, while religious felt that they had been heard. In the course of these reflections on the twenty years of renewal, a number of common themes emerged. The commission identified these ten positive factors:

1. rediscovery of the charism of the foundress or founder;
2. deepening of and more authentic spirituality;
3. new understanding of apostolic religious life;
4. new understanding of, and provision for, the uniqueness of the individual in religious life;
5. participation by religious in the decision-making processes of their order;
6. new awareness of the universality of the church's mission;
7. growing appreciation of the feminine;
8. deeper sense of solidarity with the church;
9. rewriting and updating constitutions;
10. new signs of hope through older and more mature vocations.[21]

The pope's initiative in inviting bishops to engage in this process was also viewed as positive.

A number of negative outcomes were also identified by religious. According to the report some stated the belief that there was a loss of identity in congregations. Some stated the belief that there was a decline in respect for the pope and the magisterium of the church. According to the report, most cited as negative:

1. loss of numbers;
2. lack of more new vocations;
3. tensions within communities;
4. increasing inability to continue some traditional works such as schools and hospitals;
5. criticism by laity and priests;
6. serious financial problems;
7. tensions in working with officials in Rome. [22]

In the next phase of the process, religious and bishops engaged in dialogue about these issues and related concerns. The material in "Essential Elements" was often incorporated into these sessions. While some religious believed that "Essential Elements" clearly stated the non-negotiable characteristics of religious life, others asserted that the summary was influenced far more by the ways in which the Code of Canon Law attempted to draw distinctions between religious life and other forms of consecrated life (for example, its insistence on the sign value of public consecration and on religious life as being separate from the world) and that conciliar statements about religious life being a historical phenomenon, the diversity of charisms and the influence of that diversity on the embodiments of those charisms were not brought forward. After these dialogues, each bishop wrote a letter to the pope summarizing the sessions and evaluating the state of religious life in his diocese.

The Quinn Commission's report noted that part of its charge was to answer why there had been such an exodus from religious life and such a steep decline in the number of people entering. The commission observed that the questions they were asked to address shaped their report. They noted, "We are not asking such questions as, how did so many religious women and men pass through so profound a period of transition with perseverance and fidelity? Not, how can we account for the basic soundness of religious life in the United States?" [23]

To answer the questions on vocations, the committee gathered data, asked experts for feedback, and then obtained responses from a number of bishops, priests, and religious. The data indicated that the increase in vocations from World War II until 1960 was abnormal and that the fall off began before Vatican II. The study attributed some of that rise in women's communities to the return of men from the war, which dislocated women from work and public service. Some women felt called to continue such service and entered religious communities in order to do so. Even with the decline, the report notes, at the time of the study the Vatican Bureau of Statistics recorded that the United States had 6 percent of the total Catholic population, but 27 percent of the religious and 32 percent of all novices.

The report identified five general influences on the decline in religious vocations:

1. cultural factors;
2. impact of the Second Vatican Council;
3. developments in the church in the United States;
4. impact of all the above on religious communities as such;
5. experiences which have affected personal choices. [24]

The commission expanded its description of each of these factors. It noted that a significant cultural shift was occurring and that two previous shifts of similar magnitude in the West (the Reformation and the French Revolution) also initiated a decline in religious life, followed by a renascence. The report concludes this section with this statement:

> Nevertheless, there are many things in the culture that run counter to a relig-
> ious vocation and it does not seem that the time of cultural shift is completed.
> And so it is likely that we are not going to see a notable increase of religious
> vocations in the foreseeable future, and the current decline in numbers should
> probably be regarded as more systemic than as deriving from the fault of
> individuals of [sic] from the lack of religious spirit. [25]

In its concluding observations, the committee noted that recent popes had called for the promotion of women. It viewed this development as positive, while acknowledging that some strands of the women's movement were incompatible with church teaching. Nonetheless, the report made this con-nection with the decline in vocations:

> It is widely believed that this is also an important factor in vocations to the
> religious life of women. For instance, there is considerable and spreading
> concern over the limited scope for participation by women in policy and deci-
> sion-making roles in the church. In view of this, some potential candidates find
> other modes of service and hesitate to enter religious life. [26]

Pope John Paul II responded to the report of the commission and to the letters of individual bishops in a letter dated February 22, 1989. Some of the issues discussed in this letter are not named in the Quinn report; unfortunate-ly, there is no way of determining how often bishops cited these issues nor the degree of gravity they were accorded.

The pope summarized the strengths identified in the report and the letters he had received as "generous and varied service, greater prayer life, eminent professional competence, a serious response to renewal." Among the weaknesses, he listed "a decline in vocations, decreasing numbers and aging membership, inadequate theological foundation, weakened presence in or absence from the traditional apostolates, insufficient public witness, cases of excessive introspection, radical feminism, and polarization." He addressed the tension between consecration and mission—words which often functioned as shorthand for two different theologies or foci of religious life—by noting that there is a necessary unity between the two. The pope also identified the need for a sound theology of religious life. He affirmed the equality of women and men while asserting that "radical feminism" does not truly support women's full dignity. [27]

Perhaps the most interesting portion of the letter, in light of subsequent developments, is the section on conferences of major superiors. The core of this section states:

> A common concern that has been expressed both in the report and by many of you individually is that of polarization, particularly among women religious. The right of all major superiors of religious institutes of women to belong to the established conference is clear. The members have a right to make their concerns heard. The conference must find realistic and equitable ways to express the concerns of all women religious. Both as individual bishops in your own dioceses and as a conference of bishops you are called to exhort the various religious to find effective ways to remove the causes of their division. They must speak to one another about the issues which divide them; they must also rediscover and build on the shared patrimony of the church's teaching. This teaching on religious life has demonstrated its vitality through the documents of the Second Vatican Council, the Code of Canon Law and the various documents of the Holy See. Dialogue among religious should thus be based on this body of church teaching. [28]

Unfortunately, the pope's exhortation was not heeded. In 1987, the major superiors of communities connected with the Institute on Religious Life had formed a Forum of Major Superiors as a distinct group within the institute. With the assistance of Cardinal Hickey, who bypassed the bishops' conference and went directly to the pope and CICLSAL, the Council of Major Superiors of Women Religious (CMSWR) received formal approval in the spring of 1992, thus setting up a situation unique in the world: two canonical conferences for women religious in the same country.

Finally, in 1995, the Synod on Consecrated Life took place. *Vita Consecrata,* the post-synodal apostolic exhortation, contained an extended meditation on the church and on religious life in terms of Trinitarian communion. [29]

Phase Four: Hermeneutics of Continuity and Discontinuity

Papal Address to the Curia

In April 2005, Cardinal Joseph Ratzinger was elected pope becoming Pope Benedict XVI. His Christmas address to the Roman Curia that year identified several themes which became hallmarks of his papacy. Noting that it had been forty years since the end of Vatican II, Pope Benedict asked, "Why has the implementation of the council, in large parts of the church, thus far been so difficult?" He answered, "Well, it all depends on the correct interpretation of the council or—as we would say today—on its proper hermeneutics, the correct key to its interpretation and application."[30] Since the council, there has been a conflict of interpretations between what he called "a hermeneutic of discontinuity and rupture" and a "hermeneutic of reform" or continuity. According to Pope Benedict, the former approach acknowledges that the texts of the council were the result of compromise and that, to discern the true spirit of the council, one needs to focus on what it had said that was new. Those who adhere to this approach understand these texts should be understood as the starting point of a trajectory that would initiate significant new developments for the church. According to the pope, adopting such an interpretation of the council leads to confusion.

The "hermeneutic of reform" focuses on continuity, seeing the church as always remaining the same, although developing over time. This interpretation "silently . . . bore and is bearing fruit." Later in his address, however, the pope looked at issues such as religious liberty and interfaith relationships, areas where the council did come to new positions without, however, abandoning core principles. Acknowledging the reality of historical developments, Benedict observed:

> It is precisely in this combination of continuity and discontinuity at different levels that the very nature of true reform consists. In this process of innovation in continuity we must learn to understand more practically than before that the church's decisions on contingent matters—for example, certain practical forms of liberalism or a free interpretation of the Bible—should necessarily be contingent themselves, precisely because they refer to a specific reality that is changeable in itself. It was necessary to learn to recognize that in these decisions it is only the principles that express the permanent aspect, since they remain as an undercurrent, motivating decisions from within.
>
> On the other hand, not so permanent are the practical forms that depend on the historical situation and are therefore subject to change. Basic decisions, therefore, continue to be well-grounded, whereas the way they are applied to new contexts can change.
>
> The Second Vatican Council, with its new definition of the relationship between the faith of the church and certain essential elements of modern thought, has reviewed or even corrected certain historical decisions, but in this

apparent discontinuity it has actually preserved and deepened her inmost nature and true identity.[31]

So in addressing polarization, it is interesting to note the questions the council addressed and which continued to be raised in the forty years since its conclusion. What needs to be changed? Are there illegitimate accommodations or a true recovery of what is most deeply at the heart of the matter and expressed differently in new historical circumstances? These were the same questions with which religious had struggled during the twenty or so years of the renewal process leading to their rewriting their constitutions. Furthermore, given the fact that religious life is a historical phenomenon, while it is a distinctive "lifeform" to use the phrase of Sandra Schneiders, IHM, there is also much about it that could be considered examples of what Benedict called "practical forms that depend on the historical situation and are therefore subject to change."[32]

Pope Benedict continued to raise these questions throughout his papacy; they were also contentious points in ongoing debates about matters liturgical (including texts), the theology of the ministerial priesthood *vis-à-vis* the priesthood of all believers, the ministry of women in the church, approaches to the study of Scripture, as well as the ongoing tensions about religious life in this country.

Stonehill College Symposium

On September 27, 2008, Stonehill College and the Fall River Diocese co-hosted a symposium on religious life titled "Apostolic Religious Life since Vatican II . . . Reclaiming the Treasure: Bishops, Theologians and Religious in Conversation." Sara Butler, MSBT, analyzed the "factions" in religious life, identifying as a key cause of polarization "different ecclesiologies," which she characterized as a hierarchically structured church versus an egalitarian community, between groups obedient to the teaching authority of the church and those who, under the influence of radical feminism, reject either hierarchical authority *per se* or certain teachings or the manner of exercising that authority. Butler asserted that the "anti-hierarchical option" seemed to be favored by some congregational leaders and by the leadership of LCWR and the Conference of Major Superiors of Men (CMSM) and she asked, "Are our institutes well served by these conferences? Is the Holy See well served? Is it time, perhaps, for a formal 'visitation'?" A little further in her speech, she asked about bishops: "Have they no interest in the spiritual well-being of religious who find themselves exiles in their own institutes? Have our bishops washed their hands of us?"[33]

At the same conference, Cardinal Rodé, then prefect of CICLSAL, gave an address titled "Reforming Religious Life with the Right Hermeneutic." Grounding his presentation in frequent references to Pope Benedict's 2005

address to the Curia, Rodé asserted, "This hermeneutics of rupture had domi-
nated the attempts at renewal of religious life." Renewal, he claimed, was far
more characterized by uncritical adaptation to contemporary conditions than
by return to what *Perfectae Caritatis* calls "the sources of all Christian life
and to the original spirit of the institutes." Furthermore, Cardinal Rodé noted
"Religious life was not an isolated battle-ground"; much so-called *aggiornamento* throughout the church was tainted with egotism, naturalism, and the
rejection of authority. Its bitter fruit has been disobedience, jettisoning of
prayer and asceticism, loss of vocations, and "social and political agitation."
Some religious, however, have chosen the path of continuity and bear good
fruit. So the appropriate renewal of religious life is key, for "the renewal of
the church in this great country, and her ability to serve, necessarily passes
through the renewal of religious life."[34]

The Apostolic Visitation

On November 17, 2008, at an audience with Pope Benedict XVI, Cardinal
Rodé received permission for the Apostolic Visitation. This investigation
was announced on January 30, 2009. In a statement issued November 3,
2009, Cardinal Rodé said, "This apostolic visitation hopes to encourage vocations and assure a better future for women religious." The following day,
in an interview on Vatican Radio, Rodé said he had been considering an
apostolic visitation before he attended the symposium at Stonehill College;
that conference helped him understand the magnitude of the problems United
States religious encountered. However, he had already heard numerous concerns from American Catholics about "some irregularities or omissions in
American religious life. Most of all, you could say, it involves a certain
secular mentality that has spread in these religious families and, perhaps, also
a certain 'feminist' spirit."[35]

IN RETROSPECT

In reviewing the remote and proximate, concrete and more theological factors which led to the Apostolic Visitation of women religious in the United
States, several important themes or issues have emerged. Many of these
issues have received far more extensive treatment elsewhere. For the purpose
of this study, six issues seem most significant.

Theology of Religious Life

According to *Lumen Gentium,* religious life is an integral part of the church's
life. Just as Christian marriage effectively witnesses to the ideal of covenantal fidelity between Christ and the church, so religious life effectively wit-

nesses to the community of those baptized into Christ as a community in mission. Religious life is not only a theological reality; it is also an historical phenomenon which has existed in a marvelous diversity of modes over the centuries. Throughout the history of the church, new forms of religious life have emerged ranging from monastic communities to communities more closely resembling what are now called "secular institutes." The question of legitimate pluralism is as old as the birth of these new ways of living Christian life. As many institutes of women religious rediscovered the spirit and intentions of their founders, they realized that their congregations had been required to conform to a more monastic form of religious life in order to obtain canonical recognition. To be true to their charism, they needed to move away from the monastic end of the spectrum toward what Sandra Schneiders, IHM, calls "ministerial religious life."[36]

Feminism

Despite repeated assurances on the part of members of the hierarchy of the value and worth of women, of women's equal dignity before God, of the need to promote women's dignity, when women religious speak and act from the same convictions, they are warned against the dangers of feminism, often modified by the adjective "radical" and connoting a stance completely antithetical to the gospel. Rarely, and perhaps never, is there an acknowledgement of the various strands and schools of feminist thought.

Reform and Renewal

In obedience to the call of the council, women religious engaged in the painful and graced process of renewal. The conciliar and post-conciliar directives that everyone should be involved in renewal were potentially revolutionary, setting up a new cycle of theory and practice. The mandate to return to the sources of Christian and religious life opened up history. In doing so, many congregations, particularly those whose roots stretched back beyond the nineteenth century, recovered models and practices of authority, obedience, and governance that differed from those exercised in what Avery Dulles, SJ, describes as the "institutional model" of church.[37] Dialogue, authority as service, participative structures and processes, mutual discernment—all of these were consonant with the call to evangelize structures and consistent with a model of the church understood as a differentiated communion in and with and through the differentiated communion of the Trinity. What some might characterize, then, as radical subjectivism, uncritical inculturation, rupture, discontinuity, rejection of authority, may often be the result of inhabiting a different—and legitimate—model of church as a result of making Christ the norm, evangelizing structures, recovering an institute's heritage, and participating in the process of renewal.

In *Evangelii Gaudium* (EG), *The Joy of the Gospel*, Pope Francis speaks of an "ecclesial renewal which cannot be deferred," a "missionary option . . . capable of transforming everything, so that the church's customs, ways of doing things, times and schedules, language and structures can be suitably channeled for the evangelization of today's world rather than for her self-preservation" (27). Such a missionary conversion must take place at every level of the church, including the diocese and the papacy, in order to foster "missionary communion." Sections 25 through 33 of this apostolic exhortation seem to parallel closely the process of renewal undertaken by many religious communities as well as their current understandings of the role and practice of authority.[38]

Autonomy and Unity

Conciliar and post-conciliar teachings acknowledge that religious institutes have a "rightful autonomy" and are not part of the hierarchical structure of the church. This autonomy exists within the communion of all the baptized, a communion served by the Petrine ministry and, in the local church, by the local ordinary. Such autonomy is also balanced by the need for collaboration and ministerial coordination. When inevitable tensions arise, too often the temptation can be to resort to a rhetoric of obedience and subordination, rather than to engage in respectful mutual dialogue and discernment. *Mutuae Relationes* was a response to such tensions; Pope Francis has indicated that that document needs to be updated to address current realities.

Reception of Vatican II

In the Catholic tradition, reception is the process in which the Spirit-filled members of the church recognize their faith in a decision, text, or council. It is not unusual for this process to be lengthy, messy, and unfortunately, even acrimonious. Most institutes of American women religious engaged early and intensely with the program of Vatican II and, in the process, underwent profound transformation. It is not surprising, then, that what they experienced internally and resolved through sustained prayer, study, experimentation, and dialogue still characterizes the ongoing reception of Vatican II within the broader ecclesial community. What religious were asked to do—return to the sources and adapt to the needs of the times, involving everyone in the process—is a task in which the whole church must engage.

Christian existence, on both personal and communal levels, is a constant conversion to the gospel. Throughout the two millennia of the church's history, reforms have been initiated by individuals and by groups, by rulers or other laity, by members of the clergy and hierarchy, and by religious. Prior to Vatican II, Pope Pius XII and the Sacred Congregation of Religious had called for reforms in religious life which were more or less heeded. The council and subsequent documents intensified and specified that mandate. As a fruit of their obedience to that call, many religious have worked in parishes, dioceses, schools, social ministries, and a wide variety of other organizations to implement that vision. If religious life can be understood as a sacrament (effective sign) of the church as a community in mission, then religious, if they have been faithful to their unique prophetic vocation as "experts in communion," have a particular competence which is, or can be, a gift for the whole church.[39] In their attempts to re-evangelize their lives and structures, religious communities have gleaned practical knowledge which may provide insights into the church's nature as a communion. Their experience of adaptation may also be helpful to the whole church and thus fulfill the innovative function of religious life, which Johannes Metz describes as creating "productive models for the church as a whole in the business of growing accustomed to living in new social, economic, intellectual, and cultural situations."[40]

Failure of Dialogue and Charity

Without apportioning blame, the split, now institutionalized and officially recognized, between women religious in the United States, is a source of pain and probably scandal. There have been attempts to resolve the differences over the years, but the division seems to be intractable. What would it mean for us all to act as "experts in communion" with our sisters in vowed life? Sister Sara Butler's words at the Stonehill College Symposium surely express the desire of most women religious: "We would like to get beyond the stress of being suspicious and being under suspicion, and enter into a realm where we are recognized as a resource, where we are needed and wanted, where we can make a corporate impact through ministerial service that is coordinated with or supplements diocesan plans."[41]

BEYOND THE IMPASSE: A NEW HERMENEUTIC?

The election of Pope Francis on March 13, 2013, seems to have inaugurated a new phase in post-conciliar history. He is the first pope since the council not to have been directly involved in Vatican II, the first pope from Latin America, and the first pope to have experienced renewal as a member of a religious institute. In his encyclical, "The Joy of the Gospel," (33) Pope Francis limns a vision of "pastoral ministry in a missionary key." Chapter 1, in which he presents this vision, concludes with these words:

I do not want a church concerned with being at the center and then ends by being caught up in a web of obsessions and procedures. If something should rightly disturb us and trouble our consciences, it is the fact that so many of our brothers and sisters are living without the strength, light and consolation born of friendship with Jesus Christ, without a community of faith to support them, without meaning and a goal in life. More than by fear of going astray, my hope is that we will be moved by the fear of remaining shut up within structures which give us a false sense of security, within rules which make us harsh judges, within habits which make us feel safe, while at our door people are starving and Jesus does not tire of saying to us: "Give them something to eat" (Mk 6:37; EG 49).

It is to this vision and this command that all of us, whatever our ecclesiology, theology, charism, conference of religious, must respond. Whatever there is in any of us that diminishes or obscures the "perfection of charity" and the joy of the gospel needs to be exorcised. In the transforming power of the Spirit, we hope that this might be the fruit of the Apostolic Visitation.

NOTES

1. Pius XII, *Fidei Donum, Encyclical of Pope Pius XII on the Present Condition of the Catholic Missions, Especially in Africa*, April 21, 1957, http://www.vatican.va/holy_father/pius_xii/encyclicals/documents/hf_p-xii_enc_21041957_fidei-donum_en.html.

2. For further understanding of the Sister Formation Movement see Mary L. Schneiders, "The Transformation of American Women Religious" (working paper, Cushwa Center for the Study of American Catholicism, University of Notre Dame, Notre Dame, IN, 1986) and "American Sisters and the Roots of Change," *U.S. Catholic Historian* 7 (Winter 1988), 55–72. This movement was significant in the pre-Vatican II emergence of a new theology among American sisters. Accordingly the post-Vatican II response of American sisters can be understood only in light of these and other pre-conciliar movements to adapt religious life to the needs of the contemporary world.

3. Paul VI, *Lumen Gentium, Dogmatic Constitution on the Church*, in *The Documents of Vatican II*, ed. Walter A. Abbott, SJ (Piscataway, NJ: America Press, 1966), 14–96. Vatican II documents are referenced by section numbers, in parenthesis.

4. Paul VI, *Perfectae Caritatis, Decree on the Appropriate Renewal of the Religious Life*, in *The Documents of Vatican II*, ed. Walter A. Abbott, SJ, 466–482.

5. Paul VI, *Sacrosanctum Concilium, Constitution on the Sacred Liturgy*, in *The Documents of Vatican II*, ed. Walter A. Abbott, SJ (Piscataway, NJ: America Press, 1966), 137–182.

6. Paul VI, *Ecclesiae Sanctae, Implementing Four Council Decrees*, August 6, 1966, http://www.papalencyclicals.net/Paul06/p6ecclss.htm.

7. The name of the Vatican congregation for religious has changed several times. Until 1967, it was Sacred Congregation of Religious; in 1967, it became Sacred Congregation for the Religious and Secular Institutes (SCRIS). In 1984, it became Congregation for the Religious and Secular Institutes. In 1988, it became Congregation for Institutes of Consecrated Life and Societies of Apostolic Life (CICLSAL).

8. Paul VI, *Evangelica Testificato, Apostolic Exhortation on the Renewal of Religious Life According to the Teaching of the Second Vatican Council*, June 29, 1971, http://www.vatican.va/holy_father/paul_vi/apost_exhortations/documents/hf_p-vi_exh_19710629_evangelica-testificatio_en.html.

9. The charism of a religious congregation refers to the distinctive spirit that animates a religious community and gives it a particular character. Embodied in an original way in the

congregation's founder or foundress, the charism becomes contagious and is caught and lived by the community's members. Throughout the unfolding history of a religious congregation its members give expression to the community's charism in the unique and ever-changing circumstances of the times.

10. Synod of Bishops, *Justice in the World*, 1971, www.cctwincities.org/document.doc?id= 69.

11. Sacred Congregation for Religious and for Secular Institutes and Sacred Congregation for Bishops, *Mutuae Relationes, Directives for Mutual Relations Between Bishops and Religious in the Church*, May 14, 1978, http://www.vatican.va/roman_curia/congregations/ccscrlife/documents/rc_con_ccscrlife_doc_14051978_mutuae-relationes_en.html.

12. Sacred Congregation for Religious and for Secular Institutes, *Religious and Human Promotion*, promulgated August 12, 1980, http://www.vatican.va/roman_curia/congregations/ccscrlife/documents/rc_con_ccscrlife_doc_12081980_religious-and-human-promotion_en.html. Plenaria of the Sacred Congregation for Religious and Secular Institutes, April 25–28, 1978.

13. Thomas S. Kuhn, *The Structure of Scientific Revolutions*, 2nd ed., International Encyclopedia of Unified Science (Chicago: University of Chicago Press, 1970), 2, no. 2:89–90.

14. Everett M. Rogers, *Diffusion of Innovations* (Glencoe, Illinois: Free Press, 1962), 150.

15. For a personal account of the story of the tension between Cardinal McIntyre and the Sisters of the Immaculate Heart of Mary, see Anita M. Caspary, *Witness to Integrity: The Crisis of the Immaculate Heart Community of California* (Collegeville, MN: Liturgical Press, 2003).

16. John Paul II, *Redemptionis Donum, Apostolic Exhortation to Men and Women Religious on their Consecration in Light of the Mystery of the Redemption*, March 25, 1984, http://www.vatican.va/holy_father/john_paul_ii/apost_exhortations/documents/hf_jp-ii_exh_25031984_redemptionis-donum_en.html.

17. Two dates are given for the initiation of this study. The commission's report states that John Paul II's letter was dated June 1984 (*Origins* 16:25 [December 4, 1986]). However, in a letter to the United States bishops dated February 22, 1989, in which the pope responds to the report of the Quinn Commission, he states that he had written on April 3, 1983 (*Origins* 18:44 [April 13, 1989]).

18. John Paul II to Bishops of the United States, April 3, 1983, http://www.vatican.va/holy_father/john_paul_ii/letters/documents/hf_jp-ii_let_03041983_us-bishops_en.html.

19. Sacred Congregation for Religious and for Secular Institutes, *Essential Elements in the Church's Teaching on Religious Life as Applied to Institutes Dedicated to Works of the Apostolate*, May 31, 1983.

20. Paul VI, *Ecclesiam Suam, Encyclical on the Church*, promulgated on August 6, 1964, http://www.vatican.va/holy_father/paul_vi/encyclicals/documents/hf_p-vi_enc_06081964_ecclesiam_en.html; John R. Quinn, Thomas C. Kelly, OP, and Raymond W. Lessard, "A Report to the Bishops of the United States on the Work of the Pontifical Commission on Religious Life," *Origins* 16, no. 25 (December 4, 1986): 467.

21. Quinn, Kelly, and Lessard, "A Report to the Bishops of the United States," 467.

22. ibid., 467–468.

23. ibid., 468.

24. ibid., 469.

25. ibid.

26. ibid.

27. John Paul II to Bishops of the United States, February 22, 1989, http://www.vatican.va/holy_father/john_paul_ii/letters/1989/documents/hf_jp-ii_let_19890222_vescovi-usa_en.html.

28. ibid.

29. John Paul II, *Vita Consecrata, Apostolic Exhortation to the Bishops and Clergy, Religious Orders and Congregations, Societies of Apostolic Life, Secular Institutes, and all the Faithful on the Consecrated Life and its Mission in the Church and in the World*, March 25, 1996, http://www.vatican.va/holy_father/john_paul_ii/apost_exhortations/documents/hf_jp-ii_exh_25031996_vita-consecrata_en.html.

30. Benedict XVI, "Address of His Holiness Benedict XVI to the Roman Curia Offering Them his Christmas Greetings," address, December 22, 2005, http://www.vatican.va/holy_

father/benedict_xvi/speeches/2005/december/documents/hf_ben_xvi_spe_20051222_roman-curia_en.html.

31. ibid.

32. Benedict XVI quoted in Sandra M. Schneiders, IHM, *Finding the Treasure: Locating Catholic Religious Life in a New Ecclesial and Cultural Context,* vol. 1, *Religious Life in a New Millennium* (New York/Mahwah, New Jersey: Paulist Press, 2000), 54–66.

33. Sara Butler, MSBT, "Apostolic Religious Life: A Public, Eccesial Vocation," speech presented at Stonehill College Symposium on Apostolic Religious Life Since Vatican II...Reclaiming the Treasure: Bishops, Theologians, and Religious in Conversation, North Easton, MA, September 27, 2012, Zenit, last modified October 13, 2012, http://www.zenit.org/en/articles/sister-butler-at-symposium-on-consecrated-life.

34. Franc Cardinal Rodé, CM, "Reforming Religious Life with the Right Hermeneutic," speech presented at Stonehill College Symposium on Apostolic Religious Life since Vatican II ... Reclaiming the Treasure: Bishops, Theologians, and Religious in Conversation, Stonehill College, North Easton, Massachusetts, U.S.A., September 27, 2008, Zenit, last modified October 13, 2008, http://www.zenit.org/en/articles/cardinal-rode-at-symposium-on-consecrated-life.

35. Franc Cardinal Rodé interview with Vatican Radio, by Cindy Wooden, "Cardinal Rodé Defends Apostolic Visitation of U.S. Nuns," Catholic News Service, last modified November 5, 2009, http://www.catholicnews.com/data/stories/cns/0904882.htm.

36. Sandra M. Schneiders, IHM, *Prophets in Their Own Country: Women Religious Bearing Witness to the Gospel in a Troubled Church* (Maryknoll, NY: Orbis Books, 2011), 7.

37. Avery Dulles, SJ, *Models of the Church* (New York: Image Books, Doubleday, 2002). In his book Avery Dulles provides an overview of the main models of church demonstrating the strengths and weaknesses of each model and integrating each model's positive contribution to form a more comprehensive model of church.

38. Francis, *Evangelii Gaudium (Joy of the Gospel) Apostolic Exhortation to the Bishops, Clergy, Consecrated Persons, and the Lay Faithful on the Proclamation of the Gospel in Today's World*, November 24, 2013, http://www.vatican.va/evangelii-gaudium/en/#1/z.

39. Congregation for Institutes of Consecrated Life and Societies of Apostolic Life, *Fraternal Life in Community,* section 10, (Vatican City: Congregation for Institutes of Consecrated Life and Societies of Apostolic Life, 1994), http://www.vatican.va/roman_curia/congregations/ccscrlife/documents/rc_con_ccscrlife_doc_02021994_fraternal-life-in-community_en.html. The entire document develops the significance of communion in the whole church and in religious life in particular.

40. Johannes B. Metz, *Followers of Christ: Perspectives on Religious Life*, trans. Thomas Linton (New York: Burns & Oates/Paulist Press, 1978), 11.

41. Butler, "Apostolic Religious Life."

Chapter Three

Tracing the Apostolic Visitation through a Chronology of Primary Sources

Jean Wincek and Nancy Reynolds

This chapter tells the story of the Apostolic Visitation by documenting the sequence of events chronologically through primary sources such as letters, news conferences, press releases, and information posted on the official Apostolic Visitation website.[1] The richness of first-hand communications on the part of the initiators of the Visitation, those officially responsible for carrying it forward, and the women religious who were the focus of the Visitation reveals the variegated texture of the event and gives a glimpse as to how the Visitation unfolded experientially from those multiple perspectives.

SIGNIFICANT EVENTS PRIOR TO THE ANNOUNCEMENT OF THE APOSTOLIC VISITATION

In the months before the announcement of the Apostolic Visitation, events occurred which gave hints of what was to come. One of these events was the annual meeting of the leadership of the Leadership Conference of Women Religious (LCWR) with various offices in Rome. The second was the Stonehill College Symposium which was part of the 200th anniversary celebration of the Boston Archdiocese.

In 2008, when the LCWR President Mary Whited, CPPS, Past President Mary Dacey, SSJ, President Elect J. Lora Dambroski, OSF, and Executive Director Carole Shinnick, SSND, went to Rome for their annual visit, they met for two hours on March 31 with Cardinal Franc Rodé, CM, of the Congregation for Institutes of Consecrated Life and Societies of Apostolic

Life (CICLSAL) and several other members of CICLSAL. The cardinal raised questions about community life, recruitment and formation of new members, and living the vows.[2] No mention was made of the possibility of an apostolic visitation at this meeting.

On September 27, 2008, at the Stonehill College Symposium, Cardinal Rodé delivered the keynote address entitled, "Apostolic Religious Life since Vatican II . . . Reclaiming the Treasure: Bishops, Theologians, and Religious in Conversation." In the speech he said, "All is not well with religious life in America. My remarks today are addressed especially to the active religious."[3] Cardinal Rodé's audience with Pope Benedict XVI was only seven weeks away and his remarks presaged the announcement of an apostolic visitation.

On November 3, 2009, Cardinal Rodé released a statement in which he asserted that the multitude and complexity of issues regarding women religious in the United States had been made clear to him at the Stonehill College Symposium. He concluded at that time that "an evaluation of the challenges facing individual religious and their congregations could benefit the church at-large as well as the sisters and institutes involved." And, he expressed his hope that a thorough analysis of the condition of religious life in the United States would be "a realistic and graced opportunity for personal and community introspection."[4]

OFFICIAL ANNOUNCEMENT OF THE APOSTOLIC VISITATION

On January 30, 2009, a news release and a news conference announced the first-ever canonical investigation of an entire class of persons—an Apostolic Visitation of institutes of women religious in the United States initiated by Cardinal Franc Rodé.[5] Citing the decree[6] issued five weeks earlier on December 22, 2008, the news release stated that the Visitation was being undertaken "in order to look into the quality of the life of religious women in the United States."[7]

Continuing to reference the decree, the news release specified that, with the faculties granted to him by Pope Benedict XVI in an audience on November 17, 2008, Cardinal Rodé had selected Mother Mary Clare Millea, ASCJ, superior general of the Apostles of the Sacred Heart of Jesus, as the Apostolic Visitator "of the General Houses, Provincial Houses and Centers of Initial Formation of the principal Religious Institutes of Women in the United States of America." The decree further advised that when the Apostolic Visitation was complete, Mother Mary Clare had the responsibility of sending a detailed report to CICLSAL. The report was to be based on the information she gathered and was to include suggestions she deemed appropriate. Additionally, the decree stated that Mother Mary Clare was to seek information from the bishops in whose dioceses the general houses, provincial houses, and centers of initial formation were located.

The news release clarified that the Visitation would be limited to apostolic institutes, "those actively engaged in service to church and society." In the news release Mother Mary Clare was quoted as saying, "I know that the object of this Visitation is to encourage and strengthen apostolic communities of women religious, for the simple reason that these communities are integral to the entire life of the Catholic Church, in the United States and beyond."[8]

On the same day as the news release, January 30, 2009, a news conference was conducted by Sister Eva-Maria Ackerman, a member of the American Province of the Sisters of St. Francis of the Martyr St. George, at the Basilica of the National Shrine of the Immaculate Conception in Washington, D.C. Sister Eva-Maria communicated that a few hours before the start of the news conference, leaders of LCWR and CMSWR had received a letter from Cardinal Rodé announcing an Apostolic Visitation of the principal religious institutes of women in the United States.

In looking into the quality of life of approximately 59,000 women religious from more than 400 religious congregations in the United States, Sister Eva-Maria said, "We hope to discover and share the vibrancy and purpose that continue to accomplish so much, as well as to understand the obstacles and challenges that inhibit these individuals and institutions, thus limiting their growth and/or re-directing their resources and outreach."[9]

Sister Eva-Maria explained that the process was expected to take two years to complete and would have several stages. First, Mother Mary Clare would invite superiors general to make personal contact with her in the United States or in Rome to give her voluntary input. In the second stage, major superiors would be asked for information such as statistics, activities, and community practices. The third stage would consist of selected on-site visits. The focus of this process was for sisters "to have the opportunity to share with visiting teams their joys and hopes, challenges and concerns about their lives as women religious in the church today." The final stage would be the compilation and delivery of "a comprehensive and confidential review by Mother Mary Clare to Cardinal Rodé."[10]

Notification of the Apostolic Visitation to individual congregations of women religious came in a letter dated February 2, 2009 from Cardinal Rodé to superiors. In addition to delineating the phases of the Visitation, he indicated that he had authorized the creation of a website, www.apostolicvisitation.org, "to communicate basic information about the Visitation to interested parties."[11] Cardinal Rodé stressed the fact that the report Mother Mary Clare would send him would be confidential, "regarding each institute that is surveyed and/or visited" and also a "composite report on the quality of women's apostolic religious life in the United States, based on the results of the three phases of the Visitation."[12] The letter gave major superiors information on the first phase of the Visitation, urging them to communicate with the Apostolic Visitor regarding their observations and hopes for their sisters in the United States. He specified that the communication with Mother Mary Clare could be made by letter, phone, or personal meeting, either in Rome or in the United States, and should be completed by July 31, 2009.

RESPONSES FROM WOMEN'S RELIGIOUS LEADERSHIP TO THE ANNOUNCEMENT OF THE APOSTOLIC VISITATION

On February 20, 2009, the LCWR issued the following statement on the Apostolic Visitation:

> The members of the National Board of the Leadership Conference of Women Religious, along with the conference's members, await further information from the Congregation for Institutes of Consecrated Life and Societies of Apostolic Life on the recently announced Visitation of U.S. women religious. The planned Visitation comes as a surprise to the conference and its purpose and implications for the lives of U.S. women religious remain unclear. With additional information leaders can better determine how their participation in the Visitation can be beneficial to U.S. religious life, the church and the world. . . . The LCWR board noted that the unanticipated news of the Visitation has evoked a variety of responses in women religious, has generated questions on what the Visitation might involve, and has prompted deliberations on how best to proceed with it. In addition to offering resources to members in preparation for the Visitation, the board encouraged leaders to reflect on the stories of heroic service and creative fidelity of their own members. . . . Noting that preparation for the Apostolic Visitation deserves time and careful thought they suggested leaders invite their members to bring the Visitation into their prayer and contemplation. [13]

Mother Mary Quentin Sheridan, RSM, chairperson of the Council of Major Superiors of Women Religious released the following statement:

> On the occasion of the Apostolic Visitation of Women Religious in the United States, the Council of Major Superiors of Women Religious would like to express gratitude to Mother Mary Clare Millea, ASCJ, and to her staff for saying "yes" to this significant work. The council welcomes the Visitation and we ask our membership to pray for this endeavor and to cooperate in whatever way necessary in order that the Visitation will be a fruitful outcome for all women religious in the United States for the sake of the church. [14]

The board of directors of the International Union of Superiors General also made a statement encouraging their members whose congregations would be engaged in this process "to cooperate fully throughout the different phases with those who will carry it out." The statement read:

> We pray that the Visitation will facilitate mutual understanding among all parties involved and illuminate both the vitality and the challenges of religious life in the United States. . . . [W]e affirm unequivocally our support for our sisters in the United States. Their response to the mandates of the Second Vatican Council, particularly as stated in *Perfectae Caritatis*, has been a great gift not only to the pluralistic society in which they live but also to the universal church."[15]

TRACING PHASE I OF THE APOSTOLIC VISITATION PROCESS

Phase 1 one-on-one appointments with Mother Mary Clare were scheduled for approximately one hour. In requesting an appointment to dialogue with Mother Mary Clare, one congregation whose leadership model was that of a team asked that, in fidelity to their team model, the entire team be included in the meeting with her. Anne Walsh, ASCJ, staff member in the Apostolic Visitation office, responded by saying that in this stage of the process, Mother Mary Clare was meeting only with the superior general of each congregation. However, Mother Mary Clare was willing to meet informally with other sisters on the leadership team after her meeting with the superior general.[16]

In a Phase 1 June update on the Apostolic Visitation website, Mother Mary Clare reported that she had had personal conversations with 127 superiors general of institutes of women religious at meeting sites in Rome, Los Angeles, St. Louis, Chicago, and Hamden, Connecticut and that about fifty other congregational leaders responded by letter. She explained that, in preparation for the meetings, the major superiors with their councils or sometimes with their whole congregation reflected on the current realities of their congregations. She affirmed,

> I believe that some of the finest Catholic women religious in the United States have shared their stories, hopes, dreams, and concerns about the sisters they love and the congregations to which they have generously given their lives . . . The superiors I have met have displayed a deep desire to articulate their congregation's commitment to serving the needs of the church today in accordance with their founding charism.[17]

The Apostolic Visitation office also posted on its website twenty-one testimonials from superiors general who visited with Mother Mary Clare. The superiors described her as personable, welcoming, cordial, curious, encouraging, and easy to be with. One superior in the St. Louis area described how, prior to their meeting with her, leaders in that area met to support one another and pray together. Another leader said that while she was visiting with Mother Mary Clare, her whole congregation came together nationally and internationally to pray a prayer prepared especially for this occasion and to sit in contemplative silence together for the hour. [18]

PHASE I AS SPRINGBOARD FOR SUBSEQUENT PHASES OF THE VISITATION

On May 19, 2009, Mother Mary Clare wrote a letter to superiors general saying that the conversations she had with them "are not only widening my understanding of the diversity of religious life, with all of its lights and shadows, but are also helping me to shape subsequent phases of the Apostolic Visitation." [19] She explained that in August each generalate and/or province of the apostolic congregations in the United States would receive a questionnaire regarding various aspects of its life and ministry. After she had carefully studied the results, she would designate various congregations for an on-site visit in 2010. In that same letter of May 19, Mother Mary Clare offered each superior general the opportunity to suggest names of potential team members. Because these team members would be acting in the name of the Apostolic See, they were also required to make a public profession of faith and take an oath of fidelity to the Apostolic See in Rome. Male religious were eligible to be appointed to teams but would only be assigned to visit congregations that indicated they would welcome a member of a men's religious congregation. Additionally, in the content of the letter, Mother Mary Clare identified the qualifications for visiting team members:

- at least twenty years of religious profession in an institute of Pontifical or Diocesan right;
- current membership in good standing in her/his own religious institute, with active and passive voice therein;
- clear and consistent witness to faithful religious living, in accord with congregational and ecclesial norms;
- spiritual, human, and practical wisdom drawn from extensive experience in interpersonal relationships, both within the community and in ministry;
- ability to respect confidentiality, listen attentively, and dialogue honestly;
- capacity for working collaboratively with a team in drawing clear and fair conclusions;
- ability to perceive, verify, and clarify essential ideas and data;
- ability to prepare a written report in a timely manner which is objective, unbiased, accurate, and succinct;
- ability to identify strengths and areas of concern based on data gathered. [20]

CARDINAL RODÉ'S ENGAGEMENT OF THE U.S. BISHOPS WITH THE APOSTOLIC VISITATION PROCESSES

On July 14, 2009, Cardinal Rodé sent a letter to the bishops of the United States expressing his pleasure that Mother Mary Clare was able to present information about the Apostolic Visitation during the spring meeting of the United States Conference of Catholic Bishops. Cardinal Rodé called for the support of the bishops in the effort to:

• look into the quality of life of apostolic women religious in the United States;
• learn more about the varied and unique ways in which apostolic women religious contribute to the welfare of the church and society;
• assist the church to strengthen and support the growth of the apostolic congregations to which approximately 59,000 women religious in the United States belong.[21]

Cardinal Rodé further stated that he had asked the Apostolic Visitator to be in communication with the bishops regarding the women religious in their dioceses. Noting that the projected budget for the three-year project is $1,100,000, he asked the bishops for help in offsetting the expenses.[22]

PREPARATION FOR PHASE 2 OF THE APOSTOLIC VISITATION

On July 28, 2009, Mother Mary Clare sent a letter to superiors of institutes of women religious outlining the content of the *Instrumentum Laboris* which consisted of two parts and contained four appendices.[23] Part A described the nature and purpose of the Apostolic Visitation, the four procedural phases of the Visitation process, and referenced documents about religious life, especially those of Vatican II and pertinent post-conciliar documents, critical to guiding all phases of the Visitation process. Part B provided topics and corresponding reflection questions on the identity of the religious institute, governance, vocation promotion, admission and formation policies, spiritual life and common life, mission and ministry, and financial information. In the letter Mother Mary Clare encouraged major superiors to make the *Instrumentum Laboris* available to every sister for reflection and conversation with other sisters in preparation for Phase 2, a written questionnaire to be completed by major superiors. The letter advised that this questionnaire was in the process of being prepared and would be available in early fall.[24]

In describing the nature and purpose of the Apostolic Visitation, the *Instrumentum Laboris* noted that the "specific task of the Visitation is to look into the quality of the life of women religious in the United States who are members of apostolic religious institutes" and

> Particular attention will be given to the significant witness of the vowed commitment given by women religious within the heritage of each institute's charism and in fidelity to the church's teachings and to the renewal indicated by Vatican Council II and post-conciliar documents. It will examine, for example, promotion and retention of vocations; initial and ongoing formation; the concrete living out of the evangelical counsels; common life and religious houses; the structures and practical application of internal governance; the soundness of doctrine held and taught by the religious; the nature and variety of apostolic works; and the overall administration of temporal goods.[25]

According to the *Instrumentum Laboris*, the Visitation was intended as a "constructive assessment and an expression of genuine concern for the quality of the life of all members of apostolic institutes of women religious in the United States" which hoped to "identify the challenges women religious face and to promote and encourage fidelity, integrity, and growth within religious life."[26]

LCWR ASSEMBLY RESPONSE TO THE UNFOLDING VISITATION PROCESSES

Following its annual assembly in New Orleans, Louisiana, the LCWR issued a press release on August 17, 2009, stating that the assembly discussed the Apostolic Visitation. The LCWR press release noted that the leaders of religious congregations believed their orders had always been fully accountable to the church and that they planned to collaborate with the Vatican in these studies. However, leaders had concerns about the lack of full disclosure regarding the motivation and funding sources for the studies. They also objected to the fact that their congregations would not see the reports that would be sent to the Vatican. The press release continued:

> Throughout the assembly, the leaders emphasized that their orders have remained faithful to the reform and renewal of their communities called for by the Second Vatican Council that urged women and men religious to adapt their lives, prayer, and work so they may most effectively fulfill their mission. They reclaimed their commitment to what they believe is the unique and needed role of religious life which includes serving at and speaking from the margins of the Catholic Church.[27]

TRACING PHASE 2 OF THE APOSTOLIC VISITATION:
QUESTIONNAIRE AND CONGREGATIONAL RESPONSES

Phase 2 of the Apostolic Visitation consisted of a *Questionnaire for Major Superiors* which was issued on September 18, 2009, and due on November 20, 2009. In her accompanying letter, Mother Mary Clare explained that the Center for Applied Research in the Apostolate (CARA) assisted in wording the questions of Part A of the questionnaire and would do a composite analysis that "may eventually be included in some public document regarding results of the Apostolic Visitation."[28] Part A asked for quantitative data on the institute itself, membership, living arrangements, governance, and sisters in ministry.[29] Major superiors were directed to send these responses to CARA. Mirroring the content of the *Instrumentum Laboris* previously circulated, Part B required narrative answers to questions regarding the identity of the religious institute, governance of the religious institute, vocation promotion, admission and formation policies, spiritual and liturgical life, common life, mission and ministry, financial administration, and any additional information the religious institute wished to write regarding its heritage, hopes, and challenges. Part C requested the submission of additional documentation: constitutions; documents such as directories and custom books; the formation plan; decisions of the last two general chapters; a list of each sister, year of birth, address, type of ministry; list of properties owned and/or (co)sponsored; most recent independent audit or last internal financial statement. Responses to Parts B and C were to be sent to the Apostolic Visitation office.[30]

Knowing that an apostolic visitation is a canonical inquiry, and understanding that the answers to some of the questions had legal implications, leaders of religious institutes had a variety of reactions and questions regarding the best way to respond. In consultation with leaders of other religious institutes, with canon lawyers, and with sisters in their own communities, leaders acted with integrity and according to their own consciences in their responses to the *Questionnaire*. Some completed the entire *Questionnaire* while others answered some of the questions. Still others sent a letter to Mother Mary Clare and a few did not respond to Phase 2 at all.[31]

On November 3, 2009, Cardinal Rodé issued a statement providing rationale for the Visitation in addition to the initial stated purpose of examining the quality of life of women religious. He said the Visitation hoped to encourage vocations and assure a better future for women religious. He explained that for many years CICLSAL had been hearing concerns from American religious, laity, clergy, and members of the hierarchy "about the welfare of religious women . . . and had been considering an Apostolic Visitation as a means to assess and constructively address these concerns." Further, he noted that "The multitude and complexity of these issues were made clear by speakers and participants at the symposium on religious life at Stonehill College in September 2008. . . . My hope is that the Apostolic Visitation will not only provide the Holy See with a thorough analysis of the condition of religious life in the United States, but also be a realistic and graced opportunity for personal and community introspection, as major superiors and sisters cooperate with this study."[32]

On November 4, 2009, in a conversation with Vatican Radio, Cardinal Rodé said that some media reported on the Visitation "as if it were an act of mistrust of American female religious congregations or as if it were a global criticism of their work. It is not." In that same interview, Cardinal Rodé noted that the "investigation was a response to concerns, including those of 'an important representative of the U.S. church' regarding 'some irregularities or omissions in American religious life. Most of all, you could say, it involves a certain secular mentality that has spread in these religious families and, perhaps, also a certain feminist spirit.'"[33]

On November 5, 2009, Mother Mary Clare sent another letter to leaders of religious institutes partially revising the initial requests included in the *Questionnaire* apparently in response to concerns expressed by "many major superiors . . . regarding confidentiality and protection of privileged information about their congregation, the sisters themselves, and their apostolate." Inviting leaders to share their questions or concerns, she noted that she would do her "best to make this task a genuinely positive experience for you and for each of your sisters." In this letter she confirmed that, although legal and canonical advisors concur that the Apostolic See has a right to all the information in the *Questionnaire*, she had determined that certain documents need not be sent to the Apostolic Visitation Office, namely the list of each sister, year of birth, address, type of ministry; list of properties owned and/or (co)sponsored; most recent independent audit or last internal financial statement.[34]

In a letter dated January 12, 2010, to major superiors, Mother Mary Clare communicated that in a recent meeting she had with Cardinal Rodé, he had assured her that Pope Benedict continued to show interest in and support of the Apostolic Visitation. Mother Mary Clare told Cardinal Rodé of the "wholehearted and genuine response" to the *Questionnaire* on the part of many congregations and registered her "sadness and disappointment" that not all congregations had responded to this phase of "dialogue with the church in a manner fully supportive of the purpose and goals of the Apostolic Visitation." Mother Mary Clare said Cardinal Rodé strongly encouraged her to ask those "who had not yet fully complied" to reconsider their response. Later in that same letter, suggesting a connection between the information provided in Phase 2 and her final report, Mother Mary Clare iterated that in the fourth phase of the Visitation, she will prepare a summary report for each institute and each institute subsequently "will receive feedback from CICL-

SAL for the purpose of promoting its charismatic identity and apostolic vitality in ongoing dialogue with the local and universal church."[35]

A letter dated April 28, 2010, from the leadership of LCWR to its members summarized the annual meeting with CICLSAL which took place in Rome on Saturday, April 24. The presidential team and the executive director explained to Cardinal Rodé that the Apostolic Visitation process had caused confusion among U.S. women religious because neither they nor the bishops were well-informed about all the aspects of the Visitation. During the meeting Cardinal Rodé expressed serious concerns about the many congregations that did not complete the entire Apostolic Visitation *Questionnaire.* Leonello Leidi, CP, a CICLSAL staff member, explained that as Visitator, Mother Mary Clare is "the vicar of the pope." Consequently, not completing the *Questionnaire* is seen as "an attitude of open opposition." Father Leidi spoke about "possible consequences for leaders who may be judged disobedient."[36]

TRACING PHASE 3 OF THE APOSTOLIC VISITATION: PREPARATION AND IMPLEMENTATION OF ON-SITE VISITS

In preparation for the third phase of the Apostolic Visitation, seventy-eight women and men religious who were selected as on-site visitors from those whose names were submitted by the leadership of their congregations and others came together for an orientation workshop in St. Louis, February 26–28, 2010. All the visitors were required to pronounce a public profession of faith as well as the oath of fidelity to the Holy See which qualified them to receive personal mandates from CICLSAL authorizing them to carry out their service in the name of the Holy See.

Keynote speakers for the visitor orientation workshop included Bishop William E. Lori of Bridgeport, who spoke of the Visitation as an expression of ecclesial communion; Mary Bendyna, OP, executive director of the Center for Applied Research in the Apostolate (CARA), who explained the CARA report on the Apostolic Visitation; and Melanie Di Pietro, SC, professor at Seton Hall University and director for the Center for Religiously Affiliated Corporations, who addressed issues of civil and canon law. Consultants to the Apostolic Visitation presented various aspects of the Visitation process. Topics included Visitation interviews, logistics of the on-site visit, and an overview of the development and contributions of women's religious congregations in the United States.[37]

The first group of on-site visits was scheduled from April 11 through June 4, 2010. A second series occurred from September 12 through December 17, 2010. Mother Mary Clare chose approximately 25 percent of the 400 institutes of women religious that were part of the Apostolic Visitation to be visited. This representative sample was based on the congregation's size and growth pattern, its principal apostolic works, and its geographical location. Both diocesan and pontifical institutes received visits. The number of sisters who wished to meet with a visitor determined the length of the visit and the size of the Visitation team.[38] Leadership of each specific congregation or province to be visited received a two-page letter along with a two-page checklist titled *Phase 3: On-Site Visit to Religious Institutes—Responsibilities of Major Superior.* As an integral part of the Visitation process, the on-site visit was intended to offer as many sisters as possible the opportunity to meet with the visitors to "freely express their vision of the joys and challenges you face in seeking to live your charismatic identity and mission." Mother Mary Clare expressed her hope that the dialogue would give the visitors "a broad and objective picture of the congregation and its impact on the local church." Leadership of each congregation to be visited was asked to duplicate a letter from the Apostolic Visitation office for each individual sister informing her of the on-site visit and inviting her to sign up for a meeting with a visitor. Sisters sent their requests for a meeting directly to the Apostolic Visitation office.[39]

The formal visit began with the visiting team meeting as a group with the leadership of the institute constituted by the major superior and her council, who, in preparation for the visit, had been asked to organize a presentation on various aspects of the institute. These included the areas originally introduced in the *Instrumentum Laboris*, and later forming a significant portion of the content of the *Questionnaire:* identity of the institute, governance, vocations and formation, spiritual and common life, mission and ministry, and financial administration. There were also required visits with vocation and formation personnel. As indicated previously in this chapter, members of the community had been invited prior to the on-site visit to request a meeting with the team; interview times were accordingly scheduled during the visit. In addition to these interviews, both required and voluntary, leadership could invite up to eight non-community members to participate in a focus group. The members of the focus groups were individuals familiar with the community life and/or ministry of the congregation who could speak knowledgeably about the ways the congregation lives its charism and mission.[40]

Specific interview questions were formulated by the Apostolic Visitation office for congregational leadership, for meetings with individual sisters and with the vocation and formation personnel, and for the focus groups. In addition to the presentation on aspects of the institute, congregational leadership addressed questions regarding strengths of the congregation, areas of concern for the congregation, vision for the future of the congregation, priorities in future plans for the congregation's mission, issues that could inhibit or threaten the congregation's future, and how the pastors of the church could assist the congregation. Individual sisters and vocation and formation personnel were asked to respond to these same questions. Focus group participants were asked to explain how they knew the sisters and how the sisters' presence and ministries have impacted their lives. Additional questions focused on strengths of the congregation, areas of most concern about the sisters' ministries, and hopes for the future work of the sisters. Focus group members were asked to identify three priorities they would recommend be included in plans for the renewal of the life and work of the sisters and three areas of concern regarding the ministry and works of the sisters.

Mother Mary Clare's letter to leaders whose congregations were scheduled for on-site visits stressed that all visitors were bound by strict confidentiality, and no visitor would "express any judgment either in writing or orally to the major superior, to any other member of the religious institute visited, or any other unauthorized person either prior to, during, or after the visit." She explained that the Visitation team would write a report articulating the accomplishments, key strengths, and challenges of the institute. The report would include whatever recommendations the visitors considered appropriate.[41]

The on-site visits took place during 2010. In that same year, at least one significant personnel change occurred at CICLSAL. On August 2, 2010, American born Joseph William Tobin, CSsR, was named as secretary of the Congregation for Institutes of Consecrated Life and Societies of Apostolic Life and assigned to Rome. Following a year's experience in the position, he said, "I believe a visitation has to have a dialogical aspect, but the way this was structured at the beginning didn't really favor that." He referred to Cardinal Rodé's decision early in the process not to share the visitors' reports with the institutes as part of the problem and noted that rumors and "some rather unscrupulous canonical advisors exploited [the situation]" by generating fear that the Vatican would force new leadership on communities or dissolve some. He further observed however that, from Rome, an atmosphere had been created in which such ideas "didn't seem to be so outlandish." Archbishop Tobin believed the Visitation process had not been as difficult as feared and stated that reconciliation was needed in and among communities of American women religious.[42]

FROM PHASE 3 TO PHASE 4:
AN INCOMPLETE PROCESS HELD IN SUSPENSION

Just after the conclusion of the on-site visits, another significant personnel change occurred. On January 4, 2011, Pope Benedict XVI accepted the resignation of Cardinal Franc Rodé, prefect of the Congregation for Institutes of Consecrated Life and Societies of Apostolic Life, who had reached the mandatory retirement age of seventy-five in August 2009. In his place, the pope appointed Archbishop João Bráz de Aviz from Brazil as prefect of the CIC-SAL office.

On March 8, 2011, the Apostolic Visitation office issued a press release communicating that Mother Mary Clare had held a concluding workshop at the U.S. provincial headquarters of the Apostles of the Sacred Heart of Jesus in Hamden, Connecticut on March 4–6, 2011, for religious who had assisted with the on-site visits. Archbishop Joseph Tobin, CSsR, attended the three-day gathering along with more than half of the women and men religious who served as on-site visitors as well as the core team and consultants for the Visitation. A total of fifty-eight persons were present. Mother Mary Clare invited the visitors to share their personal impressions of their on-site experiences and their observations of common hopes, challenges, and concerns that women religious face. The press release stated that the group "offered suggestions for further promoting respectful dialogue and collaboration among religious congregations and within the church."[43]

Mother Mary Clare said that Archbishop Tobin "listened attentively to the heartfelt sharing of the participants. He expressed his deep understanding of our reality and conveyed the continued support of the Congregation for Consecrated Life in fostering the ongoing revitalization of religious life in the United States." Mother Mary Clare reflected that

> this gathering has been a great grace and joy and gave me much with which to enhance my final reports. Even more important, the deepened bonds of mutual understanding and collaboration among us and with CICLSAL do much to promote the vitality of religious life in the context of respectful dialogue and ecclesial communion.[44]

Ten months later, on January 9, 2012, in a press release issued from the Apostolic Visitation office, Mother Mary Clare confirmed that she had presented an overall summary of her findings to Archbishop Tobin. In addition to the comprehensive report, which fulfills the mandate's original decree, she had submitted most of the individual reports for each of the nearly 400 religious institutes that were part of the Apostolic Visitation and added that the remaining institute reports would be completed in spring 2012. Mother Mary Clare added that the three-year charge was "demanding, but equally refreshing." She concluded, "Although there are concerns in religious life that warrant support and attention, the enduring reality is one of fidelity, joy, and hope."[45] The news release further stipulated that CICLSAL had not yet specified when it would announce its conclusions pertaining to the Apostolic Visitation. A January 11, 2012, article from the *Catholic News Service* quotes Jesuit Father Federico Lombardi, Vatican spokesman, as confirming that the reports have been received and the Congregation for Institutes of Consecrated Life and Societies for Apostolic Life "is now studying them."

The Vatican spokesman said CICLSAL is expected "to make known its evaluation of the results of the visit" at some future date.[46]

On October 12, 2012, Archbishop Joseph Tobin was appointed to the Archdiocese of Indianapolis, Indiana, leaving his post at the Congregation for Institutes of Consecrated Life and Societies for Apostolic Life. The first curial appointment made by Pope Francis on April 7, 2013, was that of Archbishop José Rodriguez Carballo, OFM, to replace Archbishop Tobin as secretary of CICLSAL.

As of June, 2014, there has been no word from CICLSAL to congregations of women religious in the United States regarding the report and recommendations which resulted from the Apostolic Visitation. However, in a January 31, 2014, press conference CICLSAL Secretary Archbishop José Rodriguez Carballo, OFM, and Cardinal João Braz de Avis, the current congregation prefect, indicated that progress on a final report was being made. According to Archbishop Carballo, "We are working intensely on a final report, and after careful study and consideration, we think it will be made public soon. We're at a good point. I think we can conclude it before the beginning of the Year for Consecrated Life."[47] The Year for Consecrated Life is 2015.

NOTES

1. The official Apostolic Visitation website is: http://www.apostolicvisitation.org.

2. Leadership Conference of Women Religious, "LCWR Officers Meet with Vatican Officials in Rome," *Update*, May 2008, 1, 4.

3. Franc Cardinal Rodé, CM, "Reforming Religious Life with the Right. Hermeneutic," speech presented at Stonehill College Symposium on Apostolic Religious Life since Vatican II . . . Reclaiming the Treasure: Bishops, Theologians, and Religious in Conversation, Stonehill College, North Easton, Massachusetts, U.S.A., September 27, 2008, Zenit, last modified October 13, 2008, http://www.zenit.org/en/articles/cardinal-rode-at-symposium-on-consecrated-life.

4. Memorandum by Franc Cardinal Rodé, CM, "Statement of the Prefect of the Congregation of Institutes of Consecrated Life and Societies of Apostolic Life, Card. Franc Rodé, C.M., on the Apostolic Visitation of Institutes of Women Religious in the U.S.A," November 3, 2009, http://www.apostolicvisitation.org/en/news/CardRodeMsg.html.

5. Eva-Maria Ackerman, FSGM. "Remarks of Sister Eva-Maria Ackerman." News release. January 30, 2009. http://www.apostolicvisitation.org/en/news/resources/conference_remarks 1302009.pdf.

6. Franc Cardinal Rodé, CM and Gianfranco A. Gardin, OMF. Conv. "Decree," Prot. N. 16805/2008. December 22, 2008. http://www.apostolicvisitation.org/en/materials/decree.pdf.

7. Apostolic Visitation of Women Religious in the United States, "Vatican Initiates Study of Catholic Sisters' Institutes in the United States," news release, January 30, 2009, http://www.apostolicvisitation.org/en/news/resources/news_release_1302009.pdf.

8. ibid.

9. Ackerman, "Remarks."

10. ibid.

11. Letter by Franc Cardinal Rodé, CM, February 2, 2009, http://www.apostolicvisitation .org/en/materials/cardinal_rode.pdf.

12. ibid.

13. Leadership Conference of Women Religious, Memorandum, "Statement by the National Board of the Leadership Conference of Women Religious on the Apostolic Visitation," February 20, 2009. http://www.apostolicvisitation.org/en/materials/lcwr.pdf.

14. Mother Mary Quentin Sheridan, RSM, Memorandum, "Statement of the Congregation of Major Superiors of Women Religious concerning the Apostolic Visitation of Women Religious in the United States," n.d. http://www.apostolicvisitation.org/en/materials/cmswr.pdf.

15. Memorandum by International Union of Superiors General, Board of Directors, "Statement of the Board of Directors, International Union of Superiors General concerning the Apostolic Visitation of Women Religious in the United States," April 23, 2009, http://www.apostolicvisitation.org/en/materials/iusg.pdf.

16. Margaret Cain McCarthy, "Apostolic Visitation Survey Analysis: The Apostolic Visitation as Experienced by Women Religious in the United States" (report, October 15, 2011).

17. Memorandum by Mother Mary Clare Millea, ASCJ, "Update on the Progress of Phase 1," n.d., http://www.apostolicvisitation.org/en/news/phase1juneupdate.html.

18. "Testimonials," Apostolic Visitation of Institutes of Women Religious in the United States, http://www.apostolicvisitation.org/en/testimonials/index.html.

19. Mother Mary Clare Millea, ASCJ, to Superiors General, May 19, 2009, http://www.apostolicvisitation.org/en/materials/letter_superiors.pdf.

20. ibid.

21. Franc Cardinal Rodé, CM, to U.S. Bishops, "Donation to the Apostolic Visitation of Institutes of Women Religious in the United States," July 14, 2009.

22. ibid.

23. Congregation for Institutes of Consecrated Life and Societies of Apostolic Life. *Instrumentum Laboris for Apostolic Visitation of the General Houses, Provincial Houses and Centers of Initial Formation of the Principal Religious Institutes of Women in the United States of America*. Prot. N. 16805/2008. Vatican: Congregation for Institutes of Consecrated Life and Societies of Apostolic Life, 2008. http://www.apostolicvisitation.org/en/news/resources/InstrumentumLaboris.pdf.

24. Letter by Mother Mary Clare Millea, ASCJ, "*Instrumentum Laboris* Message," July 28, 2009, http://www.apostolicvisitation.org/en/news/InstrumentumLaborisLetter.html.

25. Congregation for Institutes of Consecrated Life and Societies of Apostolic Life. *Instrumentum Laboris,* 2.

26. ibid.

27. Leadership Conference of Women Religious, "Leadership Conference of Women Religious Explores Critical Issues Against Backdrop of Vatican Studies," news release, August 17, 2009.

28. Letter by Mother Mary Clare Millea, ASCJ, "Questionnaire Letter to Major Superiors," September 18, 2009, http://www.apostolicvisitation.org/en/materials/ques_ltr.pdf.

29. Apostolic Visitation of Institutes of Women Religious in the United States. "Questionnaire for Major Superiors, Part A," n.d. http://www.apostolicvisitation.org/en/materials/ques_A.pdf.

30. Apostolic Visitation of Institutes of Women Religious in the United States. "Questionnaire for Major Superiors, Parts B and C," n.d. http://www.apostolicvisitation.org/en/materials/ques_BC.pdf.

31. McCarthy, "Apostolic Visitation Survey Analysis."

32. Memorandum by Rodé, "Statement of the Prefect."

33. Franc Cardinal Rodé, CM, interview with Vatican Radio, by Cindy Wooden, "Cardinal Rodé Defends Apostolic Visitation of U.S. Nuns," Catholic News Service, last modified November 5, 2009, http://www.catholicnews.com/data/stories/cns/0904882.htm.

34. Letter by Mother Mary Clare Millea, ASCJ, November 5, 2009, http://www.apostolicvisitation.org/en/materials/MajorSupLtr-11052009.pdf.

35. Letter by Mother Mary Clare Millea, ASCJ, January 12, 2010, http://www.apostolicvisitation.org/iw-cc/command/en/materials/letter_1-12.pdf.

36. Marlene Weisenbeck, FSPA, J. Lora Dambroski, OSF, and Jane Burke, SSND to LCWR Membership, April 28, 2010.

37. Apostolic Visitation of Institutes of Women Religious in the United States, "Apostolic Visitation Gathers Religious in Preparation for On-Site Visits," news release, March 1, 2010, http://www.apostolicvisitation.org/en/materials/AV_news_release_03-01-10.pdf.

38. Apostolic Visitation Begins Phase 3, http://www.apostolicvisitation.org/en/materials/av_phase_begins.pdf.

39. Letter by Mother Mary Clare Millea, ASCJ, "Phase 3: On-Site Visit to Religious Institutes, Responsibilities of Major Superior," May 15, 2010.

40. ibid.

41. ibid.

42. Archbishop Joseph W. Tobin, CSsR, quoted in Cindy Wooden, "Vatican Aims to Regain Trust of U.S. Religious Women, Official Says," Catholic News Service, last modified August 10, 2011, http://www.catholicnews.com/data/stories/cns/1103169.htm.

43. Apostolic Visitation of Women Religious in the United States. "Apostolic Visitation Gathers Religious in Review of On-Site Visits." News release. March 8, 2011. http://www.apostolicvisitation.org/en/materials/av_news_releases_03-07-11.pdf.

44. ibid.

45. Apostolic Visitation of Institutes of Women Religious in the United States. "Apostolic Visitation Closes with Final Report Submission," news release, January 9, 2012. http://www.apostolicvisitation.org/en/materials/close.pdf.

46. Dennis Sadowski, "Three-Year Study of Women Religious Completed; Vatican Reviews Results," Catholic News Service, last modified January 11, 2012, http://www.catholicnews.com/data/stories/cns/1200112.htm.

47. Archbishop José Rodriguez Carbello, OFM, news conference, by Cindy Wooden, "Officials Say Final Report on Visitation of U.S. Nuns Expected Soon," Catholic News Service, last modified January 31, 2014, http://www.catholicnews.com/data/stories/cns/1400434.htm.

Chapter Four

Experiencing the Apostolic Visitation

Part One of the Apostolic Visitation Survey

Margaret Cain McCarthy

The Apostolic Visitation of Institutes of Women Religious in the United States was initiated by Cardinal Franc Rodé, CM, prefect of the Vatican Congregation for Institutes of Consecrated Life and Societies of Apostolic Life (CICLSAL) on December 22, 2008. In January, 2012, Mother Mary Clare Millea, ASCJ, reported that she had presented an overall summary of her findings to CICLSAL.

The Visitation consisted of four phases:

- Phase 1: the invitation to superiors general to share "joys, concerns, and other observations" with the Apostolic Visitator, Mother Mary Clare Millea, ASCJ, Superior General of the Apostles of the Sacred Heart of Jesus;
- Phase 2: the solicitation via a *Questionnaire* of "empirical data as well as observations and aspirations" from major superiors in the United States;
- Phase 3: onsite visits to selected institutes across the United States;
- Phase 4: the compilation and delivery of a comprehensive report to the prefect of the Congregation for Institutes of Consecrated Life. [1]

THE APOSTOLIC VISITATION SURVEY

The experience of the Visitation has been captured through a survey which was designed and distributed by a group of women religious in the spring of 2011, as the Visitation was proceeding. Referring to themselves as the "Grassroots Group," they represented a variety of institutes across the United

States. The Apostolic Visitation Survey (survey) was composed of two parts: Part One was designed to gather information related to each of the first three phases of the Apostolic Visitation; Part Two was designed to gather thoughts, feelings, and experiences across the entire Visitation process. While some questions required a quantitative response, the majority of questions allowed a qualitative response and so generated a wealth of information.[2] Invitations to complete the survey were extended to 328 presidents or major superiors in the Leadership Conference of Women Religious[3] (one per congregation); of that number 143 returned valid surveys for a response rate of approximately 44 percent. An invitation to participate was extended to the Council of Major Superiors of Women Religious (CMSWR) but the invitation was declined and, as a result, their voices and experiences are not reflected here.[4] Survey responses, analyzed by Margaret Cain McCarthy and reported to the members of the Grassroots Group in the fall of 2011, present a rich picture of the impact of the Visitation on the women who participated. One hundred forty-three individuals returned the eighteen-question survey, generating approximately 2,500 discrete responses. In order to accurately communicate the significant volume of data the survey generated, recurring themes have been identified through qualitative content analysis of responses to individual questions. These themes are outlined below and illustrated by representative samples of survey responses in order to faithfully report the experience in the words of the sisters themselves. Approximately ten percent of responses to each question are offered and, including material in both Chapter 4 and Chapter 5, all 143 participants are represented by one or more sample responses. These examples do not necessarily characterize every individual response and are not intended to highlight either the most articulate or the most unusual.

Given the nature of a qualitative response, readers are cautioned *not* to assume that *only* those who mentioned a specific issue experienced it. Additionally, multiple themes were often expressed by individual respondents. Not surprisingly, all survey participants did not answer every question; therefore, percentages noted in the text refer to the percentage of respondents to a specific question. Generally, themes expressed by five or fewer respondents are not included in this review. Identification of institutes and/or individuals has been avoided; identifiers have been redacted and replaced with "xxx."

Survey responses to questions four through eighteen are examined in *Chapter 5: Experiencing the Apostolic Visitation: Part Two of the Apostolic Visitation Survey.* Part 1 of the survey includes questions one through three; those responses are offered here.

APOSTOLIC VISITATION SURVEY: RESPONSES TO PART ONE

Part One of the Apostolic Visitation Survey was designed to gather information on how participation in the first three phases of the Visitation occurred and to identify the reasons decisions were made to participate (or not) in a particular way.

Phase 1 of the Apostolic Visitation: The Invitation

In Phase 1 of the Apostolic Visitation, Cardinal Rodé, CM, invited and encouraged superiors general "to communicate with the Apostolic Visitator regarding your observations and hopes for your sisters in the United States." He noted that this "exchange may be made by letter, by phone, or by personal meeting with her, either in Rome or in the United States."[5]

Question 1a: Regarding the invitation to meet (either in person or by telephone) with Mother Mary Clare

   •*We accepted this invitation*
   •*We did not accept this invitation*

Including all forms of response, 117 (82%) survey respondents indicated they accepted the invitation to participate and twenty-four (17%) did not; two (1%) did not respond to questions 1a, 1b, or 1c.

Question 1b: If you did accept this invitation, please describe your experience.

Of the 117 respondents who indicated they accepted the invitation, seventy-eight (67%) reported that the form of response was a personal interaction; thirty-six responded to Mother Mary Clare in writing and ten of these written responses were made by a superior outside the United States; the form of response could not be determined for three survey respondents.

The seventy-eight who reported a personal interaction with Mother Mary Clare noted it occurred at a meeting or via telephone or electronically. Of these seventy-eight respondents, the vast majority (86%) indicated that interaction was positive and characterized the interaction using language such as *cordial, open, professional,* or *respectful.*

* Twelve of the seventy-eight respondents (15%) indicated that they wanted or hoped that more than one person would have been able to represent the institute in the meeting with Mother Mary Clare.
* Of the seventy-eight respondents who reported a personal interaction with Mother Mary Clare, seven (9%) discussed issues related to the process and hope/need/expectation for transparency or feedback.

- Of the seventy-eight, only six (8%) noted they were nervous or anxious about the meeting. However, these respondents did not indicate the experience was a negative one.

Of the 117 respondents to this question, thirty-six (31%) participated in Phase 1 through a written response. Most described their experience very succinctly, simply noting that they responded to the invitation to participate in writing with no further explanation. Other respondents briefly commented on their reasons for participating in writing or their experience.

- Of these thirty-six, nine (25%) indicated that their written response included information on their institute's charism, hopes, history, ministries, and/or constitutions.
- Eight respondents who answered Mother Mary Clare's invitation in writing indicated their reasons for choosing this option were related to travel, scheduling, or health issues.
- Five indicated they chose to respond in writing because it provided a sense of control and/or security.

Sample responses of the 117 who accepted the invitation to participate in Phase 1:

- *Mother Mary Clare was very friendly, a good listener, and I found the experience to be very positive.*
- *It was an open, engaging, encouraging experience. Mother Mary Clare is a good listener. I was nervous going into it but she set a very comfortable tone. My preference would have been to have had other members of my team present with me.*
- *I was happy to tell her about our community. I was not willing to travel to meet with her for one hour, so we met electronically. I prepared by reflecting on our history and charism, which is always a good exercise for me. She seemed to be listening, only asking questions about any new members we have. It was cordial and not very interactive.*
- *It was a very positive experience. Sister [Mother Mary Clare] was very cordial and assured me of her hope that U.S. religious women would receive information from her report. I would have preferred if [the] whole leadership team could have participated in this meeting.*
- *We are part of an international congregation and our general superior in Rome met with Mother Mary Clare along with the sister from the U.S. who is on the general council. We understand it was a good meeting.*
- *Our superior general had a meeting with Mother Clare and she found her very cordial. We all believed it was our responsibility to accept the invitation.*

- *The experience was positive but difficult because of the nature of this being an investigation rather than a conversation to learn more about what was happening in religious life among women's congregations. Mother Clare listened carefully to my hopes and challenges.*
- *The rationale for doing the onsite interview was simply that a "face to face" interview was preferred to a written response or phone interview. The ability to engage in a "face to face" conversation gives one the opportunity for real dialogue. It was a very pleasant exchange, with a few good chuckles and plenty of healthy exchange on the information shared.*
- *[Mother] Mary Clare was gracious and hospitable. Throughout the conversation she appeared interested and noted several times that our practices were consistent with her own congregation's. She reviewed the phases of the process. She did tell me she had been deeply impressed by the presidents who had elected to visit her and that she would convey to the Holy See all the good that is being done. She closed the meeting with me by asking what my dream was for my congregation.*
- *Since we are a pontifical community, our general minister responded by letter—writing to Mother Mary Clare.*
- *We are an international community with North America representing one of six units in the congregation. Our (superior general) is in London. She chose to write to Mother Mary Clare in response to the invitation a several-page reflection integrating: our constitution; the express intent and quotes from our foundress; her personal experience of having "formally" spent seven weeks with us in the U.S. the year before, visiting extensively.*
- *We accepted the invitation but put our response in writing. We felt that this was the best way to control our response. We felt it gave us the advantage to tell our story as it needed to be told rather than hope that [Mother] Mary Clare would ask questions to give us the opportunity to tell our real story. I am now concerned that it has been three years since Phase 1. We have worked very hard during that time on our charism, structures, ministries, etc. None of this will be reflected in our report.*

Question 1c: If you did not accept this invitation, please explain why not.

Twenty-four respondents implied institute non-participation in Phase 1.

- Eleven members of this group (46%) indicated the community made a conscious decision not to participate for reasons including insufficient time, not enough information, they were dealing with other more important matters, the institute was small, they did not believe the effort was valuable, or they were not interested.
- Seven respondents (29%) stated they did not participate because there was a question about whether or not their type of institute (i.e., monastic) was

expected/required to participate and Phase I passed before the issue was clarified and they learned they were expected to participate.
• Six respondents (25%) noted they did not respond due to one of several factors related to communication.

Sample responses to Question 1c:

• *The invitation was optional, and we chose not to meet because of the distance to travel and because we had very serious congregational matters to address and needed to focus our presence and energy on those matters at the time.*
• *We were not interested.*
• *It was not mandatory. We did not think it would be valuable.*
• *At the time we, those of us in monastic communities, were not clear if the invitation was extended to us.*

Phase 2 of the Apostolic Visitation: The Questionnaire

The purpose of Phase 2 of the Apostolic Visitation was to solicit input (empirical data as well as observations and aspirations) from U.S. major superiors through the *Questionnaire for Major Superiors*. In a letter dated September 18, 2009, Mother Mary Clare noted the "extremely important role" of the *Questionnaire* and explained the process:

> As stated in the *Instrumentum Laboris*, all major superiors who are responsible for an institute, province or house of initial formation of women religious in the United States will be asked to provide written information in response to the *Questionnaire*. The completed *Questionnaire* is due no later than November 20, 2009, together with a copy of fundamental congregational documents. We are pleased that the Center for Applied Research in the Apostolate (CARA) is assisting in this effort to gain a clear picture of women religious in our country today.[6]

In addition to assisting with the wording of questions on Part A of the *Questionnaire*, CARA received Part A responses and prepared a composite analysis of all participating religious institutes in the United States. Individual institute responses to Part A were submitted to Mother Mary Clare following the CARA analysis. Conscious of the need for confidentiality, Mother Mary Clare noted that:

> All responses to Part B and Part C of the *Questionnaire* are to be sent directly to the Apostolic Visitation Office where they will be reviewed exclusively by persons authorized by me. Online responses to Part B of the *Questionnaire* will also be sent directly to the Apostolic Visitation Office. Those directly involved in the analysis and evaluation of any data received from the religious

institutes are bound by strict confidentiality. Data regarding any participating institutes or individuals will not be shared with anyone except those whom I judge it necessary to consult directly to assist in fulfilling my appointment by Cardinal Rodé as Apostolic Visitator.[7]

It is important to note that the expectations for the Apostolic Visitation *Questionnaire* changed during the course of the Visitation. The letter from Mother Mary Clare dated September 18, 2009, informed superiors that the *Questionnaire* (Parts A, B, and C) was available and gave instructions for completing and returning the documents (the due date was November 20, 2009). However, on November 5, she wrote again reiterating the purpose of the Visitation and encouraging participation. At this point, she also referenced concerns "regarding confidentiality and protection of privileged information" and informed the superiors that three of the documents which were requested in Part C of the *Questionnaire* should not be submitted. If the documents had already been submitted, they would be returned. Those documents included:

- Part C. 5. A list of each sister, year of birth, address and type of ministry (full time/part time).
- Part C. 6. A list of properties owned and/or (co)sponsored by your unit.
- Part C. 7. A complete copy of the most recent independent audit of your religious unit or your last internal financial statement if an external audit has not been made. This should include a statement of financial position, statement of activity, statement of changes in net assets and statement of cash flows.[8]

Mother Mary Clare noted that "this change in the design of the *Questionnaire* was made after listening to your concerns and after considerable prayer and counsel. I have every confidence that the purpose of this phase of the Apostolic Visitation can be satisfactorily achieved with the data provided in Parts A, B, and the first four documents listed in Part C of the *Questionnaire*."[9]

The survey requested information about how institutes responded to the *Questionnaire* and why they chose to respond as they did. Respondents who indicated that they completed the entire *Questionnaire* except for financial data or a list of sisters are counted as having completed the entire *Questionnaire* since institutes were eventually directed not to send that information.

Q 2a: Response to the Questionnaire

- *We completed the entire Questionnaire*
- *We answered some of the questions on the Questionnaire*
- *We sent a letter to Mother Mary Clare instead of completing the Questionnaire*

• *We did not respond at all in Phase 2*

Of the 143 respondents to the Apostolic Visitation Survey, sixty-four (45%) answered some of the questions on the *Questionnaire*; fifty-five (38%) sent a letter to Mother Mary Clare instead of completing the *Questionnaire*; twenty-two (15%) completed the entire *Questionnaire*; and two (1%) indicated they did not respond at all in Phase II of the Apostolic Visitation.

Q2b: Please explain your reasons for taking the action you did in response to the Questionnaire.

The majority of respondents (n=64; 45%) indicated they elected to answer some, but not all, of the questions on the *Questionnaire*. Some of the respondents noted that not all questions were answered due to confidentiality concerns. It cannot be determined whether or not the elimination of the three documents originally requested in Part C satisfied these concerns and/or if all other questions were answered. Based on responses to the survey, a variety of reasons were offered for choosing to answer some but not all of the questions on the *Questionnaire*:

- Thirty-three (52%) of the sixty-four respondents felt the questions were unclear, ambiguous, did not fit with the stated purpose of the Visitation, and/or were inappropriate.
- Twenty-two (34%) indicated legal advice and/or the advice of canon lawyers influenced their decision to answer some but not all of the questions on the *Questionnaire.*
- Twenty-eight percent (n=18) did not want to answer questions related to finances. [10]
- Twenty-seven percent (n=17) noted that they answered the questions according to their rule or constitutions.
- Twelve (19%) noted that they chose not to answer questions which they believed to be an invasion of privacy, were intrusive, or requested sensitive data.
- Twelve (19%) indicated they chose to answer only some of the questions because they were concerned about how the answers would be used or interpreted.
- Nine (14%) chose to answer some of the questions because they wanted to be cooperative, had nothing to hide, viewed the *Questionnaire* as on opportunity, and/or out of respect for the church.

A minority (n=55; 38%) sent a letter in response to Mother Mary Clare instead of completing the *Questionnaire*. A variety of explanations for taking this course of action were offered. In response to this question, and others throughout the survey, some respondents offered more than one reason.

- The majority (n=39; 71%) referenced in the letter, or sent, their constitution to Mother Mary Clare rather than respond to the *Questionnaire*. Many noted their constitution had been approved by Rome and that all appropriate responses to the *Questionnaire* could be found there.
- More than half (n=30; 55%) expressed one or more concerns about the questions: the questions suggested a norm or ideal of religious life that did not fit with their lived reality; the questions did not apply; the questions had a pre-Vatican II bias; the questions were ambiguous, intrusive, insulting, a matter of conscience; and/or the questions did not fit the stated purpose of the Visitation.
- Twenty-three respondents (42%) noted that their decision was influenced by consultation with other religious, religious leaders, and/or canon lawyers.
- For fourteen respondents (25%), the decision was influenced by a desire to act in solidarity with others.
- Six respondents (11%) were concerned that the information gathered by the *Questionnaire* might be misinterpreted and/or they were unsure how it would be used and/or that they did not feel comfortable answering.
- Five (9%) noted the *Questionnaire* was a canonical document of inquiry or part of a canonical investigation.

Not all of the twenty-two respondents (15%) who completed the entire *Questionnaire* offered their reasons for doing so; some offered more than one: eight indicated they acted in the spirit of cooperation, openness, and/or faithfulness; six indicated that completing the *Questionnaire* was simply a matter of course, an obligation, or a responsibility; and five indicated they completed the entire *Questionnaire* because they valued telling their story and/or communicating their charism and/or identity.

The two respondents (1%) who did not participate in Phase 2 at all had very different reasons. One did not receive the *Questionnaire*; the other noted that the community reflected on their status as a religious organization which falls under the jurisdiction of their diocesan bishop.

Sample responses to Question 2b:

- *We completed everything except questions relating to the conscience of sisters—about five questions. We completed it because we were asked to and we felt we had nothing to hide. We are a small community and leadership team and wanted to complete this as quickly as possible so that it didn't interfere with our other obligations.*
- *Respect for the church and desire to be cooperative. We declined to provide sensitive data for legal and privacy reasons with regard to some of the questions, however.*

- *We did not answer some questions because they did not apply to our congregation or were open to misinterpretation. Others violated our sisters' confidentiality.*
- *Our team felt we could answer a few questions by stating directly from our constitutions. However, most of the questions we did not answer because we did not know how what we said might be misinterpreted. We also thought that many questions asked were beyond the scope of the purpose of the investigation.*
- *We left a few questions blank that were unclear or not applicable. We responded to the questions with quotations from our constitution. We knew that Rome had a right to ask for a response even though we disagreed with the process and did not think it was right. We held the whole congregation in our discernment about whether or not to answer the Questionnaire knowing that there would be consequences not just for the United States but for us as an international congregation.*
- *We saw the Questionnaire as an opportunity to offer information about our sisters, our ministries, and our living of and commitment to the ideals of our constitution. We did not answer questions which were ambiguous, invasive, or apparently asked with another purpose in mind.*
- *Originally our general council divided the questions and answered most of them mindful of the advice given at the national LCWR Assembly to use our community constitutions as our primary resource. Further advice from canon lawyers helped to educate us to the implications of this canonical inquiry for our own and all other religious congregations. Our response was also influenced by the following: our lives are governed by our constitutions and Rome has already approved them; many questions seemed inappropriate, unclear, and/or intrusive (matters of conscience); we feared that the responses would not be understood or interpreted correctly; the purpose and use of the inquiry was unclear; the process appeared to be biased from its inception (Cardinal Rodé's public comments); our congregation regularly reflects upon and evaluates our fidelity to the gospel and our constitutions; the process was imposed, not collaborative. In light of all of this our decision was to send a letter to Mother Clare.*
- *We spent a great deal of time praying, reflecting, meeting with each other and other members of our congregation and with other leaders of women's institutes, and seeking professional advice about the meaning of such a canonical investigation and the implications our responses might have for our own congregation and/or for the whole class of "apostolic congregations of women religious in the United States" that was under investigation. Our leader, along with other leaders of institutes of women religious in our archdiocese, met with our cardinal archbishop to express our concerns and to seek better understanding of the intent of the investigation*

and ways to respond. We experienced a great deal of pain in all of this, in common with all the women religious with whom we spoke. Although we drafted responses to the questions, we ultimately decided to simply send our constitutions along with a respectful letter instead. Our constitutions are concise and well written and had already been reviewed and approved.

- *We felt the questions were too intrusive. We also objected to the financial questions. We thought our constitutions already stated how we live religious life.*

- *We became aware that the so-called "Questionnaire" was a canonical document of inquiry. Given the ambiguity, some questions' inappropriateness and lack of clarity, we could not reconcile it with the stated purpose of the Apostolic Visitation and wished to protect the rights of our members. We believe our constitution and complementary document offered the most appropriate response.*

- *I chose not to answer the questions because I felt it was intrusive and many of the questions were "leading questions"; they were stated in such a way that they expected certain answers. Also, I wanted to be in solidarity with so many of my sisters who chose to do the same.*

- *It was a good opportunity to look at how we are living religious life and it provided good dialogue among our sisters as they shared in groups and with the council their reflections on the Instrumentum Laboris that helped us prepare the Questionnaire. I also thought it would be good to have such statistics on religious life in the U.S. and the Questionnaire provided that opportunity. It was also a request from the Holy See and therefore it was important for us to answer the Questionnaire honestly and completely.*

- *As a papal congregation the church, CICLSAL has a right to evaluate us. We were not happy with the process but we felt it was our responsibility to cooperate with the Visitation.*

- *We responded to each section in paragraph form rather than a single line per question. It was important to tell our story in a more narrative way than to answer each question separately. Our religious life is rich and not a cold hard fact.*

- *Between Phase 1 and Phase 2, we reflected on our status as a religious institute of diocesan rite. We fall under the jurisdiction of our diocesan bishop, not the prefect of CICLSAL. We have never dealt directly with Rome, and we decided to make no further response to the Apostolic Visitation.*

Phase 3: The Visit

In addition to collecting information on *The Invitation* and *The Questionnaire*, the Apostolic Visitation Survey also requested data on *The Visit*, which was the third phase of the Apostolic Visitation. Mother Mary Clare anticipated selecting "approximately 25 percent of the congregations involved in the Visitation to receive an on-site visit."[11] Survey questions and responses presented here provide basic information about the visit and reaction to the news that a particular institute was selected for a visit or not.

Question 3a: We did receive an on-site visit. Number of days our visit lasted:___

Question 3b: If you responded "Other," please indicate the number of days here:___

Of the 143 survey respondents, fifty-six (39%) participated in a visit. Six of these respondents indicated the visit was conducted by telephone, Skype, or involved travel to a central location to participate in an interview which lasted about 90–120 minutes. For most (n=36) of those who participated in a visit, the visit lasted four or five days; the visit lasted two or three days for nine respondents; and six days for three respondents. The question was not answered, or it was not possible to determine the length of the visit for two respondents.

Question 3c: The number of visitors we had:____

Question 3d: If you responded "Other," please indicate the number of visitors here.____

Twenty-five (45%) of the fifty-six who participated in a visit reported that two visitors conducted the visit. Seventeen (30%) reported three visitors; four reported four visitors; four reported five visitors; and for six respondents, the number of visitors was unknown or the question was left unanswered.

Question 3e: We did not receive an on-site visit. Please describe your feelings about this.

Eighty-seven (61%) of the 143 survey respondents did not receive an on-site visit. Of those who described their feelings, many expressed relief. The words "relief" and/or "relieved" were used more often than any other descriptors and appeared in fifty-seven (66%) of the eighty-seven responses to this question.

• The vast majority (n=73; 84%) of the eighty-seven who did not receive a visit expressed feelings of relief, happiness, or gratitude, or more simply noted they were "not upset" or were "very comfortable" with not being selected for a visit. Twenty-five noted *time* as the primary reason, or one of the primary reasons, they were grateful not to have been selected. Other reasons mentioned were: the small size of their institute; leadership was in transition; concern about the amount of energy it would require or the stress it might cause; and/or concerns about the process.

- Twenty-four respondents (28%) who were not selected for an on-site visit reported mixed feelings. In some cases, individuals in the same institute reflected different feelings, perspectives changed over time as word of positive visits spread, or the press of responsibilities worked in tension with the desire to share the story of community life. Many in this group felt that, had they been visited, they would have welcomed the opportunity to share and/or been well prepared to tell the story of their institute and work.
- Six (7%) of the eighty-seven not selected for a visit noted that they remained in solidarity with those who were selected and/or supported them through prayer.
- Three respondents (4%) would have welcomed a visit, without reservation.

Sample responses to Question 3e:

- *Relief, unadulterated relief, both on the part of leadership and membership.*
- *We were relieved and happy because of the additional preparation and work that would be involved in meeting with the visitors and scheduling the sisters.*
- *In the summer of 2010, we experienced transfer in leadership and we were most happy that we did not have to handle a visitation at that time.*
- *We were relieved although we were prepared to respond to a visit.*
- *Although we were relieved to know that we were not chosen for an on-site visit, we were prepared to host the apostolic visitators and felt that we had a long history of commitment to ministry in the church and world to share. We were grateful not to have been chosen for a visit because preparations would have taken time and attention from urgent community and ministry needs.*
- *Generally we were relieved; the idea of a visit seemed artificial as we had little trust in the process.*
- *We are a small province and had general visitation at the time of the Apostolic Visitation site visits, so we were happy not to have to be distracted from our work and the general visitation to get ready all that was expected of the Apostolic Visitation site visit.*
- *I would have liked an on-site visit. Many of the sisters and I gave a great deal of time reflecting on this Apostolic Questionnaire. I am very proud of*

our community, our mission, ministries, and who we are as xxx in the church—I would have liked to have shared this personally.

- *No site visit. We would have welcomed on-site visitors as our sisters were ready to talk about our quality of life as xxx. However, we weren't exactly disappointed that we weren't selected for an on-site visit.*
- *The greatest feeling was relief. We are extremely small here in the U.S. and very spread out. Entertaining and making sisters available for inter-views would have taken an exorbitant amount of time that we did not feel was worth it.*
- *We have mixed feelings. On one level, we felt at peace that we were not selected for a visit. On another level, it is disconcerting to know that a report will be made about us based only on a Questionnaire and other written materials submitted. We are a small congregation, who are doing great work in the church, and the process in no way provided [an] oppor-tunity for us to tell this story. The entire process felt disrespectful! The motives for the Visitation were never honestly communicated, and the motives that were given changed as the process progressed.*
- *We did not receive an on-site visit. There was definitely some relief be-cause we did not have to do the lengthy preparation and experience the emotional stress, especially on our aging sisters, that the Visitation would have caused because of its unclear purpose. However, it would have been an opportunity for our congregation to speak openly about the wonderful accomplishments religious are making today in the church. We did involve our sisters with the prayer for the Visitation and especially for each con-gregation that was involved in it.*

Institutes responded to the invitation to participate, and experienced the first three phases of the Visitation in a variety of ways, consistent with their charism, their role in the church, and in relationship with their sisters. Chap-ter 5 examines responses to survey questions four through eighteen and re-veals the thoughts, feelings, and experiences of participants across the entire Visitation process.

NOTES

1. "Our Approach," Apostolic Visitation of Women Religious in the United States, http://www.apostolicvisitation.org/en/approach/index.html.

2. Margaret Cain McCarthy, "Apostolic Visitation Survey Analysis: The Apostolic Visita-tion as Experienced by Women Religious in the United States" (report, October 15, 2011).

3. The Leadership Conference of Women Religious has more than 1,400 members who represent more than 80 percent of the approximately 51,000 women religious in the United States. According to the Center for Applied Research in the Apostolate, there were 51,247 women religious in the United States in 2013, http://cara.georgetown.edu/CARAServices/re-questedchurchstats.html.

4. Citing the fact that the Apostolic Visitation had not yet come to a conclusion, the Council of Major Superiors of Women Religious declined to participate in the Apostolic Visitation Survey.

5. Letter by Franc Cardinal Rodé, CM, February 2, 2009, http://www.apostolicvisitation .org/en/materials/cardinal_rode.pdf.

6. Letter by Mother Mary Clare Millea, ASCJ, "Questionnaire Letter to Major Superiors," September 18, 2009, http://www.apostolicvisitation.org/en/materials/ques_ltr.pdf. In a canonical visitation, the *Instrumentum Laboris* defines the content and procedure for the visitation.

7. ibid.

8. Letter by Mother Mary Clare Millea, ASCJ, November 5, 2009, http://www.apostolic visitation.org/en/materials/MajorSupLtr-11052009.pdf.

9. ibid.

10. On November 5, 2009 Mother Mary Clare announced that responses related to finances were no longer required. See letter by Mother Mary Clare Millea, ASCJ, November 5, 2009.

11. Apostolic Visitation Begins Phase 3, http://www.apostolicvisitation.org/en/materials/ av_phase_begins.pdf.

Chapter Five

Experiencing the Apostolic Visitation

Part Two of the Apostolic Visitation Survey

Margaret Cain McCarthy

APOSTOLIC VISITATION SURVEY: RESPONSES TO PART 2

Part 2 of the Apostolic Visitation Survey (survey) was designed to gather thoughts, feelings, and experiences across the entire Visitation process.[1] The majority of responses were qualitative, providing a rich portrait of the Visitation as it unfolded. Survey responses to Part 2, analyzed by Margaret Cain McCarthy and reported to the members of the Grassroots Group in the fall of 2011, detailed the emotional, spiritual, and practical impact of the Visitation on the women who participated.

Approximately 2,500 discrete responses were generated by the 143 individual leaders who returned the eighteen-question survey. Recurring themes have been identified through qualitative content analysis of responses to individual questions. Sample responses are offered for each question in order to illustrate the experience in the words of the participants.[2] Where several descriptors are included to express a theme, it should not be assumed that all responses included each descriptor and many narrative responses expressed multiple themes. Percentages noted in the text refer to the percentage of respondents to a specific question. Generally, themes expressed by five or fewer respondents are not included in this review. Identification of institutes and/or individuals has been avoided; identifiers have been redacted and replaced with "xxx."

Survey responses to questions one through three are examined in *Chapter 4: Experiencing the Apostolic Visitation: Part One of the Apostolic Visitation Survey*. Part 2 of the survey includes questions four through eighteen; those responses are offered here.

Part 2 of the Apostolic Visitation Survey: The Visitation Experience as it Unfolded

Question 4: As the leader(s) of your congregation/province, what were some of your thoughts and feelings in January of 2009 when you learned that U.S. women religious would become the subject of an Apostolic Visitation?

All 143 survey participants responded to this question. One hundred twenty-three (86%) individuals expressed thoughts and feelings that can be characterized as having a generally negative tone. Others (n= 9; 6%) were neutral; five (4%) primarily expressed concern; three (2%) responses were mixed; and three (2%) were generally accepting or positive.

- Although the words *anger/angry* were most common, other words expressing similar dissatisfaction were also used including *disappointment, fear, shock, resentment, unjust, sadness, indignation*, and/or *stress*. Altogether, 110 respondents (77%) expressed this general theme. Seventy-one respondents in this group included the specific words *anger* and/or *angry* at some point in their response to this question. In some cases, it was the initial response; in other cases anger emerged as more information regarding the Apostolic Visitation became known.
- Ninety-four respondents (66%) expressed concern about the purpose of the Apostolic Visitation and/or its outcome.
- Almost one-third (32%) of the respondents noted their surprise or confusion regarding the announcement of the Apostolic Visitation.
- Forty-two respondents (29%) expressed the view that the Visitation reflected a lack of respect for, or a betrayal of, women religious. Some reported that they felt women religious were not supported or valued by the hierarchy/male hierarchy of the church; these feelings ranged from disappointment to a sense of oppression.
- Initial concerns regarding the announcement of the Apostolic Visitation included the perception that it would be a distraction from the important work of ministry and/or would be a waste of time and money that could be better spent addressing the multitude of problems facing the church and the world. Thirty-four respondents (24%) expressed this theme.
- Although the tone of the responses varied, nineteen respondents (13%) noted their willingness to cooperate or determination to use the opportunity to share the truth about their lives and ministries. Some simply took the Visitation in stride while some witnessed the movement of the Spirit or viewed it as an opportunity to look thoughtfully at religious life or to be part of an important story.
- Fifteen respondents (10%) expressed a sense of sadness, injustice, or offense noting specifically the significant contributions of women religious

to the development of the church and/or their long fidelity to the church on a personal or communal level.

- Twelve respondents (8%) mentioned the Stonehill College Symposium and wondered what role it had played in the development of the Visitation.
- Some respondents (8%) questioned the Visitation in light of the sex abuse scandals.

Sample responses to Question 4:

- *We were incredulous, angry, resentful, cautious, and fearful. We were astonished that we learned of the Apostolic Visitation, first through the public media and then through an initial communication addressed to "The Major Superior." We were expected to check the Apostolic Visitation website daily to learn of developments. We were resentful that so much time and energy was taken from our ministry to our budding new congregation. We were deeply offended that the church we love and serve so faithfully initiated such a humiliating public process.*
- *We were shocked, scandalized, confused, and questioned why the hierarchy, especially the U.S.A. bishops, thought so little of all our sisters. These are women who have given so much and who had worked hard to intentionally follow the directions of the hierarchy during the renewal of the last 40+ years. Our sisters had renewed according to church documents and with church approval every step of the way. We wondered why the women religious were being put through such an embarrassing, belittling procedure instead of the U.S.A. bishops with the problems they have contributed to in their actions in the sexual abuse situations. We felt anger, distrusted, disheartened, and oppressed by the hierarchy without due cause.*
- *I immediately felt disrespected and continued to feel that way throughout the process—imagine holding a press conference about U.S. women religious being investigated without having the common courtesy to notify the congregations first. It was a full month before we received an official notification in a letter from Rome. I think it took another month or two for the Instrumentum Laboris to arrive. According to church procedures this document should have arrived at the same time the Apostolic Visitation was announced. Throughout the entire process I felt like each step was being made up as we went along. It was clearly not a well thought out process. Mother Clare obviously did not even have a complete list of all U.S. congregations—some never received any of the communications!!!*
- *Rage, then anger and a sadness that will not go away. We have been faithful to our calling and continue to actively discern our fidelity. I still feel oppressed by my own church.*

- *My first reaction was a feeling of deep sadness, especially for our elderly sisters who have given their lives in service of the church and then suddenly and inexplicably found themselves under investigation by the church. I was also concerned that the investigation was initiated with no prior consultation with LCWR, CMSWR, and U.S. Catholic bishops, leaving me to wonder who asked for it and why.*

- *As the xxx whose order has served the church and the people of God faithfully for over 1,500 years I deeply resented any attempt to silence or control the Spirit speaking in and through us. I strongly felt that the matter was poorly conceived and even more poorly executed and communicated.*

- *I was a new xxx and felt significant anxiety as well as anger, confusion, and sadness. It was so not how we are accustomed to operating. There was also a sense of being betrayed by the church to whom and for whom we have given so much. Yet, in the midst of all of those negative feelings, I so wanted us to respond from the best of who we are, from integrity and honesty.*

- *We had mixed feelings. God works everything to our good, so the good that came out of it all was the solidarity among the women religious, the courageous generosity of our canon lawyer friends (they know who they are), and our willingness to look at ourselves as a group.*

- *Initially I was startled and surprised and wondered really why this was occurring. I also was willing to be cooperative and thus made the appointment to visit with Mother Clare because I wanted to meet face to face and see what the investigation was all about.*

- *Questions arose: What has prompted the Apostolic Visitation? Is there a hidden agenda? Why only U.S. apostolic women religious? As a leader I felt disrespected that we found out through a press conference. We were angry about the secrecy and unfairness of the process, lack of dialogue. The process felt paternalistic and un-pastoral. We felt betrayed by the church—we had done what the church asked us to do at Vatican II. I was shocked at the comments of Cardinal Rodé and Sara Butler. As president, I was anxious about my response and the consequences to my community. I thought the Apostolic Visitation was a manifestation of sexism. That was painful. I was fearful the [Visitation] would be divisive within our community. I felt overwhelmed by another major item on my plate.*

- *Our first thought was one of sadness and great disappointment. Sadness because we were learning that usually an Apostolic Visitation means there is something seriously amiss and something that needs correcting. We were at a loss to know what the women religious had done to warrant such a visitation. We checked out the Stonehill papers which we understood were accepted by Cardinal Rodé as accurate descriptions of current practices of religious life in the United States. We continued to search for information which might lead us to some validation of what was reported*

in those presentations at Stonehill. None could be found. The disappointment bordered on anger about the way this information was received by
Cardinal Rodé and some of the American cardinals and bishops.

- *Initially I was concerned about the intent of it because of the lack of
  information as to its sources. The lack of consultation was unfortunate
  and to some degree harmful. I was also concerned about the time and
  energy this would require especially for leadership and its impact on other
  important matters facing the congregation. I was also concerned about
  some elements of the process and the lack of consultation prior to this
  announcement.*
- *In retrospect, the enormous contributions of women religious have shaped
  the American church. This force for good is diminishing, dying—not surprising, therefore, that the hierarchy are aware of the church's loss and
  are asking us to reflect on it.*
- *A little bit of curiosity/anxiety. We put the issue in perspective and did not
  over-react. Just took it in stride and did not spend a great deal of energy
  individually or corporately.*

*Question 5a: Have your [refers to the individual completing the
questionnaire] thoughts and feelings about the Apostolic Visitation changed
over time?*

Question 5b: If you answered "Yes," please describe how they have changed.

As the Apostolic Visitation proceeded, most (71%) of the 143 survey respondents reported that their own thoughts and feelings about the Visitation
changed over time. Of the 101 respondent leaders who reported a change, 50
percent described thoughts and feelings that moved in a more positive direction. For about one-third (36%), the response was a mix of both negative and
positive as negative feelings remained but had softened to some degree and
they were able to identify one or more positive outcomes of the Visitation.
For others (8%), initial negative thoughts and feelings persisted or intensified. A few (7%) offered neutral responses or did not address the question
directly.

   Based on the statements of the 101 respondents who reported a change in
thoughts and feelings, a more detailed analysis is offered to capture the range
of views they expressed.

- The most commonly expressed change was the development and growth
  of solidarity with other women religious, regionally and nationally. Forty-
  eight of the 101 respondents (48%) noted this change.
- While some respondents noted the theme of solidarity among and between
  women religious of different institutes, the recognition of the Visitation as

an opportunity for growth, collaboration, strengthening, and development of individual religious communities was also noted, sometimes in spite of a continued belief in the injustice of the Visitation itself. Forty-five respondents (45%) reported this change.

- Of the thirty-six respondents (36%) who expressed a mixed change in thoughts and feelings, twenty-eight reported a sense of consolation or joy due to the growth of solidarity among women religious, a positive impact on their own institute, gratitude for the outpouring of support from the laity and some male religious or bishops, relief that Rome seemed to back down a bit, and/or easing of anger and anxiety. However, all thirty-six respondents noted negative feelings about the Visitation, citing continued secrecy regarding its inception or purpose and/or a continuing or deepened sense of concern or distrust regarding the outcome.

- Overall, twenty respondents (20%) who noted a change in thoughts and feelings expressed appreciation for the support of the lay community and/or priests and religious orders of men and/or some bishops.

- Sixteen respondents (16%) noted that anger, fear and/or other negative feelings had eased. Some felt less threatened or more relaxed/hopeful. Several noted their trust in God to bring some good from the Visitation experience.

- Comments throughout the survey responses were repeatedly complimentary regarding interactions with, and the leadership of, Mother Mary Clare Millea. Additionally, polite, positive treatment of communities during visits seemed to move respondents to view the Visitation in a more optimistic light. Fourteen respondents (14%) expressed this view in response to this survey question.

- Thirteen respondents (13%) noted that Rome listened and, over time, the focus of the Apostolic Visitation changed somewhat. For some, the addition of an American male religious, Archbishop Joseph Tobin, SSsR, to the Congregation for Institutes of Consecrated Life and Societies of Apostolic Life (CICLSAL) as its secretary was viewed as a positive development.

- The eight respondents (8%) whose thoughts or feelings remained generally negative noted that mistrust or skepticism had deepened and/or anger, resentment, or sadness had remained or intensified.

Sample responses of those who answered "yes" to Question 5b:

- *There was a great movement of the Holy Spirit between the time the Questionnaire arrived and the deadline for answering. A great solidarity of leaders developed. Because of this solidarity . . . I was able to let go of a lot of negative feelings and anxiety about the possible consequences of the Apostolic Visitation. As a community we approached the Apostolic Visita-*

tion as an opportunity to reflect on our journey since Vatican II and articulate who we had become; i.e., religious life for us now. We could see positive aspects of the Apostolic Visitation. The appointment of Tobin has created a more positive feeling about what may happen when the reports are sent to Rome.

- Yes. Our feelings have eased somewhat because of the tremendous experience of collaboration and mutual support from canonists and leaders of other religious congregations. Also, the replacement of Rodé has had an effect on the intensity of feeling. Finally, we have deepened the sense of our own self-determination and integrity in relationship to who we are in the church.

- Despite our initial questions and frustration about it all from the beginning, we were inclined to participate so that we could share our story and express how proud we are to be women religious in the U.S. today. The process promoted much good dialogue and continued to shed light on the gift that religious life is to our country, the church, and the world. We also felt very encouraged with the appointment of Archbishop Tobin.

- On a positive side, some unintended results of the Apostolic Visitation give me great hope—the tremendous solidarity forged among women religious across the world and the terrific support of us from our lay brothers and sisters and the appointment of Joe Tobin to the Roman dicastery were all signs of "something new happening." I still have feelings of anger that so much energy was spent on this process. I feel sad that this institutional church structure wastes its time on things like the Apostolic Visitation. It seems to be a futile effort of a decaying structure which, probably not in my lifetime, is headed for significant changes.

- My hope is that women religious will help to create a transformed reality in our church reflective of the gospel in the future. The initial awful sense of assault on our integrity and fidelity as women religious deeply committed to the church has subsided over time. Anger and resentment gave way to deepening bonds of solidarity and support among our various congregations, both at the regional and national level. The experience has unified and strengthened us in our core. We received so many expressions of support from the laity, and especially from our colleagues in ministry, as well as from many priests and religious orders of men. We were buoyed by the public statements of support from UISG [International Union of Superiors General], the Conference of Women Religious in Asia, Bishop Dowling from South Africa, and countless other individuals, groups, and agencies in the United States.

- I found the experience much more open and engaging than I had thought. I am most grateful for the collaboration, the deepening unity that happened among us as women religious. I am delighted in the response of the faithful who rose up in support of the gift of women religious in all of our *diversity to this church of ours. Grace did prevail, and I refuse to be concerned about the "report" to come.*

- *As I began to see the religious women RISE UP to the challenge with dignity, courage and great creativity, I felt my anger dissipate somewhat, although the sadness remained for a while. As we took up our own "agenda-with-the agenda" it began to become a learning [experience] for us. We felt affirmed and confirmed: the U.S. apostolic women religious are a diverse, alive, and responsive voice of light in the ecclesial body. Our sadness expanded to a new-found awareness and pride, bringing new solidarity and communion to us as a group on a national level.*

- *Interaction with Mother Mary Clare Millea both personally and in phone conversation has alleviated some of the fear. Speaking with some of the members of communities who had on-site visits and hearing how positive they were and what good has come as a result, as well as experiencing the support of other religious brothers and sisters nationally and internationally, as well as the rest of the lay faithful has brought peace. However there is still some anxiety because the purpose is still not clear and the outcome is unknown.*

- *The ground rules kept shifting, layers were added, there was contradictory information; information was hard to get except in the media. We tried to make the best of an unjust situation. Anger persists but unanticipated positive results have emerged: greater unity among our members; greater unity among women religious. For some, trust in, and regard for, those exercising church authority greatly diminished.*

- *We remain grateful for the unintended consequences—deeper communion among us as congregation, greater solidarity among women and men religious in the U.S. and around the world. Public comments from the office of CICLSAL compounded the feelings of anger and angst and confusion. We were concerned and discontent with what seemed to be the "cross-purposes" in what was stated. This made the gap between members of the hierarchy and women religious in the U.S. even more evident. It also raised questions about a general lack of understanding about the varied, valid expressions of lived religious life.*

- *Our thoughts and feelings have changed somewhat because our experience was positive. However, it was totally unnecessary: a waste of time and money. Many attitudes softened as a result of the visit.*

Question 6: What thoughts and feelings of yours [refers to the individual completing the questionnaire] have remained constant over time about the Apostolic Visitation? If none have remained constant, please simply enter "none."

One hundred thirty-three (93%) of the 143 survey participants described thoughts and feelings about the Apostolic Visitation that remained constant over time.

- Overwhelmingly, the common thread among the 133 was continued questioning of the rationale behind the Visitation and belief that the Visitation was unjust, unnecessary, or wrong. Some noted continuing anger, disappointment, or anxiety; some continued to believe it was a waste of resources, based on mistrust, demonstrated a lack of understanding of religious life in the United States and/or was based on a pre-Vatican II mentality and/or was promoted by the male hierarchy of the church. One hundred six respondents (80%) of the 133 expressed this common theme.
- Fifty-one respondents (38%) noted that questions and/or concerns regarding the process and/or the lack of transparency remained constant.
- For some, faith and trust in God and/or a focus on the gospel remained constant. Others mentioned confidence/pride in their work and the importance of their response or gratitude for being able to participate. Thirty-seven (28%) of the 133 respondents who reported feelings that remained constant are included in this category.
- Nineteen respondents (14%) noted the support of the laity, male clergy and/or canon lawyers and/or solidarity with other women religious as constants throughout the Visitation.

Sample responses to Question 6:

- *Some feelings of apprehension and caution remained constant. Despite various attempts by Mother Mary Clare and others to "explain" the Visitation and paint it in a positive light we remain skeptical and we regret, for the sake of the church, that it ever happened. But for our part, we feel the end result was unexpectedly positive.*
- *The purpose of the Visitation was unclear. The whole thing was a waste of time. We felt we were going to be judged. We did not know the criteria for the visit. We do not know what happens to the data gathered. We never wavered on our commitment to the monastic way of life. We stayed committed to the support of other women religious.*
- *Uncertainty about the purpose. Unfairness of the process. The Apostolic Visitation as a manifestation of a sexist system. There is an effort by some in power to curtail the spirit of Vatican II. The importance of the response*

of women religious for the entire church. Still somewhat apprehensive about the possible outcomes.

- *We have been wondering if we will receive a report regarding our congregation after the process is completed. We are still curious as to why the Apostolic Visitation was initiated. We continue to be grateful for the opportunity to participate in this historic moment.*
- *We have nothing to hide! We have a great story to share, both as an individual congregation and as women religious throughout the U.S. Anger, frustration, and questioning were constant. We felt the whole process was a waste of time and the church could have made better use of funds that were spent in this project.*
- *Concern for what will be done with the report, for its purpose, and how it will be interpreted/misinterpreted at many different levels.*
- *Deep concern about the secrecy and lack of trust exhibited by CICLSAL. Lack of respect on the part of those who initiated and conducted the Apostolic Visitation for collaboration, participation, subsidiarity. Vatican does not understand religious life and culture in the U.S.*
- *I remain cautious and mistrustful since they seem to be hiding the real reasons for the Visitation by not giving a full explanation. Even though Mother Clare now seems to be saying that each congregation will receive a copy of what is submitted, this is not enough. It has been a waste of time, energy, and money.*
- *Still questioning regarding the purpose of this and what will be the result of it.*
- *Excitement at being involved in something meaningful; challenged; peaceful; led by the Spirit; united with many of my sisters in leadership as we were led together by the Spirit and we listened and responded.*
- *We continue to believe that the amount of time, energy, and money spent on this entire process could have been more fruitfully applied to a process of dialogue that would have engaged apostolic women religious in a collaborative process concerning religious life in our culture at this time in history.*
- *We have remained with the attitude that the church/CICLSAL has the right to evaluate us and we have the responsibility to cooperate with the process. We remain with the question "what will be the final outcome of this?" We have also consistently felt the burden of the amount of time and effort we have put into this process.*
- *Constant thought was that we, women religious, place our faith in God's providence on a daily basis. I found peace in that.*

Q7a: Did you engage your sisters throughout the Apostolic process?

Of the 143 survey respondents, 133 (93%) reported that they did engage their sisters throughout the Apostolic process. Nine (6%) reported that they did not; one (1%) did not respond to the question.

Q7b: If you answered "Yes" [to Q7a], please indicate when and how.

One hundred thirty-three respondents reported that they did engage their sisters throughout the Apostolic Visitation process. Some provided substantial information on their engagement activities during certain phases and much less during other phases. Further, institutes that did not receive a visit may appear to have had less engagement with their sisters when, in fact, they may have been strongly engaged but only in Phase 2 (*Questionnaire*). Respondents mentioned many types and forms of engagement, but it cannot be determined whether or not they each mentioned *all* of the types and forms in which they engaged. Therefore, general conclusions based on the information presented below should be cautiously considered.

- Of the 133 who responded to this question, 114 (86%) noted that they kept their sisters engaged through: sharing the *Questionnaire* and Visitation material; informing the sisters and/or sending updates via websites; correspondence; and/or electronic communication.
- A majority (62%) mentioned the collaborative nature of the engagement: sisters were invited to consider/respond to/reflect on the questionnaire; were invited to discussions; were requested to provide input or feedback; and/or to share thoughts and feelings.
- Eighty-two (62%) indicated they held meetings, conference calls, and/or worked in committees.
- Thirty-one respondents (23%) specifically mentioned that sisters were engaged through prayer or prayerful reflection. Some noted that prayers were offered for other institutes on the day of the visit.
- Twenty-one respondents (16%) specifically mentioned efforts to engage the sisters in the visit itself or in reflection afterward.
- Eighteen respondents (14%) shared information from canonists or cannon lawyers.
- Eleven (8%) shared articles or other information with their sisters.

Sample responses to Question 7b indicate various forms and levels of engagement:

- *Our team kept the sisters informed at each juncture: (a) as letters were received and sent; (b) in reading all material and encouraging visiting the Apostolic Visitation website; (c) in learning about the nature of apostolic visitation from a canon lawyer at our provincial chapter; (d) in inviting sisters and the focus group to meet with a canon lawyer; (e) invitation to all sisters to attend the opening prayer and ritual of blessing of visitors and participants; (f) collaboration of the provincial team in preparing and hosting the Visitation; (g) in having a debriefing with the entire province the Saturday after the Visitation (in person, video, and audio conference); (h) in crafting a statement about the Visitation that could be used by the sisters if asked.*

- *Leadership gave in-person explanations to members about the way we chose to respond to Phase 2. We arranged to have canon lawyers prepare sisters who volunteered to be interviewed. Communication as appropriate occurred throughout the process. After the Visitation, we held a debriefing conference call open to our sisters around the U.S. Approximately seventy-five sisters agreed to be interviewed while others served as escorts for visitors.*

- *In October and November of 2009, we brought our sisters together to distribute a copy of the Questionnaire and explain the process. In November we brought them together to inform them how we responded. We received a standing ovation!*

- *In responding to Mother Mary Clare's requests to send out the Questionnaire, called a meeting to discuss and clarify.*

- *Letters, readings, regional meetings, small group meetings. Consultation with canon lawyers. Assembly presentations. Much time was put into this.*

- *At each new juncture, we kept the sisters informed of what leadership was doing and how we were handling it. We shared the questions with the sisters so that they knew what we were being asked. There was discussion among the members at our community meetings.*

- *During Phase 1 and 2 we kept the sisters informed of the process and how we were responding through letters. Once we knew we would have an on-site visit we met face-to-face with sisters at our three centers. The visitors stayed at one of our centers and had numerous opportunities to interact with the sisters. After the visitors left we provided sisters who had been part of the visit [an opportunity] to process their experiences.*

- *We shared information right from the start and met with all the members to explain about the Apostolic Visitation and why we had decided to respond as we did to the Questionnaire. In preparation for the on-site visit we again met with all members in the region being visited and, as far as possible, with members in other regions. We also gathered all who had signed up for a personal or group meeting with the visitors and spoke with them—this was at their request and to respond to their questions and concerns; we did not wish to influence them and made it clear that they were free to speak as they wished. All these meetings were important as we held the tension between, on the one hand, those members who ob-*

jected very strongly to the Apostolic Visitation and felt we ought not collaborate in what they regarded as an abusive and unjust process, and, on the other, those who would not think of questioning the process, much less refusing to cooperate. The bulk of the members fell between these extremes.

- *By detailed email, I communicated information received from Mother Clare as it arrived. At an assembly of the congregation in November 2009, I explained to the congregation why we decided not to answer the Questionnaire.*
- *Every step of the way our sisters were engaged in the process and communicated with. There was frequent and honest communication with the members of the congregation.*
- *We engaged our sisters in communication regarding the Apostolic Visitation, keeping them informed of events as they occurred. We were not visited; thus communication occurred as opposed to active engagement.*
- *I informed the community as soon as possible (same day) and shared every communication from Mother Mary Clare's office. I put out the Instrumentum Laboris, the Questionnaire and my responses. At our regular chapter meetings (6–8 a year) I kept them informed. They were involved in the prep for the actual on-site visit. The prep was a refresher course for us and helped us put into words for the visitors what we take for granted about our life.*
- *Theological reflection, discernment, listening sessions, communication, and prayer. Invited sisters to write to leadership expressing their concerns, views, feelings. Sisters affirmed our decision not to answer Questionnaire.*

Q7c: If you answered "No" [to Q7a], please indicate why.

Four of the nine respondents who answered "no" to Question 7a, indicating they did not engage their sisters in the Visitation process noted, however, that they did keep the sisters informed or generally informed. One of these four reported that there were other issues of importance to the institute at the time. The remaining five offered a variety of reasons for not engaging the sisters including: they were not visited (mentioned by two respondents); not engaging them was the decision of the leader or approved by the leadership team (mentioned by two respondents); such engagement might cause division (one respondent); the sisters were aged (one respondent); did not want to disturb sisters' lives (one respondent); the membership was scattered (one respondent). [Note: one survey participant did not respond to Question 7a, 7b, or 7c.]

Q8: How would you describe the thoughts and feelings of your sisters (as individuals and as a community) during these two years of this Apostolic Visitation?

In some cases, a variety of adjectives described the thoughts and feelings of both groups of sisters and individual sisters over the two year period. In some responses, change over time was noted; in other responses it was not. Most responses expressed more than one theme as the respondent attempted to describe the experiences of many individuals. One hundred thirty-eight participants responded to this question.

- Ninety-six (70%) expressed concern about the process and/or the outcome. These expressions included worry, fear, apprehension, suspicion, discontent, offense, and/or distrust.
- More than half (59%) of the 138 respondents noted that the sisters experienced feelings of anger, outrage, frustration, betrayal, and/or resentment.
- Almost half (49%) reported that the sisters were engaged, developed a deeper appreciation of themselves, were supportive of leadership, experienced internal solidarity, and/or were interested in sharing their institute's story with Rome and others.
- Twenty-seven respondents (20%) wrote that the sisters were upset, hurt, disappointed, and/or saddened by the Visitation.
- Others (23%) were surprised and/or curious about it.
- Some (19%) took it in stride, did not feel it was a concern, or felt that it was not important. Some in this group simply paid no attention.
- Seventeen respondents (12%) noted that some sisters were pleased by the external support and the sense of solidarity they felt with other religious/laity.
- A few sisters (n=6; 4%) expressed support for the idea of the Apostolic Visitation and/or believed it was needed.

Sample responses to *Question 8*:

- *When they first heard of the Apostolic Visitation many sisters indicated that they experienced a range of emotions including anger, fear, sadness, hurt, confusion, and surprise. Through a variety of processes including prayer, study, reading, preparation, communication, dialogue, and presentations as well as through the guidance of leadership, most felt movement to a different place. This was described in various ways: they became more aware of the work of the Spirit; they witnessed a greater depth of oneness within the congregation and with other women religious; they appreciated the goodness and commitment of the congregation and the blessings of being a member; they experienced pride and confidence in the [leadership team] and their sisters; they felt greater peace, calm, faith, and trust; they were called to deeper prayer and thought; they were challenged to play an active part in the transformation of the church.*

- *As individuals, they had various thoughts and feelings, ranging from outrage, anger and fear, to submission to "whatever Rome wants." As a congregation, they listened to the information provided for them by leadership, read information that came out in the media, and studied the materials recommended by LCWR and the Apostolic Visitation websites. They supported the decisions that leadership made regarding our response to the various phases of the Apostolic Visitation.*

- *In most ways, our sisters' reactions were very similar to ours. Because they weren't attending as many meetings with other congregations and canonical consultants as we were, they constantly expressed interest, concern, anger at the hierarchy and desire to understand what seemed incredible. They reminded each other to pray and to maintain a nonviolent stance. Some expressed a sense of "betrayal" by the church which they had loved and tried to serve so faithfully all their lives. Some remained fearful about the outcome, what it might mean in the end. Many heard from friends in other congregations that their leadership had not openly shared information as we had—and they expressed feeling proud of themselves and our community for the trust shared among us. Many are still wondering, "What next?"*

- *Initially our women were angry and questioned the "why" of the process. They were supportive of our response. Sisters attending the introductory session of the onsite visit asked insightful and pointed questions. The openness of the visitators diffused some of the anger. Sisters were engaged via articles in the NCR* [National Catholic Reporter], *especially those by Sandra Schneiders.*

- *Our sisters, especially some of our elders, were confused about why the church would do this to us and why an Apostolic Visitation was needed to assess the quality of our lives. Some expressed fear about reprisals from the Vatican but, after reviewing the Questionnaire, they too could see that the questions did not fit our way of life. As a result, trust in the hierarchy waned. Our members were extremely supportive of the leadership team, especially our decision not to fill out the Questionnaire. Our sisters expressed pride and confidence in how we are living religious life and in the vibrancy of our new congregation. They were angry—not about how we are living religious life—but that the Questionnaire was so skewed towards the particular form of religious life of more conservative congregations.*

- *I would say our sister's feelings ran the gamut of feeling and reactions mostly along liberal and conservative lines. The liberals expressed anger, a sense of being misunderstood by Rome again, and wanting to not coop-*

*erate. Our conservatives expressed confusion about why this was happen-
ing and why it seemed to come at us without warning but urged that we
participate as best we could. I must say that our leadership team's final
decision on how we responded was affirmed by both groups. We received
great support from our sisters.*

- *The initial feelings of anger and dismay have dissipated somewhat but the
  disbelief about the way the entire process happened still remains. The fear
  that the Apostolic Visitation engendered in the older members was the
  most disturbing thing to me. Many of them felt that their vowed lives of 50,
  60, 70 years were being questioned. The preparation and pride of the
  sisters in speaking our truth during the on-site visit gave us a sense of
  strength and confidence. There was energy of the Spirit. Once we were
  able to integrate how we wanted to respond and be women of integrity in
  the Apostolic Visitation we experienced a sense of freedom from the oppression of the process.*

- *They expressed a movement from anger to the reality of our goodness with
  nothing to hide. Amazement with all the real problems that the church has
  now that they would go after us. Shock that the spiritual lives of so many
  faithful sisters was being questioned. Lack of dialogue led to many misunderstandings. Real feeling that [Cardinal] Rodé was trying to distract
  the public from the very real problems in the church and that this was a
  smokescreen.*

- *We did a check on this several times during the two years of this Apostolic
  Visitation. We have a five-page list of what our sisters said in a questionnaire we gave them after the on-site visit. We included a question much
  like the one above. One third of the group that responded to our questionnaire were sisters who live at our retirement home. The most frequently
  mentioned word was "anger"—anger at the church, anger at the secrecy,
  anger at not getting feedback, anger at the unfairness of it all. The second
  most frequent word was "waste"—waste of time, money, and energy. The
  third most frequently mentioned word was "fear"—primarily fear of what
  could happen. The next concern was about "why"—the question of the
  purpose of it all—what were they looking for? Why us? Some of their
  concerns were alleviated by the open discussions we had and by the infor-
  mative reading. Some sisters said that despite their feelings, they found the
  Visitation to be a time of grace for the province as it came together . . .*

- *Confused as to why this is happening now. Willing to enter into a process
  to prepare for a visit. Relieved it is over, if it is really over. Glad for the
  support of the laity and our local ordinary. They were offended by the
  process. They were eager to tell the real story of religious life. They
  cooperated fully and used this as a grace-filled moment.*

- *Some sisters agreed with the Visitation and were supportive of Rome;
  others were not and others did not really feel affected by it.*

- *In the beginning apprehension. Later a sense of support from U.S. Catholics and a sense of solidarity across congregations. Also a clearer awareness of how much we have evolved since Vatican II and the major differences many of us have with traditional communities.*
- *The feelings of the sisters were mixed. Some expressed sadness at the thought of their long lives of faithfulness being questioned. Others were anxious to assist the visitators in understanding our way of life. Some individuals looked at this with the wisdom of experience, responding with a heart-felt "trust in Divine Providence." We did this as a community as well. Some individuals felt anger and concern; we (leadership team) spent time with them to process.*

Q9a. Did the thoughts and feelings of your sisters (as individuals and as a community) shift over the course of these two years?

Forty-eight (34%) of the 140 respondents to this question indicated that the thoughts and feelings of their sisters did *not* change over the course of the two years of the Apostolic Visitation. The majority (n=92; 66%) of the 140, however, indicated that the thoughts and feelings of their sisters did shift over the course of the Visitation.

Q9b. If you responded "Yes" [to Q9a], please describe below.

Of the ninety-two who indicated the thoughts and feelings of their sisters did shift over the course of the Visitation, the majority (n=65; 71%) noted a general shift toward more positive thoughts and feelings, although the shift may not have been experienced by all the institute's sisters. Some respondents (n=14; 15%) described a mixed change. Ten responses (11%) were inconclusive in terms of indicating the direction of the change. Three (3%) expressed a general shift toward more negative thoughts and feelings.

   Multiple reasons were offered to explain the generally positive shift experienced by the majority:

- Thirty-nine percent of these sixty-five, noted that the sense of unity they experienced, the sense of solidarity within the institute, and/or the expanded sense of ownership in their charism, mission, or work resulted in a more positive feeling about the Visitation.
- Nearly as many (33%) noted the positive sense of external solidarity with other women religious, the clergy, and/or the laity.
- Some respondents (19%) felt more positive simply because time had passed, they had returned to their primary/important work, and/or had lost interest.
- Some (14%) expressed the view that the attitudes of their leaders and/or the faith they had in their leaders generated more positive feelings.

- Other comments included the observation that the Visitation process had improved, leadership in Rome had changed, that visits had been positive, and/or that the respondent's institute had not been selected for a visit.

Sample responses to Question 9b:

- *A mellowing and acceptance, the resignation of [Cardinal] Rodé and appointment of [Archbishop] Tobin with a sense that he will be supportive is a sign of hope. We recognized our solidarity with other religious communities.*
- *The positive experience of the visit was very significant for us. When I first talked with our visit coordinator I asked us to make a pact to make this a positive experience for our sisters. Our visiting team was delightful and affirming. Our sisters didn't want them to leave. We had a special blessing for them at the beginning and end of their time with us.*
- *Like myself, they became more positive and worked through their anger. We were choosing to focus on the positive and to trust God in all of this.*
- *As with us, their negative reactions have faded in intensity. Although still not happy about it, they are peaceful. They are proud of themselves, their leadership, and all the women religious who have maintained dignity, composure, and integrity and not allowed ourselves to be demeaned by this. Some sisters, having heard stories from friends about how "nice" the visitators were when on site have begun to forget the fact that it is still an official visitation to correct perceived abuses and not just a friendly visit by a few other religious.*
- *I think that the thoughts and feelings of the sisters shifted to a more positive and hopeful stance over the course of these two years because of the new leadership that has come into the top levels of the Congregation for Religious. The kinds of reports that came from congregations which were visited were more positive than expected and I think that this began to relieve the fear and negativity of the sisters and the community as a whole. At this point almost no one refers to the Apostolic Visitation anymore. We are just watching and waiting with more hope and positive expectation than I think we even thought we could or would be able to have at the beginning.*
- *A full range of emotion was experienced by our sisters. In a general way, as sisters became more educated about the nature and purpose of this Visitation, they moved from initial anxiety, to freedom in claiming their religious identity, (along with some anger and/or indignation about the Visitation and process.) At this point, most sisters no longer care about the outcome, as they are focused on their religious life of prayer, community, and ministry to the people of God.*

- *The sisters became clearer and more confident about describing our identity. A sense of solidarity with other women religious in the U.S. became stronger as conversations took place among members of different congregations.*
- *Certainly, after personal experience in our own visits, or among the sisters who served as visitors, our positive perspective was confirmed. Gradually reading about positive experiences among other congregations strengthened our hope for real growth among all U.S. religious. The warm personal contacts among women religious of various congregations have definitely been the most effective influence in strengthening our commitment to continue working toward greater authenticity and collaboration despite the negativity experience in media, etc., early on.*
- *There was less distress about it. As time went on the sisters were more focused on their daily ministries and the Apostolic Visitation took a back seat except for the ongoing press communications, which often raised some rather energizing and positive communication about religious life.*
- *Yes, after the initial shock and disbelief, the sisters closed ranks and went to a deep place of trust in their own integrity, appreciation for their call to religious life, belief in and love for the congregation and its charism, gratitude for the vocation of every member, living and deceased, whose lives have contributed in countless and profound ways to the life and mission of the church in the U.S. and around the world. The sisters expressed, time and again, their heartfelt support for the stance of leadership—how we chose to respond in the various phases—that we maintained a positive attitude, not allowing ourselves to become demoralized or mired in negativity and defensiveness.*
- *Though there was some constancy, gradually the thoughts and discussions moved into greater skepticism about the entire investigation, concern about the secrecy and lack of transparency, and anxiety about the anticipated future actions of the Vatican which would follow the reports of Phase 4.*
- *Anxiety increased over time, especially as we learned of the on-site visit. When faced with the personal choice of an interview, some were concerned that they respond in a way that represented the congregation well and others were glad and grateful to be able to tell our congregational story and share their experience in their own words. As we began to participate, there was a sense of togetherness among us, and a growing solidarity with other women religious.*
- *The sisters' interest and concern waned. We were not visited. Leadership remained calm and confident.*
- *This is mixed. There remains a fundamental disagreement with the process and a desire to know what will become of the materials shared during*

the process. There is a growing sense of solidarity with other religious and the laity who have supported women religious during the process.

Q10. What remained constant for your sisters (as individuals and as a community) during these two years of the Apostolic Visitation?

Of the 136 valid responses to this question, the majority (n=90; 66%) expressed a theme of consistency that described faith in God and a sense of certainty in the integrity of their lives. These elements were identified in a variety of ways including: trust in God; prayer; service; commitment to mission; a sense of pride in their work; the desire to make the Visitation a positive experience; and/or the solidarity/integrity of their own institute. About half (n=46) of these ninety expressed only this theme.

- Fifty-six (41%) of the 136 respondents to this question noted that concerns and questions about the Visitation remained constant. For example, they cited frustration, resentment, and/or concerns about secrecy/the process/ wastefulness/the institutional church, and/or concerns about why the Visitation was initiated and/or fear of the outcome.
- Thirty four (25%) of the respondents noted that a sense of solidarity remained constant. This was expressed as support for and from other U.S. institutes and other congregations around the world, trust in one another, gratitude for women religious and/or prayer for one another.
- A theme expressed by seventeen respondents (13%) was that support for leadership and or the consistency of leadership remained a constant during the Visitation.
- Smaller numbers of respondents expressed the following themes as constants: interest in the Visitation and/or media reports about it (n=9; 7%); anger (n=7; 5%); confusion for those not involved and/or a lack of interest (n= 5; 4%); sadness and/or hurt and/or dismay (n=5; 4%).

Sample responses to Question 10:

- *What remained constant was the belief that the Spirit would win out in the end and all that we have lived would be vindicated.*
- *What remained constant was our own fidelity to our call and its lived expression. We were moving toward our general and provincial chapters and, as always, we hoped to ask some of the deeper questions of ourselves. We did not appreciate being forced to consider the quality of our lives based on the Vatican concerns. Rather we looked forward to exploring together where our God calls us as we move into a new and unknown future.*

- *I quote from our 2004 (repeated in 2010) general chapter enactments, ". . . as women of the church, the people of God . . . we are called to rise again and again, not to give up on a vision of church that is a humbler, truer sign of God's inclusive and reconciling love, not to abandon the wounded, broken church we experience."*

- *What remained constant over the two years is a conviction that, whether or not the institutional church acknowledges the contribution of our lives and mission as women religious, our sisters know from a deep place that the members of our congregation, throughout our long history and true to our founding charism, have entered deeply into the lives and needs of people; that individually and collectively we have made a difference for good in the world, and no one can ever take that away or say it isn't so. Our foundresses went through a lot grief with members of the hierarchy to be able to found the congregation, but they never gave up. It hurts to have your integrity called into question, but we know the truth of our lives. We will get through this and be stronger for it.*

- *Our affection for one another and our love for God and the people of God. Our support and affirmation of leadership, awareness of the importance of women religious to the church, appreciation for our forebears, renewed appreciation for our constitutions, keen awareness of the support of women religious in the U.S., around the world, and of so many of the laity who count on us to bring about a renewed Vatican II vision of the church. The conviction that we are following the charism of our foundress, adapting and interpreting it as we read the signs of the times. Our belief that the Spirit is moving with us and that we live our lives for and in God.*

- *The feeling of uncertainty, mixed messages, and suspicion remained constant. Sisters were confused since we told them that this was a canonical inquiry process and a formal visitation and the lead visitor told them publically that this was a sister-to-sister process. The pride that we were standing strong with our congregation and with all U.S. women religious was a constant. The anger our sisters felt did not affect how they responded to the three visitors. They were received with gracious hospitality. What remained constant is our willingness to treat people with dignity no matter what their personal beliefs are.*

- *Feelings of justified anger, resentment, and insult have remained constant for many of our sisters. At the same time, we have all become aware of common bonds with other religious, and of the mutual respect between ourselves and many of the congregations who choose more traditional living of the vows.*

- *Solidarity and a belief in our prophetic role and our good works: the hallmark of our life remains our commitment to the poor. We stayed focused on who we are.*

- *Our prayer for the good of the process and for those being visited was a constant. We also confirmed our belief that we as a congregation have been faithful to our call, community life, prayer, and have been good stewards of our resources and ministries. Leadership felt a support from all the sisters.*
- *What remained constant for our sisters during the two years of the Apostolic Visitation is an ongoing support and trust in their leaders, a deep seated knowledge that, as ecclesial women, they have remained loyal to the church in the midst of calling it to greater fidelity. For the most part, during the two years, sisters have gone about their ministry and engaged in the same community life and prayer life that they always have.*
- *I think most sisters trusted that leadership was participating in the process in a responsible manner. There was consistent interest in the information and analysis given in public accounts in the Catholic press and other media. There was growing solidarity and prayers with and for all religious women engaged in the process.*
- *The sisters have kept this intention in prayer, but are anxious about the possible outcomes. The negative comments from the Vatican, especially at the beginning were stressful to membership. The questions most frequently asked are, "When will it be over?" and "How will our lives be changed?"*
- *A deep sense of solidarity, confidence and trust in God, a belief in the goodness of their lives as women religious, and a desire to live our mission fully and freely. There was also a shared vulnerability as a result of what appeared to be a lack of trust and appreciation on the part of the hierarchical church.*
- *The solidarity and support; love for our congregation and our call to religious life; the question about "why"; the belief that the process was unjust.*

Q11a. During these two years, did you participate in gatherings with leaders of other religious institutes in which the Apostolic Visitation was discussed?

All but one of the 143 respondents (99%) stated that she participated in gatherings with leaders of other religious institutes in which the Apostolic Visitation was discussed. The one respondent who did not noted that, in retrospect, she wishes she had.

Q11b. If you attended them, how did these gatherings impact your thoughts and feelings about the Apostolic Visitation?

Eighty percent (n=114) of the 142 respondents who participated in gatherings with leaders of other religious institutes in which the Apostolic Visitation was discussed noted that these gatherings provided strength and support through solidarity, appreciation for religious life, affirmation and/or confirmation of the direction they were taking; and/or confidence/courage. Fifty-six percent (n=80) cited that they gained knowledge/clarity, they shared wisdom and/or experiences; and/or they gathered useful information about the *Questionnaire*.

- Thirty-five respondents (25%) appreciated the peaceful, contemplative stance they witnessed at gatherings and/or the opportunity to process feelings/thoughts/hurt/anger and/or discern a response. For some in this group, gatherings helped to dissipate suspicion/anger and some noted that the gatherings offered prayerful support.
- Thirty-one respondents (22%) valued the opportunity to learn about canon law and/or their rights and responsibilities through these gatherings.
- For some (n=16; 11%), the gatherings raised or instilled fear, suspicion, and/or anger. Some individuals in this group felt the gatherings were divisive or a distraction and, for some, the gatherings deepened their anger or strengthened the belief that the Visitation was a flawed process and/or reinforced concerns regarding motives for the Apostolic Visitation.
- The opportunity to learn about and/or support or appreciate different approaches to, and perspectives on, the Visitation was noted by thirteen respondents (9%).

Sample responses to Question 11b:

- *We were deeply enriched, challenged, humbled, and inspired by the gatherings. The overall strong spirit of support and networking which only grew stronger each month continues today. We experienced an American sisterhood emerging instead of individual congregations and courage to speak up for the integrity of our lives. Solidarity among the women religious, especially in the U.S.A., and non-violent, contemplative status grew even as congregations responded in different ways to the procedure.*
- *These gatherings renewed our hope in the church as the people of God who were in solidarity with each other. We grew in admiration of LCWR leadership at this time of crisis and this witness gave us courage. LCWR displayed a professional manner. They maintained a quiet dignity.*
- *They [the gatherings] helped us formulate questions, identify options, explore alternatives for response, and gather the information we needed for discernment of our actions. They also helped us to remember that we are together in this experience—together as U.S. communities, and united globally with so many other women religious as well. This was a very powerful experience of solidarity.*
- *It [gave] witness to the integrity and solidarity among women religious. It also demonstrated the love for the church despite the negative experience. We look at our rights and responsibilities as vowed women of the church.*

- *I participated in gatherings of prioresses of other autonomous monasteries, with leaders of apostolic institutes, and with our local diocesan bishop. These meetings were supportive, helped clarify the questions in the Questionnaire and helped me not take the process personally. The collaboration with others in both monastic and apostolic traditions increased our collaboration and respect for different charisms and community life. They lessened the sense of isolation and resistance for a process that I did not understand, like, or really want to do.*
- *I found them extremely helpful in sorting through our options. It was good to feel solidarity with so many other women religious. Just speaking my feeling out loud proved to be helpful, since I could not do this with my sisters for fear of alarming them.*
- *I felt a great unity in how we women religious were feeling about the process, and how we were strengthened in claiming our own identity and charism as gift to the church and the world. There was a great sense of mutual support, as well as clarity about the decisions we needed to make as we responded to the Questionnaire.*
- *They impacted our sense of solidarity. They made us reflect more on the theological groundings in our lives. Many of us read the articles by Sandra Schneiders in the NCR and felt they described our evolution.*
- *Yes, meeting and talking with others was very helpful in expanding our understanding of the implications of answering some of the questions. This clarified for me the dangers in being transparent and how hurtful the results could be for religious in the U.S. (This is still a worry but I have faith that [Archbishop] Tobin will conduct the conclusion of this with respect, dignity, and affirmation.)*
- *These gatherings and conference calls were extremely helpful. It seems that many of the questions had different meanings than face value interpretation. They also helped dissipate some of the anger and suspicion that was felt. These gatherings also brought us more together as committed religious from different congregations.*
- *The gatherings presented vital new insights into the process of an Apostolic Visitation and our options on how to respond. Canon lawyers, our federation and regional federation gatherings were also very helpful and supportive as we collaborated with each other in deeper ways.*
- *The first consultation was with a canon lawyer whose information about the Visitation and possible outcomes surprised and frightened us. Meetings with members of regional and national LCWR and xxx reassured us, because we experienced our shared purpose, we learned from each other, and we made explicit our intention to support each other. Meetings with several bishops were also reassuring because of their support.*
- *Although we understood (and to some extent shared) the initial hesitation among religious due to the unprecedented nature of this Visitation (and*

unfortunate remarks by Cardinal Rodé), we were appalled at the concerted efforts to instill fear and suspicion among women religious toward the Vatican outreach. If anything, these meetings/calls reinforced our sense of the necessity of such a Visitation to explore the tensions, attitudes, and fidelity of U.S. religious toward the universal church.

- *The gatherings reinforced my own beliefs that the motives and purposes of the Visitation were never honestly acknowledged and that CICLSAL was abusing its canonical authority and insulting American women religious. The gatherings also reinforced my own belief that responding in anger and resentment does not contribute to resolution.*

Q12. During these two years what role, if any, did canonical input/advice play in your approach to the Apostolic Visitation?

The vast majority (n=122; 85%) of the 143 respondents described the assistance of canonists as generally or very positive, supportive, helpful, significant, important, or critical. Most of these responses included additional information on the type of assistance offered. A few, however, simply stated their gratitude for the assistance. Nineteen respondents (13%) noted the receipt of canonical input/advice but did not characterize it as either positive or negative. Two respondents (1%) indicated that canonical input/advice did not play a role in their approach to the Visitation. Most respondents noted the receipt of canonical input/advice and described the type of input/advice they received.

- Ninety-four (66%) of the 143 respondents noted that the canonist(s): explained rights and/or responsibilities; presented options for responding or not responding; presented options and/or information on the questionnaire; and/or helped the respondent (and/or the institute) make an informed, articulate response.
- Forty respondents (28%) noted that the canonist(s): united and/or protected sisters; helped respondents to speak their truth and/or share their charism; strengthened courage or confidence; were affirming; and/or reduced fear/anxiety.
- The canonist(s) promoted an understanding of the Apostolic Visitation, the process, and/or the stakes for thirty respondents (21%).
- Ten respondents (7%) stated that the canonist(s) reviewed their materials and/or reviewed the *Questionnaire* prior to submission.

Sample responses to Question 12:

- *Canonical input/advice was extremely important. Among other things it presented us with options as to how we might answer (or not answer) the*

Questionnaire. We became aware of the canonical implications and seri-
ousness of the Visitation.
- I consulted our canon lawyer when we first received the announcement
  about the Apostolic Visitation and the visit with Mother Clare. There has
  been no further input since then.
- We utilized canonical input mostly for the financial/real estate section.
- A major role. We were carefully guided in understanding that this was a
  legal document, not just a questionnaire, and how the response of any
  given congregation would impact all other congregations. It was a great
  call to solidarity and mutual support. We clearly understood our responsibility as we moved through this process.
- Canon lawyers helped to bring a balance between the gravity of the event
  and the sincere living out of our community charism. We appreciated the
  expertise and generosity of canon lawyers who provided counsel.
- Canonical advice was very important to us. It provided an understanding
  of the Apostolic Visitation as a juridical process and we learned about the
  potential outcomes. It helped us to understand, appreciate, and act from a
  sense of our rights and responsibilities as congregations and leaders. The
  advice and encouragement of a number of canon lawyers helped us to
  speak out truth.
- I participated in talks about the Questionnaire given by canonical lawyers. Our answers to the Questionnaire were read by a canon lawyer and
  we changed a few responses upon his advice.
- Significant amount, thank goodness. Without this input, we would not have
  been as sure and peaceful about all the options and responsibilities we
  had to each other. Because of the injustice we were experiencing
  [through] the Apostolic Visitation, we sought canonical and civil counsel
  that led us to act not as one congregation, but as a collective sisterhood in
  the U.S.A. and perhaps the world.
- I took all the canonical advice I could get and valued every bit of it. It has
  a calming influence for me. It left me with some reassurance that the
  process could be just.
- I looked at the questions more critically. Sometimes they seemed to be
  more paranoid than the situation warranted, but we'll see when the results
  of the Visitation appear.
- The information was very helpful. It helped me take the matter more
  seriously and ultimately more peacefully.
- We deeply appreciated the input at RCRI [Resource Center for Religious
  Institutes] and at LCWR from canon lawyers. They gave us a solid sense of
  our rights within our church. They made us aware of the very radical
  choice that Rome made in undertaking this visitation process.
- Very much and all was very positive. Never did any canonical lawyer try
  to direct or tell us what to do, but each one was extremely helpful to all of

us who asked for help. They gave such wise advice. Personally, I was truly grateful and in sharing with other women religious this was a real common thread—we were so blessed to have such good canon lawyers.
- *Promoted understanding and appreciation of what was at stake. Taught us the incongruities within the questions; gave us confidence to follow our own wisdom.*

Q13. *During these two years, who or what has been a source of support or inspiration for you?*

A significant majority (n=126; 88%) of the 143 respondents to this question cited regional and/or global women religious, their organizations, and/or their leaders. About 50 percent of this group mentioned the LCWR specifically. Eighty-three respondents (58%) noted that support or inspiration came from members of her own religious institute, the constitutions of the institute, their patron(s)/ founder/ foundress(es), and/or pioneer sisters. Multiple other sources of support and inspiration were noted:

- For many (n=69; 48%), the response of the laity was a source of inspiration or support. A subset of this group, eleven respondents, specifically mentioned the members of focus groups who participated in the Visitation as a source of inspiration or support. Lay associates were noted by five respondents.
- The canonists were noted as a source of inspiration or support by forty-nine respondents (34%).
- Twenty-eight respondents (20%) noted a source of support or inspiration during the course of the two years was God/the Spirit, prayer, and/or belief in vocation/religious life.
- Members of the clergy were noted as a source of support or inspiration for thirty-two respondents (22%), and twenty-four respondents (17%) mentioned the bishop/archbishop/cardinal.
- Sixteen respondents (11%) specifically mentioned Sandra Schneiders, IHM, and/or her work as a source of support or inspiration.
- Nine respondents (6%) mentioned media support.

Sample responses to Question 13:

- *Other women religious in the U.S. and across the globe, clergy. and laity; the Catholic and secular press. LCWR responded well to the requests of its members; canon lawyers; and RCRI staff. The prayer support organized among the leadership for those experiencing on-site visits was an inspiration and support. Regional and national LCWR gatherings. Our lay colleagues who were part of the group dialogue with the visitors.*

- *Prayer about the experience has been a constant source of support. We chose to respond out of love of God, integrity, and our truth, not out of anger. Our members totally trusted leadership to respond with integrity, no matter the consequences. The solidarity of women religious and the support of our lay partners was truly an inspiration. We were also grateful that NCR kept the issues in front of the public and impressed how they tried not to sensationalize but to tell the truth of what was happening. Tom Fox is to be commended.*
- *Leaders of congregations across the country; the two on-site visitors; LCWR nationally and regionally.*
- *The community and I received tremendous support from the laity with whom we serve, our families, friends, and xxx. The members of the focus group were most supportive. When I met with them to explain what the Apostolic Visitation was about and required of us, I felt very "exposed" and vulnerable—almost defensive with a group of supporters. I wanted them to know whatever they might not already know about us that could be asked of them by the visitors. I had the feeling that I was taking them into the community's private life. Once again I tried to defend the church who "was doing this to us." It was quite an emotional roller coaster experience for me.*
- *Other religious women. Some of our great theologians . . . Sister Sandra Schneiders for an example. Her understanding of the history of religious life is very helpful.*
- *LCWR at all levels; other women religious; the canon lawyers. Also the support of the laity and the appointment of [Archbishop] Joe Tobin.*
- *Our pioneer sisters set the example of strength of women religious, LCWR leadership—xxx, public support, our bishop, and associates.*
- *Prayer!! More prayer!! And the prayers and support of our sisters. Other friends of mine who are general superiors. The weight of this Visitation clearly fell to us. It helped me a lot to have confidential conversations with them to share our feelings and how we were going to respond. Many of us found that our council members could not understand the added pressure that was on the general superior throughout this entire process. It was consoling as well as supporting to talk to other general superiors who felt as I did the weight of putting one's signature on these documents on behalf of your entire congregation.*
- *The canon lawyers who consulted with us and were always available; our archbishop who was very supportive to all of us women religious in our archdiocese; the congregations that were visited and their positive approach to their visits were all a source of inspiration. We were greatly encouraged by the outpouring of support from bishops and clergy, conferences of religious, both male and female, from all over the world as well as the laity.*

- *The support of other congregational leaders and our own community sisters. Also, the surprising groundswell of support from local clergy— priests and bishops—as well as past pupils of our schools.*
- *The ever present love of my God, my sisters. The willingness of so many good people, especially the canon lawyers who took such a risk to be of assistance to us. The constancy of LCWR and the presidency. The out- standing sense of solidarity with all of the religious men and women from around the world. The outspoken support of so many of the laity.*
- *Mother Clare, Archbishop xxx, other religious who have visited us, or whom we have visited.*
- *We are heartened by the quality of our response to the whole process and by the integrity of the way we went about approaching the Apostolic Visitation. We worked hard on the presentations we gave to our sisters. We were strengthened by the support of our congregational leadership team and the leadership teams in our other provinces and vice-province. The very best came out from our sisters who were behind us all the way. This whole process has had unintended consequences: strengthening our commitment to mission; strengthening the bonds among U.S. women relig- ious and women all over the world—we can come through something like this not denying the pain but walking through it with dignity and integrity, strong in our identity. Coming to these realizations is a source of support and inspiration for us.*
- *We found inspiration and support in one another, in the members of our institute leadership conference, and among the members in general. Our founder, Catherine McAuley, continued to inspire us and we often prayed for guidance from her and from the Spirit. There was also support in the solidarity that developed among women religious across the U.S.*

Q14. Have any particular Scripture passages or stories from your congregation's history been particularly meaningful for you during these two years?

One hundred thirty-five individuals responded to this question. One hundred twenty-five (93%) offered one or more Scripture passages and/or stories of the congregation; thirty-five respondents included both. Seven individuals (5%) responded to the question but not with a Scripture passage or congrega- tional story. Only three (2%) indicated that there was no particular Scripture passage or story from the congregation that had been particularly meaningful during the Visitation.

- Ninety-five respondents (70%) of the 135 respondents identified a story from their congregation's history as particularly meaningful during the Visitation. These inspirational short stories focus primarily on struggle, challenge, discouragement, and tremendous difficulty but illustrate that ultimately success is achieved through perseverance, hope, and deep faith in God.

- Sixty-five respondents (48%) described Scripture passages which reflected many themes including faith and trust in God's will even when we don't comprehend God's plan for us and the understanding that, at times, we may suffer for our faith but that we are following God's plan for us.
- Seven individuals (5%) responded to the question but did not identify specific Scripture passages or congregation stories. Among their responses, they noted Vatican II, the mission of Jesus, trust in God, and several individuals.

While each response to Question 14 is truly unique, a few examples are offered here to illustrate the rich variety of meaningful Scripture passages and congregational stories gathered from the respondents.

- *The Prayer of St. Francis de Sales; St Paul's "do not worry" and the Magnificat.*
- *Isaiah 43:1—I have called you by name; Ephesians 4:2 - 3 Bear with one another charitably. "We do not have a mission—the mission has us" story of our congregation. God's dominion and grace will prevail.*
- *Forgive them for they know not what they do; what our sisters went through during the French Revolution and the expulsion of religious in the early 1900s. God took care of them and they came out stronger. God never gives us more than we can bear.*
- *In our early history the sisters did knitting and embroidery work to raise money for their living expenses so that education could be offered free. The merchants were jealous of their work and they were brought to court. The sisters handled this situation with tranquil daring as did our first missionaries—so now it was our turn to do the same. "God will bring to completion the good work he has begun in you" Philippians [1:6].*
- *Our congregation has a long tradition of praying, "Providence can provide; Providence did provide; Providence will provide." We continue that prayer in the context of the Visitation and in the context of our numerical diminishment. When confronted with things hard to understand, I pray with the Scripture passage, "For my thoughts are not your thoughts, nor are your way my ways, says the Lord" (Isaiah 55:8).*
- *Scripture: "Always be prepared to give an answer to everyone who asks you to give the reason for your hope" I Peter 3:15. "I am doing something new, can you not see it?"*
- *In the darkest of times, our foundress never lost hope. She is quoted as saying, "I have placed all my hope in God and I will not be confounded." Also, "One must, in this stormy time, have one's eyes raised continually to*

the Star of the Sea and go often to the source of living waters so as not to be shaken and to keep the middle of the road."

- *In 2004, our congregation was formed as a result of the union of three former communities of the same heritage. In 2007, another congregation merged with our union, also of the same heritage. Our prayer throughout this time of union and merger was taken from Jeremiah 29: 11 - 14. Stories from our history remind us that we all share a common foundation and the same founder and foundresses. Throughout our history, it was always in responding to the needs of the church in different dioceses that brought us to different branches of the same heritage. Our ancestors were always ready to respond to the needs of the times in the church and for God's people, whatever and wherever they might be. As such, our story of responding to the needs of the Hawaiian people and those with Hansen's Disease also stands out as a sign of our willingness to minister to God's people.*

- *1 Corinthians 14, 4 "There are many gifts but it is always the same Spirit . . ." Deuteronomy 30, 19 "I am offering you life or death, blessing or curse. Choose life, then, so that you and your descendants may live."*

- *Isaiah 49, 3 "Behold, I am doing something new. Do you not perceive it?" The foundress of our order began in France in 1625. Her life was one of struggling with bishops and cardinals who resented her as a woman and didn't believe that a woman could be knowledgeable in theology, spirituality, or Scripture. Yet, she founded an order that extends itself today—more than 400 years later—on six continents.*

- *A Scripture passage that resonated during this time is Matthew 10: 16: "Behold, I am sending you like sheep in the midst of wolves; so be wise as serpents and gentle as doves." Our foundress worked closely with bishops and members of the clergy and occasionally had some practical difficulties. Her examples of respecting clerical authority and speaking her views have been meaningful to us.*

- *I found comfort in lamentation psalms which had never meant much to me before, like the De Profundis and in the story of Jesus in the Garden of Gethsemane. And the story of the first leader of our local community, who was excommunicated by the pastor for refusing to burn books, was a consolation.*

- *Luke 4:16 - 21 A text important to the congregation, Micah 6:8 This is what Yahweh asks of you/us . . ., Luke 24:13 - 35 Emmaus story. Our early history is one of conflict with the bishop leading to a division in the congregation—we survived; "we have been here before."*

- *The Emmaus story has been pivotal for us during this time. The day before the visitors arrived we had a province assembly which was a day of reflection on this story. A sister from another congregation led us through this day, and sisters were touched profoundly. Also, in the ritual we had as the opening of the Apostolic Visitation on-site visit, we prepared a litany which named the leaders of our congregation and of our provinces, ending with current leaders. This was profoundly touching. Also in that ritual, Mary Magdalene, Mary of Guadalupe, and our founder were central. All of these women reflect the essence of the Emmaus story—telling the story of what was happening for them, recognizing Jesus in the breaking of the bread, then going back and telling others what they saw and learned.*

- *Hildegard of Bingen (whose community was put under interdict for doing what they believed was a corporal work of mercy) comes to mind as well as the words, "Thy will be done."*
- *God works all things to our good. After all was said and done, the hierarchical replacement for Cardinal Rodé is a man who would promote dialogue and transparency. Dare I say, "Go figure." Our patron saint's words ring true: "Let nothing trouble you, let nothing frighten you, all things are passing . . . God alone is enough" (St. Teresa of Jesus).*
- *Our early years as an international congregation were filled with Vatican appointed visitators who were unable to understand the vision and charism of our foundation. So the experiences and responses of Father Francis Jordan and Blessed Mary of the Apostles became especially important to us as we discerned our responses and lived through the experience.*
- *Our founder was often misunderstood by the papacy. He was never disobedient but would use every means available to give the Spirit a voice that could be understood by the hierarchy.*
- *We were intrigued by the fact that during the founding of our order nearly 400 years ago, our foundress, Jeanne Chezard de Matel, was the subject of an apostolic visitation.*
- *We have a history as "pioneer women," having left the founding country as well as several states as need and circumstances dictated. Our history reveals many changes and adaptations. After Vatican II we had widespread involvement of our sisters in renewal beginning in 1966. The Spirit was evident in the many ways in which our members responded to the "signs of the times" in developing new ministries. We anticipate having the resilience to change and adapt to whatever comes from this Apostolic Visitation.*
- *We were celebrating a congregational anniversary when the Visitation occurred so many stories surfaced; the story of the Visitation [of Mary to Elizabeth] itself is a central one for our congregation; the courage of our leaders in the past—their ability to take risks.*
- *Yes, when we Ursulines were founded in 1535, our foundress, St. Angela Merici, did not place us in a specific ministry. We were to live among the people being like yeast, doing whatever was needed for the time and place. Within a few years there was the Council of Trent and Ursulines did not "fit" the form of religious life, so the Vatican placed us in monaster-*

ies. It took until Vatican II to reclaim the vision of St. Angela Merici. The difference? We were able to talk with each other; distances no longer were a hindrance nor a division to realizing we were not "alone."

- *I believe that Jeremiah's statement (29), "you know not the plans I have in mind for you" is always helpful to me when I am struggling with the unknown. I also rely on Jesus' promise to always be with us—even in the difficult and challenging times—I have not felt abandoned by our loving and compassionate God. Also from Micah, "this is what God asks of you . . ." which I believe I am always trying to live faithfully.*
- *Our founder emphasized our dependence on God and God's providence for us. He asked that we be patient with opposition and learn from it.*
- *Mary journeying to greet Elizabeth to acknowledge the life in her womb— to be present to one another. This is what we did for and with one another these past years. It has been a rich journey!*

Q15. *If you have any fears about the outcomes of this Apostolic Visitation, what are they?*

Of the 139 respondents to this question, sixty-nine (50%) identified concerns that the report may not accurately represent them and/or there was no opportunity to review or respond to the information that was gathered. This aligns with concerns due to the lack of transparency and the fear that there is a hidden agenda behind the Visitation. Some expressed one or more of these ideas as a "concern" rather than a "fear" or simply noted it was "unfortunate."

- Nearly half (n=66; 47%) expressed concerns about the impact of the Visitation and the potential for new rules/sanctions to be imposed by the church hierarchy and/or whether decisions will be based on pre-conceived or outdated notions of religious life. Some feared a loss of diversity.
- Twenty-seven respondents (19%) reported that they had few/less/no fears. Some decided to take a wait-and-see attitude.
- Fourteen respondents (10%) noted that they feared polarization or divisiveness between sisters and/or institutes or a resistance to collaboration.
- Thirteen (9%) noted issues related to the relationship between women religious and the church hierarchy and/or the image of the church/religious life.

Sample responses to Question 15:

- *The continuing lack of transparency by the authors of the Visitation, and consequent uncertainty, fear of sanctions of any kind; the possibility of selected congregations being harshly treated as a lesson to all. We have no idea of the content of the report from the visitors or of the content of the report on our congregation to Rome. We are also concerned about a lingering cloud of suspicion that hangs over women religious in the U.S. because the Visitation implies an offense on our part. We grow increasingly concerned that the image of our church has suffered—yet one more failure to treat women as equals, to respect persons, to inspire rather than to exert power over.*

• *We have a concern that the outcome and the message that will come from the Visitation office will not be an accurate representation of women's apostolic religious life in the U.S. This concern is based upon the reality that reports have been sent by visiting teams without the feedback or knowledge of those whose lives they are reporting about. We have a concern that there can be no real authentic representation of our life made in the report because of the lack of transparency in the Visitation process. We have a concern that the hierarchy of the church will use the outcome as another occasion to use or assert their authority in inappropriate ways.*

• *Our concern is that the outcome—the report—will not be able to justly represent all congregations. We also have a concern regarding the ultra-conservative approaches to community life and the vows that do not promote adult commitment to God and to ministry. We fear some ways of being and living will be imposed on us. We fear that there might be some repercussions as a result of the manner in which we responded to the [Questionnaire]. We are concerned about the lack of transparency that continues to prevail in the institutional church.*

• *The outcome—what will be done with all this information? That there will be a move to return to the notion that one description of religious life will fit all, without regard for our charisms and the challenges of Vatican II. Since it was so public, some laity are now suspicious of religious. Hopefully, this telling of our story will do away with any lingering suspicions.*

• *I fear that there may be a return to the structures of the past and see that as an impossible task. In my mind, it would be counter to where we are and to where the Spirit is leading us.*

• *A constant concern was that the questions did not fit our monastic life. Our fear is that all women religious will be lumped together with no distinctions made for unique charisms. That we may have to invest more time and energy in responding to whatever comes from Rome. That the Apostolic Visitation process will drag on for years to come.*

• *I have no fears or concerns at this point. I believe that God is in control so I wait patiently for the outcome.*

• *That the results will include all women religious and not be based on facts, but on perceptions. The questions were biased and the fear is that the responses will be filtered through a pre-conceived notion of religious life in the U.S. The fear that in choosing to wait for our invitation to participate we will be expected to live with the results of the study without being included.*

- *I have a fear that the diversity that is present in religious life today will not be respected in the report.*
- *We did have some concern and fears about the outcomes initially, but these have lessened significantly because we trust that the Visitation will go nowhere. Our first concern was that the Sacred Congregation could use the Apostolic Visitation to promulgate directives about our life and ministry that could lead to some very difficult and potentially divisive choices, such as remaining canonical or not.*
- *I had been told that if I refused to cooperate fully, there was (at least in theory) the possibility that I would be removed from office or even excommunicated, but that was never really an issue for me. My major fear was that my community would come under some sort of sanction and I guess that concern has not been entirely alleviated. The most frightening thing about this whole experience has been the fear of the unknown, the fear that events are out of our hands and that we are in someone else's power—that someone has the power to hurt my sisters.*
- *As we now have different people in the office in Rome I don't have the same concerns or fears. We were afraid that Rome would take over our congregations here in the U.S. and take us back to before Vatican II. Now, I think the new officials understand religious life in the U.S. and will work with us to bring about the quality of life all of us want and are striving for.*
- *That someone who does not know and appreciate us will try to regulate our lives; the lack of trust in us as we respond to the Spirit's call; that we will not receive feedback; the concern that all of the time, effort, and money spent on this will minimize the opportunities for doing ministry; that relationships between hierarchy and women religious will never be mutual due to the lack of transparency and trust; that any written reports will be inaccurate, biased, or lead to punitive measures. Concern that the outcome will lead to further divisions between CMSWR and LCWR.*
- *Going forward many concerns, feelings, hopes, and expectations remain. If we are misrepresented or judged not good enough, sisters expressed a fear that they may have to choose between what God is calling them to and what the church is asking of them. This could affect others around them in the church. Some felt that their honesty and integrity will prevail and therefore there was no need for these concerns. While much of the anger and fear was transformed, some remains, as well as sadness and dismay that the hierarchy may not understand us and may continue to operate in ways not consistent with just treatment of women religious. Balanced with this is the trust that sisters did the best they could and they can rejoice to be living at this historic moment in time.*

Q16. If you have any hopes for the outcomes of this Apostolic Visitation, what are they?

One hundred forty-one individuals responded to this question. Many (n=93; 66%) expressed the hope that there would be some positive outcomes from the Visitation including: an improved relationship between the sisters and Rome/the hierarchy; that there would be an acknowledgement of, respect for, or appreciation of the work and contributions of women religious from Rome/the hierarchy; and/or that a dialogue would be opened.

- About one-third (n=48) hope for continued communication and/or growth of solidarity among women religious.
- One-third (n=46) expressed hopes that religious life and/or diverse charisms are affirmed and/or strengthened and/or that there be an increase in vocations.
- Eleven percent (n=16) of the respondents hope for greater respect and/or visibility for women and/or women religious in the church.
- Eleven percent (n=16) reported the hope that the report submitted by Mother Mary Clare will be an honest representation of their work and/or that it will be made public and/or that it will be a positive report. Some in this group hope that American women religious will see the reports on their institutes and/or that there will be meaningful communication regarding them.
- Others hope the reports will be lost forever and/or that Apostolic Visitation will be forgotten. Some noted that they hope it will never happen again and/or that women religious can continue with their mission without interference. These themes were identified by twelve respondents (9%).
- Nine respondents (6%) expressed hopes for a positive public response and greater understanding and/or that the laity will be inspired and strengthened.

Sample responses to Question 16:

- *One of my hopes has already happened: that we are united as women religious leaders. My other hope is that we continue to deepen our vocation in the only One that really matters. That we grow in knowing that our vocation is one given by God, not by a church, and that the only one we owe allegiance to is God, and that we live with respect towards all as we live from our integrity.*
- *That the U.S. women religious will be respected, trusted, and appreciated by the Vatican for who we are and our role in the church. That religious in no other country experience what we have. That we be faithful in doing what Vatican II asked of us without being reprimanded and that the arms*

of the church be wide enough to embrace diversity in living religious life faithful to their charism and mission.

- *The women who came to us as visitors were normal, healthy religious, who understood the problems and issues we face in a pluralistic society and a divided church. They conducted their process well and respectfully. If the same happens as the info goes upward it could produce good results.*
- *That the life and mission of U.S. religious women will be affirmed.*
- *Religious women of the U.S. and throughout the world are better understood and valued for their contribution to the church—that this be a stepping stone to more equality, recognition, and rightful position of women in the church and the world. That there be a change in the leadership (in Rome) in terms of recognizing and valuing religious women, signaled by affirmation and encouragement. Continued renewal of communities, gaining confidence in the power we have. Increasing sense of mutuality for all religious women's communities. That the two U.S. women's conferences continue to work together.*
- *That Rome will realize we are educated women who value dialogue and the principal of subsidiarity. That Rome will believe in our capacity to evaluate ourselves—we do this as a regular part of our lives in our general chapters. That Rome not operate out of fear but openness and trust in the Spirit. That no one group has all the answers. It is time within the church to be open to dialogue—the hierarchy is not the church—the church becomes inclusive.*
- *The solidarity among women religious will deepen. Our lay counterparts will feel empowered by observing how we responded and they will speak their truth and be heard. Rome will realize the need to collaborate before they begin a program that will affect others. Rome will grow in their realization that being heavy handed is not how Jesus wants us to be in relationship.*
- *The national and international solidarity that the Visitation birthed is a strong gift to carry into the future. We hope the Vatican learns greater prudence in following the perceptions of a few persons as the congregations conduct their work. We hope the Vatican will begin to openly promote women's participation in the church at all levels, in all ministries.*
- *Just as the Women and Spirit exhibit displayed in a positive manner the values, charisms, challenges, "living" history, spirituality, etc. of the United States of America's sisters may Rome come to acknowledge, accept, and respect who we are as women religious. We are not a threat but rather co-workers in the vineyard. We are dedicated religious women.*
- *We would hope for transparency and dialogue in any future efforts like this from the Congregation for Institutes of Consecrated Life and Societies of Apostolic Life.*

- *My hope is that this experience will have encouraged us to recognize who we have become since Vatican II. I hope that we can strengthen the identity that we have been shaping over all these years and that we can celebrate the power that we have when we know who we are and work together.*
- *I hope there will be better, more open dialogue with the Vatican, and a better understanding of religious life in the U.S. I also hope the final report will be published for all to read.*
- *We hope that the hierarchy will recognize the diversity of charisms and the variety of ways in which we answer the gospel call, all of which are gift to the church. We would hope that they will acknowledge the diversity of ways in which religious in the U.S. have responded to the call of Vatican II with honest searching and prayer and embraced the gospel call, returned to our charism and studied the signs of the times.*
- *I hope that we will all feel more empowered to move forward, to live the gospel message, each congregation with its own charism and gifts and not all expected to mold together or to look alike.*

Q17. Assume for a moment that U.S. women religious will be able to write and share the story of the Apostolic Visitation in our own words. From your experience of it, what is the most important part of this story to convey?

Many respondents expressed more than one "most important part of the story." About two-thirds (n=93; 65%) of the 143 respondents to this question noted the importance of faithfulness and/or fidelity to the church and/or their mission. They would like to convey the idea that their lives have been affirmed and/or they are committed to Vatican II and to responding to the times. They have made a substantial contribution to the life of the church in the U.S. and/or the world, yet remain willing to examine themselves.

- The most important part of the story for almost half of the respondents (n=69; 48%) is the development and strengthening of solidarity and unity among and within diverse institutes of women religious.
- Forty-four respondents (31%) identified the model or integrity of their response and/or their respect for the diversity they collectively represent.
- For twenty-one respondents (15%) an important part of the story is the relationship of the sisters and the laity, especially in terms of the support given and received. Some view the Visitation experience as a model for the laity and/or women to claim their voice.
- Nineteen respondents (13%) believe that problematic issues related to the institutional church are an important part of the story. This was expressed in a variety of ways, including: as a sense of the disconnect between the

church and sisters; as negativity about the Apostolic Visitation and/or its process; and/or as the devaluing of women.

- For ten respondents (7%) the value of, and/or need for, dialogue and collaboration is a very important part of the story.
- Some respondents noted the recognition that there are many ways to serve Christ in this world and/or the importance of respecting other ways and cultures. Nine respondents (6%) offered this perspective.
- Eight respondents (6%) expressed the importance of trust in God and/or the importance of transforming a negative into a positive.
- The same number (n=8; 6%) noted the supportive effort of the clergy and male religious as an important part of the story.

Sample responses to Question 17:

- *Our commitment to the mission of the church.*
- *It is important for the story to convey that the women religious in the U.S. have given faithful service throughout the history of our country, and that our dedication today remains strong. Often religious women have seen a need in our society and forged ahead to meet the need, even with minimal resources available. This continues to happen today as we read the signs of the times and follow God's call to serve out of love, looking especially to stand with the marginalized and disenfranchised. It is important to recognize that the role of women religious in the church is a prophetic role.*
- *I would not like it to be a rebuttal of their accusations, but a sincere, transparent image of who we are and all that we do.*
- *Willingness to examine aspects of our life as women religious, to discern the presence of God in the experience and to re-commit to the values expressed by our vows. The faithfulness of women religious to ongoing transformation of religious life during a period of societal upheaval; growing sense of sisterhood and mutual support among congregations.*
- *That we remained faithful to our mission, charism, and the church. We answered with our integrity intact. We did what we saw was best for the common good. Our strength and solidarity together which did bring about some changes in the process of the Apostolic Visitation. We are grateful for the amazing support from so many that we received throughout the process. Our sense that the Vatican totally overlooked and/or ignored the amazing contributions of women religious in . . . our church in the U.S. The sense of great disconnect of the Vatican officials regarding women religious and who we really are in the U.S.*
- *While the Apostolic Visitation was heavy-handed and disrespectful, women religious (with an average median age of 75+) are, as a result, experiencing new life in: our coming together to discuss and decide our re-*

sponse, thus renewing a strong solidarity among us; our courageous and non-violent refusal to participate in the process as it was given to us (the Questionnaire); our recognition that we could not act out of self-protection—that we had to take risks on behalf of all women who labor in the church but do not have the safety net which women religious have; the growing trust we re-discovered in our own insights about religious life and where authority resides; our communal reflection on our prophetic identity and mission as women religious; the personal and collective freedom we experienced by speaking our truth in solidarity and love.

- *That U.S. women religious have been faithful to living and spreading the gospel in the church and in our world. That we have been faithful to the challenges and calls of Vatican II to refound our congregations; to deepen our understanding of the vows; to live out the values called forth by our charisms and constitutions. That, just as Jesus lived in, and responded to, the culture of his time, we also live, respond to, and minister in a unique culture and are impacted by it.*

- *The experience of solidarity and the commitment to speaking and living our truth.*

- *That the announcement of the Apostolic Visitation was a surprise with no dialogue with women religious before it was announced. If the congregations to be investigated had been involved in the development of the Visitation from the start, the implementation may have resulted in fewer or milder emotions than it engendered in its expected compliance. That women religious continue to be faithful to their call and to the church and have responded to the Visitation with prayer, thoughtfulness, and solidarity with one another.*

- *The most important part of the story, from our perspective, is the unintended consequences. These include a growing sense of our unity with one another, the deepening sense of partnership with the laity, the recognition of our development since Vatican II, and an appropriate sense of our freedom and self-direction. We are proud of the fact that throughout the process we chose to respond out of our charism. We might have been angry, but we did not respond in anger. There were priests and bishops who supported us, which opened up growing opportunities for dialogue.*

- *We are all very human and in the absence of information, we are often quick to assume the negative. However, given times of prayer, reflection, and dialogue, we come to realize that God can be found even in something like an apostolic visitation.*

- *The Apostolic Visitation brought religious communities into greater solidarity; that we grew in an understanding of our role in the church and world affirmed by our brothers and sisters lay, religious, and clergy; that we stand on our integrity and fidelity to the gospel and to the teachings of Vatican II. The Visitation also resulted in our modeling an approach to*

Rome that represented a balance between hierarchical authority and inner authority.

• *That women religious are committed and dedicated to live religious life authentically in their time and that they will not return to abuse structures.*

• *Of course we don't know the end of the story yet, but here's my preferred ending: this peaceful, non-violent stand against the institutional violence of the church against women was a turning point in the relationship of the church and women, when the women risked everything—their relationship with their church, perhaps even their resources and their future "identity" (Mother Mary Clare suggested to one group that they might consider becoming a secular institute)—suddenly the church and the laity saw them in a new light, not just as useful cogs in the machinery of church service, but as real persons with courage and integrity, intelligence, and rights. It would be wonderful to write in the history books that this was the beginning of true equity in the church, true inclusion of women as equal partners.*

Q18. As we move forward from this experience what difference, if any, might your experience of the Apostolic Visitation make in how you function as a leader of a religious institute?

One hundred thirty-eight individuals responded to this question.

• Sixty-four respondents (46%) mentioned the importance of outside organizations and support; and/or collaboration/communication with other religious/other publics including the bishop and/or the laity; and/or the general theme of valuing inclusiveness.

• Forty-three percent (n=59) of the respondents to this question believe that they will be more committed and/or have a clearer sense of mission/fidelity to the gospel. For some, this will be expressed through a stronger appreciation of diversity, an increased focus on internal communication/dialogue/collaboration and/or heightened transparency.

• For some respondents (n= 36; 26%), the experience of the Visitation has strengthened them as a leader. They expect to be more confident or courageous, more willing to speak out/step up/share truth/share wisdom, and/or to be a voice in the church or the world. Some noted an increased pride in their sisters and their work.

• Twenty respondents (14%) stated that they expected no real change in how they function as a leader as a result of the Visitation. Some noted they will continue as servant leaders and/or continue to follow their mission or charism.

• Twenty-one respondents (15%) noted that they have a greater understanding and/or appreciation of the role/importance/power of leadership. Some noted that they are more aware of the value of service leadership and have a greater awareness of the challenges of leadership.

- Twenty-one respondents (15%) voiced a focused attention to listening to the Spirit and/or the importance of discernment/prayer and/or faith and trust in God.
- Eight respondents (6%) noted that the Visitation experience moved them to become more aware, as leaders, of their rights, the canons on religious life, ecclesial power, their place/role in the church, and the way the church functions.
- Seven respondents (5%) noted that they expect to be more cautious and/or less trusting as a result of the Visitation experience.

Sample responses to Question 18:

- *A heightened awareness of the challenge of leadership to relate to and effectively lead a very diverse membership. A desire to be as transparent as possible to the members; to operate with the trust and mutuality that felt absent from the Apostolic Visitation process. A deepened commitment to ongoing discernment of the promptings of the Holy Spirit in all that we do as leaders in these challenging and complex times. A deepened desire to articulate and share the values expressed by our religious commitment with the laity.*
- *I am not sure how to answer this one; I definitely am less trusting in and supportive of our hierarchy. That has made it more difficult to help the sisters who struggle with fidelity to the masculine structure of the church in our diocese.*
- *The difference that it makes to us is that it has increased our awareness of the public nature of religious leadership at this time in our church and society. It calls us to greater transparency and courage in our own leadership. It confirms our belief in the role of and need for authentic dialogue in any setting and among any type of group, particularly when there are multiple perspectives and experiences. This experience has given us courage and firm grounding from which to seek and create opportunities for dialogue in those places where none exist.*
- *Our dialogues with other religious leaders have taken on a new depth and profound sharing. We have found a new corporate public voice and will have the courage to use it. And we've come to a greater appreciation of the complementarity of the charisms and are open to exploring new ways of collaborating with one another and connecting in diverse ways. We are not alone as leaders of institutes—we are truly sisters together.*
- *I will always attempt to share my piece of the truth with those to whom God sends me.*

- *We carry on as we did before—faithful to our mission, ever challenging, ever striving to keep the lines of communication open with church leaders.*
- *We have deepened our conviction that we ARE faithful; we have enhanced our connections with other religious leaders; we have greater appreciation that our role as leaders in our congregation is important to the larger church.*
- *I hope to seek out ways to boldly act in solidarity with other women religious about the most pressing needs of our times. As a leader it is important to be dialogical and prophetic within the church. I think I've developed a greater sense that we're all in this together and that I, as leader, am not the only one responsible. I've learned how to more easily let go of consequences and do what we have to do. Hopefully, to more boldly live the gospel!*
- *It is obviously important that religious leadership will be conscious of appreciating and encouraging their sisters and religious in other congregations as they live out their mission and ministry. Hopefully, it will continue to deepen the bonds between religious institutes so that we can even more effectively witness to the gift that religious life is in the church and in the world today!*
- *None. I am the same as I was before and will continue to be.*
- *I feel that we must try our best to be in unity with our ordinaries; that we must be the ones to communicate our gifts to the local church; that we must continue to be the voice for the most vulnerable and that we stay united as women religious even if things are difficult.*
- *Awakened us to our place in the church and in relationship with church hierarchy. Commonality with other religious and our need for collaboration. Collective engagement of our sisters. Power of collective discernment. Awareness of our public image. The church is watching us.*
- *I think any leader that went through this experience surely gained confidence and courage, having survived what may have been the hardest [experience] of her career—a decision that risked not only her personal status, but the welfare of her community.*
- *The experience of the Apostolic Visitation moved us to greater unity and solidarity within the congregation and with others in the church and world. The vowed life we are living holds the threads needed to create a future unknown to us at the present time. The process of creating this future will be transformative and needs to be based on these key values: solidarity with the poor, community, prayer, discernment, deeper awareness of the vowed life, responsiveness to the signs of the times. Foundational to this process is the belief that those living the vowed life have a role and responsibility for the future of the church and world. We are called to respond to the marginalized, including those needing education, health care, eldercare, and welcoming communities (immigrants, mi-*

grants) in new mission territory found in the urban and rural settings.
There will be a cost to living the gospel radically which will bring us to a
new awareness of who we are and who we are called to be.

CONCLUSION

The experience of the Apostolic Visitation by women religious in the United
States, as described by the participants in this study, is one of tremendous
dedication and resolve. Although there were many questions about the Visitation, its purpose, the process, and the possible consequences, women religious moved through it as valuable colleagues, as collaborators, and as sisters.
The end result for many was a reaffirmation of their shared charisms, a
recommitment to their mission, constitutions and founding principles, and
the realization that they have a truly powerful gift in each other.

NOTES

1. Margaret Cain McCarthy, "Apostolic Visitation Survey Analysis: The Apostolic Visitation as Experienced by Women Religious in the United States" (report, October 15, 2011).
Invitations to complete the Apostolic Visitation survey were extended to 328 presidents or
major superiors in the Leadership Conference of Women Religious (one per congregation). Of
that number, 143 returned a valid survey resulting in a response rate of approximately 44
percent. The Leadership Conference of Women Religious has more than 1,400 members who
represent more than 80 percent of the approximately 51,000 women religious in the United
States. An invitation to participate was extended to the Council of Major Superiors of Women
Religious (CMSWR). Citing the fact that the Apostolic Visitation had not yet come to a
conclusion, the CMSWR declined to participate and, as a result, their voices and experiences
are not reflected here.

2. Approximately 10 percent of responses to each question are offered as sample responses. Including material in both Chapter 4 and Chapter 5, all 143 participants are represented in one or more sample responses. These examples do not necessarily characterize every
individual response and are not intended to highlight either the most articulate or most unusual
responses.

Chapter Six

Living It Twice

Sources of Support and Inspiration

Marcia Allen

INTRODUCTION

A Chinese Proverb goes something like this: "To recreate something in words is like being alive twice." The Apostolic Visitation is not something any congregation of women religious is eager to live twice; however, there's a side to this story that bears repeating not just once but many times. It is the story of solidarity, of how thousands of sisters came together in their communities and across communities; the story of how their associates and co-workers came together around them and with them; the story of how family, friends, and veritable strangers all created a network of communication that held together through the months of uncertainty, creating a new reality of support and inspiration.

This new web of relationships is a story of discovery, a discovery of a wealth of new wisdom and courage, humor and understanding, resolution and commitment, tenacity, and clarity of purpose. This network created for women religious the consolation and strength to do what they needed to do. The unexpected faith and resilience they found in one another and the testimony of those who knew them, who wished them well and counted on them, all converged to carry them through the unexpected and unknown territory called the Apostolic Visitation.

For the majority of sisters, the most immediate response to the announcement of the Visitation was curiosity. Most did not realize that it was an announcement of a formal canonical instrument of the Congregation of Institutes of Consecrated Life and Societies of Apostolic Life (CICLSAL), which that office would use to test the integrity of women living religious life as well as that of the communal life itself. Almost immediately, canonists and those familiar with the term apostolic visitation as it has been applied to other institutions, disabused them of their naiveté and stronger emotions ensued.

Women religious, true to form, took in that steep learning curve quickly and adroitly. They immediately gathered together within communities and across communities through friends and leadership groups. Together they processed the mystery of this situation. To have been accused of abusing their constitutions and commitment to a way of gospel living by those who, by very reason of their existence, would have known better was both unbelievable and unacceptable.

Sisters were bewildered that the announcement came without warning. Its provision for secrecy was even more mystifying. Anger was a typical response with frustration at not being able even to advocate for themselves. As they increasingly understood this as a sheer abuse of authority in which they were the victims of unjust accusations that protected the accuser, communities of women religious became bastions of resistance. Decades of ministering to and counseling women suffering from abuse had taught them how to recognize abuse of women when they saw it. Now that they were experiencing it, they applied what they had learned: they made known what was happening and they established support systems.

SOURCES OF SUPPORT AND INSPIRATION

The majority of respondents (88%) in the Apostolic Visitation Survey (survey) named as their main sources of support and inspiration other women religious, their organizations, and/or leaders. Many in this group also cited pride in their own history and charism as well as the realization of their own gift to the life of the church and world. Fifty-eight percent of the respondents mentioned their own congregations, their founders, and histories. Nearly half of the respondents (48%) named various groups of laity, including focus groups and associates; twenty-two percent listed members of the clergy; twenty percent noted that God/the Spirit, prayer, and/or belief in religious life had been a constant source of support and inspiration; thirty-four percent cited the canonists who assisted them in interpreting the questions or who accompanied them during their actual on-site Visitation. [1]

In Chapter 7, the Visitation experience is examined from the perspective of theological reflection and many congregational stories and Scripture passages which provided inspiration and support are described in detail there. The other general sources of support and inspiration will be discussed here in four categories:

1. the congregations, their founding histories, their own self-organized manner of proceeding, their leadership;
2. global friends and allies;
3. local friends and allies, some of whom were associates and clergy, but most of whom were laity; and,
4. a brief word about the canonists who assisted.

The Congregations

Actions of Congregational Leaders

Leaders of communities activated their various networks in order to see what others were planning to do. Because Phase 1 of the Visitation provided for personal contact with Mother Mary Clare Millea, ASCJ, through a letter, a phone call or visit, leaders met through phone or social media networks to coordinate what information they would share, how they would prepare, and plan to share transportation or arrive at a Visitation site together. Once they had visited with Mother Millea by phone or in person, they reported on their impression of her and the questions she asked and the responses she appeared to take notes on. Simultaneously, leadership councils and teams were strategizing about how to proceed.

Leaders then met with members to share information about the Visitation as well as to educate members on the nature of an apostolic visitation. Communities quickly settled into the process of discerning how to ready themselves for the various steps in the Visitation. Although each community discerned according to processes and practices within its particular heritage, it is safe to say that they shared many of the values underlying their discernment in common.

As an example, the Ongoing Formation Committee of the United States Federation of Sisters of St. Joseph put together a list of these values for its member congregations. This list captures how all wished to conduct ourselves throughout this difficult time. The questions of how to contact Mother Millea, whether to write up a report to be given to her following one's contact, whether to participate in Phase 2, the *Questionnaire,* or how to go about preparing for the visitors, should their name be chosen—all these and others were weighed in the balance of these values:

• commitment to a dialogue that is respectful and honest;
• deep love for the religious life we are living;
• profound commitment to the church;
• appreciation for all we have learned in these post-Vatican II years;
• confidence in the power of our charism;

- commitment to insertion in the world as adult women, responding to the signs of the times, seeking to inform our consciences and our corporate conscience as sisters of St. Joseph. [2]

Peter Block, well-known author and consultant on successful organizational communication, added his wisdom. [3] He advised leaders to adopt an attitude of compassion and to be honest but not provide more information than asked for. Another strategy he recommended was that they plan how they would set the course of their conversations. By taking charge of the conversation they would be able to communicate what they thought was most important.

As communities talked with each other, they realized differences in ecclesiologies or understandings of church, and the theologies of religious life, but they also came to understand that what united them was the realization of a shared charism, passion for their lives, dedication to the gospel and service to God's creation. This inner strength surfaced as concrete testimony of their ability to weather the current storm.

Spirit of Founders, Foundresses, and Constitutions

At the same time they called on their founders and foundresses. Stories of origins, difficulties surmounted, successful and enduring foundations were told and retold. History revealed that their origins had indeed called for stalwart women, fully committed to live according to the charismatic meaning of the life to which they were called. This life was often founded amid difficulty, most often with bishops or pastors unwilling to tolerate innovation, especially innovation led by women. Communities raised up larger-than-life women who had braved hardship, conflict, and persecution in order to fulfill a vision of what was necessary for the good of the people they came to serve. These early models served as mentors in the contemporary milieu.

In addition to their heritage and founders' courage, the sisters relied on the wisdom in their constitutions. Vatican II, calling as it did for the renewal of religious life that could only be lived by mature adults, enabled women religious to examine their lifestyle in light of their founding charisms, the gospel, and the signs of the times. This renewal of life is reflected in post-Vatican II constitutions.

These constitutions were a source of strength. They describe the way of life, its commitment and articulation through prayer, works of service, and fidelity. Constitutions offer a pattern for how the Holy Spirit leads a community and how obedience to that same Spirit is lived out. They show how the faithful life is lived. And, to note the obvious, constitutions for communities of women religious have all been approved either by Rome or by a local bishop. Sisters know they are not living outside of a church-approved way of life!

Solidarity within and among Congregations

It could be that the Roman Visitation hoped to find some source of dissension within communities. They urged private conversations with the visitors or invited confidential letters sent to CICLSAL. But for the most part the Visitation did the opposite; rather than dividing communities, it created tighter bonds among the sisters.

Eighty-eight percent of the survey respondents agreed that "deepened solidarity and communion among other women religious and especially among the elected leaders of our religious communities have been supporting and encouraging."[4] Although many sisters felt an alienation from the institutional church and readily acknowledged this, they felt stronger ties with their sisters in community and with the purpose and meaning of their communal life.

Community assemblies of various kinds provided opportunities for sisters to speak candidly about the effects of the Visitation on them and their community. They worked through anger, disappointment, frustration, and hurt to a newfound clarity about the role that they were meant to play as the Visitation process unfolded. They became more and more convinced in the power of the gift of women religious to the life of the church and the world. They took pride in their history and in their current engagement in the ministries to which their communities were committed. They not only drew consolation from the charism that had first attracted them, but also conviction about the way it was meeting the needs of the twenty-first century.

At the same time, sisters singly and as a whole established networks of information, both formal and informal, that sprang up overnight. They mentored one another with shared wisdom about how to speak with Mother Millea, for example, or how to remain true to who they really are as a religious community, how to maintain an awareness of the power that they have, how to retain what is theirs and not capitulate to fear or not grow disrespectful of those who disrespect them, how not to respond to condemnation in kind.

Conference calls blanketed the country. First of all, they enabled leaders to discern together how they would respond to the *Questionnaire;* then when Phase 3 began, they shared reports of who the visitors were, what questions were asked, how they conducted their investigation, etc. By the time half of the first cycle of communities had been visited, nearly everyone else in the country had pretty much been prepped for a Visitation should they be chosen. No one was isolated; those who networked felt a part of a very large community of wisdom and focused intentionality.

Voices of Wisdom among Women Religious

Respondents also cited voices of universal wisdom among women religious. These women reminded sisters of the critical nature of an apostolic visitation and, as they negotiated its processes, kept them mindful of the evolution of religious life through the centuries and its current significance as it unfolds in this era of the church. Continuously recognizing the context for their life in its historical development, many women religious saw and claimed with greater clarity how their contemporary lives fit into the life of the church at this time. The meaning of religious life, its particular charism, and what it contributes when the church is in a critical era of its own history enabled them to see themselves in the larger picture.

One such voice was Sandra Schneiders, IHM, of Monroe, Michigan, theologian and scripture scholar, professor emerita of New Testament Studies and Christian Spirituality at the Jesuit School of Theology/Graduate Theological Union, Berkeley. Schneiders wrote a series of essays on the Apostolic Visitation and religious life, originally published in the *National Catholic Reporter* January 4–8, 2010, and later compiled into the book *Prophets in Their Own Country: Women Religious Bearing Witness to the Gospel in a Troubled Church.*

In her work Schneiders carefully and thoroughly explained the nature of an apostolic visitation. Women religious were not only astounded but amazed that such a process should be used against them. That they were judged guilty of "serious types of moral, religious, spiritual, doctrinal, financial, civil, or other types of misconduct or conflict whose solution the unit in question cannot, or will not, undertake on its own" was simply unbelievable.[5] Coming to understand the nature of a Visitation and then comprehend the unjust manner in which it was to be carried out added to the clarity about their situation. Citing theology and scripture, Schneiders clarified the evolving character of active apostolic life since Vatican II.[6]

Schneiders also addressed the role of prophet and its relationship to the very nature of religious life throughout history. The prophet lives and speaks the reality of the times. She suggests that religious life is a "prophetic lifeform" in the church.[7] As such, it will by its very nature, constitutions, and ministry live in contradiction to systems and institutions that eventually take the low road of stability, security, and acceptance of the status quo, even if such violates the very reason for their existence.

In an earlier era Johannes B. Metz wrote in his book *Followers of Christ,* translated and published in 1977, that the role of religious life is to make interventions in the life of the church so that it will be reminded of its mission to live out the following of Christ.[8] The following of Christ is incumbent on every Christian; however, members of religious communities have vowed it in a special way.

Schneiders freshened this concept in her work through a thorough explanation of the biblical dimensions of the prophetic impetus and its importance in today's church. Her scholarly delineation of the work of the prophet in the church as a work invariably in tension with the prevailing institutional reality assisted women religious in understanding better the context of the Apostolic Visitation. Moreover, it enabled them to see anew how their lives and work are an exercise of obedience to the Holy Spirit mediated by their constitutions and charism and lived out in community. [9]

Sisters welcomed Schneiders' exposition of religious life for active apostolic women because they saw it mirroring the life they are living. The confusion caused by the unexpected and harsh judgment rendered by the authors of the Apostolic Visitation dissipated and sisters went back to their lives with determination and clarity. Schneiders' gift to religious life for women was honored by the Leadership Conference of Women Religious when they presented her with their annual Outstanding Leadership Award for significant contributions to religious life for women in August 2012. [10]

Another important voice of encouragement was that of Joan Chittister, OSB. Her ability to describe an issue with clarity and humor carried sisters into the maelstrom of debate with an understanding of the circumstances and principles that invalidate the process. In a *National Catholic Reporter* (NCR) article published April 24, 2009, Chittister presented comparisons between the moral violations within dioceses that go without visitations and the life of religious communities of women that do not need a visitation, but have one. [11] She showed the incongruity of the Apostolic Visitation for women religious in such a way that illustrated the irrationality of the current process. This was Chittister's gift: pointing out the illogical and irrational process of the Apostolic Visitation for women religious.

With her usual asperity, Chittister put her pen right at the nub of the issue. In an NCR essay of March 6, 2013, she described how the church could benefit from what communities of religious life learned in their post-Vatican II renewal. According to Chittister, renewal "was a matter of demystification, integration and relevance." [12] This work did not come easily or quickly and it has taken sisters a good fifty years not only to understand it, but to articulate their experience of it. Now, as mature religious communities, sisters have moved into a sense of identity and purpose understood by women religious but not understood by many of the members of the hierarchy.

A veritable litany of wisdom figures universally known and acknowledged by women religious around the country spoke publicly or wrote for the media about the effects of the Apostolic Visitation or how to move through it with integrity. These women's words and passion for religious life served as guides for many sisters.

Theresa Kane, RSM, former LCWR president, spoke to the National Coalition of American Nuns (NCAN) on the occasion of its fortieth anniversary.

Kane emphasized that women religious must take the one chance they have—their one life—and live hope and endurance. In the face of what she called the hierarchy's "dictatorial mindset and spiritual violence," she said that "our hope comes from solidarity between women religious and laywomen."[13]

Nadine Foley, OP, past president of LCWR, wrote an article titled "Negotiation with Rome: A Reflection on Possibility" for the LCWR *Occasional Papers*. Written in 2001, this article was circulated again during the early days of the Apostolic Visitation. Although nearly a decade old, Foley's cogent analysis of the probability of successful negotiation between the women religious in the United States and their ecclesiastical accusers illuminated the reasons why such hoped-for strategies might fail. More accurately, Foley suggested that they would indeed fail. She cited two requirements for successful negotiation: information and power. Her argument was that women religious, thanks to extraordinary ministerial experience and years of education, definitely had sufficient information with which to enter negotiation. The question of power, of course, is where the challenge lies. Foley argued that power for women religious lay in the fact that their charism is for the church and is always under the power and leadership of the Holy Spirit. Although this should be power enough, gender differences intrude on the process. Foley's conclusion is that the threat of "feminism" overshadows "attitudes toward women," and leads to "reluctance to share information and an unexamined assumption about religious life as charism in the church. . . ." This, she concludes, causes her to believe that "there is little or no possibility of true negotiation between women religious and the Vatican."[14]

This is not her final conclusion, however. She admits the power of grace that creates possibility for those with determination and commitment as well as knowledge of the various documents and statements within recent history that call for dialogue and equality for women.

Doris Gottemoeller, RSM, in an article in *America* took the position, based on an analogy of any service institution with those responsible for its quality and adherence to its professed values, that the church had the right to evaluate communities of women religious. She also warned the visitors, saying that "not to disclose the findings is to suggest that there is another agenda—some sort of sanction, for example, against a congregation or group of congregations expected to be found deficient—that underlies the study."[15] She went on to say that a respectful reception of an "instruction" would depend on the transparency of shared information.

Anne Marie Mongoven, OP, of Sinsinawa, Wisconsin and professor emerita at Santa Clara University in California outlined the process of emergent religious life for women from 1950 to the present.[16] Citing Pius XII's meeting with leaders of women's orders in Rome in 1950, she quoted his request to modernize their orders to accomplish "not only greater dignity but also greater efficacy" in their missions and congregations. She suggests that our "modernization" began before Vatican II and made women religious ready for the urgings of renewal imbedded in the documents of the council. For many, the fact that Pius XII had called for the renewal of religious life for women was a startling revelation. It gave a greater sense of rootedness in the renewal and reform that had transpired during the last sixty-plus years.

Coinciding with the announcement of the Visitation was the opening of the now-famous exhibit "Women and Spirit: Catholic Sisters in America." This brilliant illumination of lives of women religious in the United States since their inception with the Ursulines in New Orleans in the early eighteenth century showed clearly the value of the life well-lived in service of others. The sense of mystery surrounding the Visitation became even more pronounced as women religious and their friends and the general public viewed the exhibit in wonder. The presentation of amazing accomplishment occurred at a time when the Vatican was clearly placing that history and its accomplishments in doubt. Viewing the exhibit enhanced the sisters' own self-confidence as they witnessed their combined history and influence on the social assistance structures of the United States. This public exhibit shored up women religious' pride in their own histories and confidence in the strength of their charisms. At the same time, this coincidence of events was one of the factors arousing the American Catholic public to come to the defense of the sisters.

Friends and Allies around the World

Leadership of National and International Conferences of Women Religious

As the purpose of the Visitation became clearer, letters of support from innumerable groups poured in. It would be impossible to list them all, but a few examples will illustrate the intent of these organizations in their solidarity with, and support of, the sisters. They present a roster of praise and promise of continued collaboration in the works of the gospel throughout the world. These allies encouraged sisters to stand fast and maintain their integrity. Some risked their own security by being aligned with women religious under suspicion.

The LCWR executive director and staff were most solicitous in their support for their member leaders. In a January 30, 2009, letter to the membership, they communicated the Apostolic Visitation, its three phases and its official visitator, Mother Mary Clare Millea.[17] They also promised continuing support, including a set of "talking points for communication" with members of communities and the press. In a letter of February 9, 2009, Executive Director Jane Burke, SSND, listed five points to consider when preparing community members for the Visitation.[18] This particular communication also included suggestions from the LCWR communication director about how to respond when contacted by the news media. Throughout the first two phases of the Visitation LCWR leadership and staff were available as support and offered various services should anyone have need.[19]

The International Union of Superiors General issued a statement of support that read, in part: "We affirm unequivocally our support for our sisters in the United States. Their response to the mandates of the Second Vatican Council particularly stated in *Perfectae Caritatis*, has been a great gift not only to the pluralistic society in which they live but also to the universal church." In solidarity they added:

> Our desire is to assist them in facing the challenges which we share. Many of us are superiors general of international congregations. The diversity of religious life that exists in the church exists also within our congregations. After decades of cross-cultural dialogue and searching together for God's will in general chapters, the unity of vision and purpose we now experience is indivisible. Therefore, as leaders, we are confident that our members all over the world join us in our prayers for success and blessing on the Apostolic Visitation of our sisters in the United States.[20]

This example of the network crisscrossing the world provided anew the sense of strength behind the communities under scrutiny in the United States.

Barbara Bolster, RSM, president of the Conference of Leaders of Religious Institutes in New South Wales, Australia wrote in a letter to Marlene Weisenbeck, FSPA, then president of the LCWR:

> [W]e hold the women religious of America in our prayer. We stand with them in solidarity in mission and ministry. We share your longing for a world where the role of women in the church is appreciated and promoted. We pray that the outcome of the Apostolic Visitation . . . is a deep and abiding gratitude in recognition of the role played by the congregations of LCWR in creating the religious, social and justice history of the United States.[21]

In the letter from officials of the Leadership Conference of Consecrated Life in South Africa, U.S. women once again heard the commitment to solidarity: "Where one part of the body suffers, the whole body feels the pain." They pledged their prayer that "Spirit Sophia" might "show her face and grant her wisdom" so that even this negative experience might be an instant of grace for all religious everywhere as well as for the church as a whole.[22]

A statement from the Conference of Major Religious Superiors of Women of Asia-Oceania meeting in Samphran, Thailand, appeared on the *National Catholic Reporter*'s website and offered solidarity and prayers for the women religious in the United States.[23] The letter represented 113 women religious from seventeen countries. They acknowledged "shared circumstances of vulnerability" of women living and working on the "margins of society, often with little support." They ended their letter with an offering of solidarity and prayers.

National and International Lay Organizations

On September 26, 2009, The Quixote Center, Women's Alliance for Theology, Ethics and Ritual (WATER), Women's Ordination Conference (WOC), Future Church, the 8th Day Center for Justice, Center of Concern, Southeast Pennsylvania Synod (SEPA), New Ways Ministry, Roman Catholic Women Priests-North America (RCWP-North America), *Pax Christi* Maine, Save Our Sacraments, *Communitas,* and NOVA Catholic Community placed an ad in the *National Catholic Reporter* signaling their solidarity with U.S. sisters whose quality of life was under Vatican investigation. These groups pledged to stand with sisters as a community and church that celebrates diverse vocations and a common commitment to love well and act justly. They also stated that the investigation of religious life for women religious is "an indictment of all of us who share your values and strive to live as a 'discipleship of equals.'" They suggested dialogue, discussion, and discernment as ways to share information and build community. They urged sisters to "be steadfast in maintaining the integrity" of their communal lives according to their constitutions. They pledged their assistance. They listed at length the contributions of U.S. women religious and, in the end, encouraged them to commit to one another and to their ministries because their love and energy are vital to a just world.

On November 8, 2009, Call to Action delegates unanimously approved a statement which addressed Catholics in the United States and around the world saying that women religious have "taught us how to live the gospel and open our arms until they embrace all God's people." Because of this they called on Catholics to put into practice all they had been taught in order to "ensure that our sisters in faith are not ripped from the church's embrace." They described women religious as the "bedrock" of the church and country. They also addressed those doing the investigation. In effect they said that their actions did not reflect those of Jesus in the gospels. They invited the investigators to "have a conversion of heart" and join with Call to Action as they stand with women religious. Once again, the dimension of prophet appears. They went on to say: "In every generation God raises up prophets to point the way toward the gospel vision of inclusion. Women religious are these prophets. Today we stand not with those who cling to the gates of exclusion but with the prophets who open the gates and call us to live as one."[24]

Communications from Men Religious

Another example of the acknowledgement that active women religious lead their lives as "authentic and effective prophets" came from a letter to the Sisters of Charity, BVM, from the Provincial Ministers of the Order of Friars Minor in the United States. They spoke for the whole Order to add their support to that of the many American Catholics who had already expressed their solidarity and support. They described the sisters as those who make the "joys and hopes, grief and anxieties of today's people their own." They listed the many ministries and works of service in which sisters are engaged all aimed at the "transformation of the world by the power of the gospel of Jesus Christ." Their letter includes the martyrs of El Salvador, the imprisoned protesters for civil disobedience and advocates for the immigrants and those otherwise disenfranchised. They underscore sisters' contributions to scholarship, their administrative skills, and their pastoral care in dioceses and parishes. The Friars end their letter by citing the tangible evidence that the laity understand what sisters have been and are now about. They mention that in 2009, the National Religious Retirement Office collected more than $26 million to care for retired religious most of whom are members of women's religious orders. And finally, the letter ends with "We owe them our love and support." [25] This letter, signed by the seven Provincials of Friars Minor, was only one among many that carried the nearly endless list of all that sisters contribute to the world around them.

Another typical communication came to Jane Burke, SSND, executive director of LCWR, from Thomas R. von Behren, CSV. He said that the Chicago province of the Viatorians "unanimously endorsed a statement of support for United States congregations of women religious during the Vatican Visitation." Furthermore, the Clerics of St. Viator expressed their prayerful support for congregations of women religious in the United States . . . and "hold our sisters in great esteem for their dedicated and innovative ministry, their commitment to the challenges of a Vatican II church and their fidelity to their particular charisms." They close their statement with the oft repeated words urging the "entire church to support these faith-filled women in their efforts to serve the church and the world." [26]

Finally, a couplet of masterful letters from Brother Peter Fitzpatrick, CFX, to Cardinal Franc Rodé, then prefect of CICLSAL, contributed a sense of the strength of the support that sisters had around the world during this event. Brother Fitzpatrick, former vicar general of the International Order of Xaverian Brothers, twice provincial of the Xaverian Brothers in Kensington, Maryland, executive director of the National Organization for the Continuing Education of Roman Catholic Clergy and co-director of the Spiritual Integration Program for Experienced Men and Women Religious in Canada, is qualified to express his concerns. In his first letter Brother Fitzpatrick offered advice to Cardinal Rodé and in doing so advised the readers about how the Apostolic Visitation might be addressed. He called the Visitation "most unjust, most unworthy" of the cardinal or anyone in his position. He said that the Visitation was "brutally oppressive of the greater majority of religious women's congregations in this country." And, he added, "Lay women especially see it as one more example of the Vatican's oppression of women throughout its long history." He called Cardinal Rodé's attention to the fact that the laity see this as abuse: "a bullying of our sisters to force them to conform to your narrow views." He describes the call to U.S. bishops to contribute $1.1 million to pay for the Visitation as the "final straw." His letter puts a fine point on the meaning of participation in the Visitation: complying with the demands of the Visitation would be "to participate in the demeaning of one's own person and that of one's congregation." Women religious, already suspecting this, could read Fitzpatrick's commentary and know that once again they were interpreting the Visitation correctly and their perception was corroborated by one whom they respected. [27]

Brother Fitzpatrick's second letter outlined in three points how Cardinal Rodé could end the Visitation process in a "peaceful resolution." In summary, he advises Cardinal Rodé to notify the U.S. congregations that the Visitation has ended and suggests that Cardinal Rodé should meet with all of the members of LCWR and find out how his office could actually be of service to women religious in the United States. [28]

On October 19, 2009, Marlene Weisenbeck, FSPA, then president of LCWR, received a letter from the Canon Law Society of America. In it, President Rev. Lawrence Jurcak, JCL, stated that in the name of the Society he volunteered their services should anyone wish to consult them. They would be glad to serve pro bono as advisers to major superiors in regard to the Visitation. [29]

Joseph Tobin, CSsR, former superior general of the Redemptorist Order and now archbishop of Indianapolis, Indiana, was appointed by Pope Benedict XVI in August, 2010, as secretary of CICLSAL. Early in December, 2010, he said that he didn't expect any "punitive" fallout from the Visitation, and that before any decisions are made, women's communities should have a chance to know the results and to respond. Tobin said that, as a matter of "justice and charity," he would "strongly advocate" for feedback and a right of reply. Tobin's clear intent was to facilitate a dialogue between CICLSAL and the American congregations of women religious. [30]

This innovative and rational approach to the whole event might have resulted in a friendlier and more trustful relationship between the women religious and CICLSAL had he remained in office. But by October, 2012, Bishop Joseph Tobin had been transferred to Indianapolis. This move by Rome was further evidence, should any be needed, that the original intent for the Visitation was to be maintained and that their assumptions were, as a matter of fact, to be proven accurate. Thus, the loss of this advocate for reason and temperance, dialogue, and mutual resolution created among women religious an attitude of watchfulness and further commitment to respond with integrity and solidarity with one another, whatever the outcome of the Visitation.

Local Friends and Allies

Forty-eight percent of the survey respondents cited support from their lay partners as providing inspiration and courage for the task ahead. Laity who had been served by, or who were working closely with, women religious quickly rallied behind the sisters. They wrote letters to the editor, posted on blogs, and communicated privately to individual sisters or congregations with whom they were closely connected.

These lay friends wrote of their support and encouraged sisters to continue the struggle to claim their identity within the church, because their own identity as laity depended on the outcome. They were outspoken in defense against what they judged an unjust attack on women religious when their exemplary ministries were supporting the lay church everywhere, at the same time that the institutional church was faltering under its own duplicity and sinfulness. This distinction was quick in coming. The laity spoke with one voice in its demands for just and fair treatment as well as redress for the ills rampant in the institutional church. One of their insights was that whatever happened to the sisters would either enhance their role in the church or stifle their voices for good.

The sisters sensed a new responsibility and it echoes in the words of one leader of an international order who summarized it succinctly: "This is an opportunity to raise a collective voice. . . . We will need to pray for the courage to live with our voice!"[31] This statement reminded women religious in the United States that they are engaged in the work of dignifying the place and role of all women and men in the church.

More often than not, these voices made themselves known in the news media. Though the voices of support and inspiration crossed religious lines, they were of one opinion when it came to the sisters. For example, a column in the January, 2010, issue of the *U.S. Catholic* creatively compared the various "bossy" women in contemporary TV series ("Law and Order," "The Closer," etc.) and the women religious who have proven that they are equal to the task of leadership as well as supervision and management. The author, Patrick McCormick, wrote that extraordinary leaders like Elizabeth Ann Seton, Catherine of Siena, Teresa of Avila, and Louise de Marillac

> founded congregations and religious orders; led reform movements; began and
> oversaw national and global networks of schools, missions, universities, and

hospitals; ran multimillion dollar institutions; and supplied much of the care for the world's poor and sick. In such a church there should be a profound and deep reverence for women's gifts for leadership. There should be a shrine to the female boss.

Were this the case, continues McCormick, those responsible for the Visitation would see "the wondrous talents and genius women leaders and bosses have brought to the Catholic Church, and all the other gifts they would have brought had we but seen their talents, brains, compassion, and skills earlier."[32]

Three lay women wrote a tribute to the sisters in Wichita, which was published in the *Wichita Eagle* on August 16, 2009. They expressed sadness that the teachers and nurses they loved and had learned from were being subjected to an investigation. They went on to say that these women were "highly educated and spiritually motivated. They use their talents and resources to feed the hungry, care for the sick, educate children and adults and tend to those standing on the margins of society. . . ." They are "shining examples of gospel values." Their care includes programs and care for the poor, the sick, the abused, the indigent, the elderly and many more who do not have the resources to care for themselves. The women end their praise of the sisters with their gratitude because the sisters have been able to manage their own resources in such a way that they have been able to provide not only for themselves but also for those in need. They are "confident the fruits of their ministries will speak for themselves."[33]

In February, 2013, *Boston Globe* reporter Ruth Graham observed:

> this upheaval and decline also come at a moment when historians and other scholars are taking a fresh look at the role of nuns in American life, and finding that nuns' contributions to the broad story of America have been, if anything, underappreciated. Nuns have served as the face of Catholicism to generations of Americans, and they've also been pioneers in health care, education and social work—fields that may sound decidedly secular today, but whose development in the United States was profoundly shaped by the labor and influence of nuns. And, as those stories come under close examination, it's becoming clear that the question of what's next for nuns affects not just fine inner workings of the church, but its future course in America.

Graham concludes that a "lack of formal power within the church, a strong intellectual component, and centuries of work with the oppressed" have formed the "foundation for their increasingly outspoken politics beginning in the 1960s."[34]

Carol Marin, *Chicago Sun-Times* columnist, posed a provocative question on July 3, 2009: "Don't these sisters know their place?" Her response:

For centuries, that place has been at the foot of the church, running schools, operating hospitals and working with the poor. While diocesan priests lived in rectories with more rooms than they could use and housekeepers to cook and clean, the sisters lived in tiny cells, did their own scrubbing and potato peeling and provided the church with a dirt-cheap work force. The diocese, in turn, gave them less than a subsistence wage with neither pensions nor health insurance.[35]

Expository articles like this did not present anything new to the sisters about whom they were written. But for many of the laity they contextualized a problem of focus in the Apostolic Visitation. Why, indeed, was a Visitation being conducted for the sisters? Lay people began asking the same question—and expecting answers. This article and many like it helped sisters formulate their own arguments for not complying with the requests of the Apostolic Visitation.

The Visitation inspired stories of how sisters made a difference in early lives of lay people and showed that difference carried through the years in loyalty to them. Testimonies of this came to light in myriad newspapers or personal letters. Sisters read a continuous stream of defense for themselves, and often these stories moved them to tears of gratitude and amazement. Always they inspired and supported. The stories brought the Chinese proverb to life. They enabled sisters to live the lives of their ancestors or their peers—or their own life all over again.

Opening the *Blade-Empire* newspaper on June 29, 2012, sisters in Concordia were startled to see themselves as the subject of a lengthy editorial written by the publisher, Brad Lowell. Seeing themselves in print because of a respected and influential member of their civic community not only startled them, but truly moved them to tears. Who would have thought that anyone outside the Catholic community would hold an opinion on the Apostolic Visitation? Sisters, taking themselves and their "place" in the town for granted, were suddenly brought up short by the observations of an "outsider." Here's the story as Mr. Lowell told it:

My first contact with the Sisters of St. Joseph was on January 26, 1938, the day that I was born at the old St. Joseph Hospital on East Fifth Street. It was a tragic day for my father because my birth mother died of complications resulting from a Caesarean-section. . . . Until my father could arrange a place for me to stay, the sisters in the nursery were my mothers. He told me later that they only charged 50 cents a day to keep me for the several months I remained in the nursery. . . . A number of years ago, [several sister friends] and my wife Lee, took me back to the old hospital and showed me where the nursery had been and the hospital room in which my mother died. We held hands and said a prayer and I had closure.

But his story of the sisters was not finished. Over the years, he wrote, he began

> observing the good works of the sisters and the progressive influence they had on the community. I'm convinced that many of the progressive projects accomplished in Concordia could not have come to fruition without the support of the sisters. How lucky we are to have the sisters located here, particularly in view of the fact there are fewer than 60,000 nuns remaining in the country.

Again, this storyteller segued into the past when the sisters became "true heroes" by taking in refugees from Guatemala. He cited their courage as they provided the basics of living for the refugees, facilitating their transition into a foreign country. And today, he described their work initiating the Year of Peace program, organizing community meetings to discuss the poverty in the area, and creating Neighbor to Neighbor as a shelter for women and children. "How great is that?" he asked. Finally, he noted that when he was diagnosed with cancer, many sisters asked about his welfare and promised prayer. "So," he wrote, "for a Protestant member of this community, I have a special place in my heart for Catholic Sisters of St. Joseph." His point in writing this personal story? He wanted to "register my voice in support of Catholic sisters all over this nation who are doing so much for the poor, the sick, the disabled, the abused and almost anyone else in need." Mr. Lowell ended his story with the words: "The goodwill that the Sisters of St. Joseph have earned in this community will live forever. The great thing is that they are not resting on their laurels and continue to seek new ways to give to the community each and every day."[36]

Another story comes from famed Catholic journalist, Moises Sandoval, who writes about his relationship with the Sisters of Our Lady of Victory Missionaries. Sandoval began his letter by saying that he would be spending several days at the motherhouse of Our Lady of Victory Missionary Sisters in Huntington, Indiana. "Because they played a key role in the history of the Hispanic church in the twentieth century and in the history of my family, I accepted their invitation to help them write about their early years. Moreover, my late mother loved them and I can think of no better way to honor her on Mother's Day than to help the sisters in any way I can." Their work, says Sandoval, "enriched the faith of millions of poor people" and responded to the needs for

> catechetical instruction, social work, and health care among the poor in isolated rural communities like the one in which I grew up. Not tied to the institutional church, the sisters of Our Lady of Victory cared for the poor with little or no access to the church's care. I met the Victory Noll catechists in the 1930s when several came to our one-room school on my grandfather's land to ac-

quaint us with the Baltimore Catechism and prepare us for our First Holy Communion.

Sandoval goes on to describe their work and how his path crossed theirs through the years. He says that even now, though fewer in numbers, they still have their characteristic virtues that led him to admire them in the first place: simplicity, hospitality, humility, and courage. He closed his letter by saying that it would be a privilege for him to be with them for a few days.[37]

Another friend, Bishop William J. Dendinger of Grand Island, Nebraska, wrote in his weekly "Bishop's Corner" column the thoughts engendered in his celebration of a funeral Mass for one of the sisters in his diocese. He couldn't help but contrast the mutual love of this sister and the people she served with the Rome-based investigation of this sister and many like her. He describes the contributions of the women religious in the United States as "monumental." He also cites the letter of support written by the bishops of California. He echoes their gratitude and acknowledges the many ministries they began and through which they continued to serve in his vast rural diocese. For ninety-seven years, he wrote, sisters have given themselves to his diocese. For him and for any bishop, this is no small thing.[38]

These stories, like many others, enabled sisters to see themselves in another light. It straightened their spines and enabled them to continue to work as never before, affirmed in the strength of self-understanding retold through another's eyes. No small thing, this favor.

Testimonies also came from associates and from the lay friends and coworkers who were asked to form focus groups in congregations who were visited. These lay friends stood loyally by the sisters as they were questioned by the visitors. One respondent to the survey described her attempts to prepare the members of the focus group for the Visitation as "an emotional roller coaster experience."[39] The task of orienting the focus group to the various aspects of congregational life while attempting to be loyal to the church created in many a leader this sort of experience. As it happened, however, the outrage created by the proceedings of the Visitation tightened the bonds the focus groups felt with the sisters. Their loyalty was solid.

Finally, Marcy Kaptur, D-OH, introduced a resolution into the House of Representatives on May 14, 2009, honoring the lives and works of sisters. The resolution, agreed to on September, 22, 2009:

H.Res.441 resolves that the House of Representatives:

• Honors and commends Catholic sisters for their humble service and courageous sacrifice throughout the history of this Nation; and
• Supports the goals of the Women & Spirit: Catholic Sisters in America Traveling Exhibit, a project sponsored by the Leadership Conference of Women Religious (LCWR) in association with Cincinnati Museum

Center and established to recognize the historical contributions of Catholic sisters in the United States.[40]

The resolution noted the "social, cultural, and political contributions of Catholic sisters" and acknowledged that they "have joined in unique forms of intentional communitarian life dedicated to prayer and service since the very beginnings of our Nation's history, fearlessly and often sacrificially committing their personal lives to teaching, healing, and social action . . ."[41]

All of this testimony enabled sisters to realize that the foundation on which they live is a strong one indeed. There, for them and for the world to see, was evidence of the difference they had made over nearly three centuries in the social and cultural life of the people of the United States.

The Canonists' Support

Another source of encouragement, both inspirational and realistic, was the Resource Center for Religious Life (RCRI). This organization of canonists, civil attorneys and financial experts immediately announced its readiness to offer advice and consultation to any congregation who asked for it. Approximately one-third of the survey respondents lauded the canon lawyers for their presence, support, and expertise. Sisters realized that the canonists put themselves at great personal risk in doing this.

In a series of phone conferences offered during 2009, RCRI members were able to advise women religious about the serious nature of the Apostolic Visitation. They assured them that this was not a friendly visit and they would be well served to temper their habitual hospitality with reserve. Because they would never see the report, they should examine the questions with care. Canonists and civil attorneys were able to show how a single question might require responses that took into consideration issues from both canon and civil law. This ambiguity in a single question could result in ambiguous responses which would skew the report. Not only did responders need to be alert to these anomalies but responses would have to be carefully nuanced.

Because each religious congregation is unique, following different rules and customs and providing a different kind of approach or spirit within the same service, communities would be best served by erring on the side of failure to comply rather than providing too much information that in the end would only count against them. Their cautions were well-taken by congregations and helped many decide that they would not respond to the questions. They were particularly cautious about Part C of Phase 2 of the Visitation. Much credit can be given to RCRI for the withdrawal of most of Part C from the *Questionnaire*.

This organization, because of their familiarity with many congregations, urged leaders to network across the country. This advice, as it turned out, served them well. Leaders quickly learned what others were doing and were able to offer mutual advice and create a common purpose in regard to the Apostolic Visitation.

These remarkable friends and allies are the people who stand by the women religious of the United States. Their witness illuminates with clarity the meaning of life for women religious and their responsibility for continuing their fidelity to the path renewal has taken them.

CONCLUSION

The Visitation offered unexpected energy and inspiration in the lives of women religious. Prone to take themselves and what they do for granted, they go about their daily lives according to a Rule of Life that calls them to deep prayer and discernment. Contemplation of their mission and purpose, those in need in the context of gospel values, the Christ whom they follow and bring to life in the world, sends them into works of service—ministries—that they embrace in a more or less matter of fact manner. This "habit" of self-giving fits like a glove; in fact it fits so well that it goes unnoticed by the woman religious herself, but seems extraordinary to those around her. The Visitation, the "Woman and Spirit" exhibit, the communications from friends and persons who wished them well all suddenly brought into sharp focus what women religious had long taken for granted: theirs is an extraordinary vocation and is seen as such by those who observed them.

This new perspective on themselves and a new perspective on their communities brought them to immediate and conscientious defense of the life they are living. The values manifested themselves: fierce love of charism and mission; fierce loyalty to one another; generous love for and loyalty to the church; absolute determination to preserve personal and communal integrity; their work in and for the world and church; a generous sisterhood across the country and around the globe; and willingness to dialogue with the Vatican until a resolution for the situation could be found. They became as passionately alive in their resolution to endure this suffering and persecution from the church with integrity as were their foremothers in comparable situations.

This story twice lived is the story of a robust identity, a deeper and tougher commitment, and best of all, a sense of unity as strong as the primordial endurance of a spider's web. It is the story of hard won integrity and solidarity—hard won together!

NOTES

1. Margaret Cain McCarthy, "Apostolic Visitation Survey Analysis: The Apostolic Visitation as Experienced by Women Religious in the United States" (report, October 15, 2011).

2. U.S. Federation of Sisters of St. Joseph Ongoing Formation Committee (Sheila Briody, SSJ; Mary Clark, CSJ; Janet Mock, CSJ; JoAnn Tabor, CSJ; Kathy McCluskey, CSJ) to Member Congregations, Sisters of St. Joseph, August 2009.

3. Peter Block to Nancy Conway, CSJ, in a private conference she shared with other congregations, 2009.

4. McCarthy, "Apostolic Visitation Survey Analysis."

5. Sandra M. Schneiders, IHM, *Prophets in Their Own Country: Women Religious Bearing Witness to the Gospel in a Troubled Church* (Maryknoll, NY: Orbis Books, 2011), 8.

6. ibid, 12.

7. ibid, 79.

8. Johannes B. Metz, *Followers of Christ: The Religious Life and the Church* (New York: Paulist Press, 1977), 26.

9. Schneiders, *Prophets in Their Own Country*, 125.

10. Leadership Conference of Women Religious, "Sandra Schneiders, IHM to Receive Outstanding Leadership Award," *Update*, May 2012, 1.

11. Joan Chittister, OSB, "The Past is a Very Living Thing: Try Not to Forget It," *National Catholic Reporter*, April 24, 2009, http://ncronline.org/blogs/where-i-stand/past-very-living-thing-try-not-forget-it.

12. Joan Chittister, OSB, "Vatican Could Learn a Thing or Two about Renewal from Women Religious," *National Catholic Reporter*, March 6, 2013, http://ncronline.org/blogs/where-i-stand/vatican-could-learn-thing-or-two-about-renewal-women-religious.

13. Thomas C. Fox, "Mercy Sister Theresa Kane Criticizes Church Hierarchy," *National Catholic Reporter*, September 30, 2009, http://ncronline.org/news/mercy-sister-theresa-kane-criticizes-church-hierarchy.

14. Nadine Foley, OP, "Negotiation with Rome: A Reflection on Possibility," *LCWR Occasional Papers*, Spring 2001, 21–28.

15. Doris Gottemoeller, RSM, "A Visitor's Guide: How the Vatican Investigation Could Prove Beneficial," *America*, November 23, 2009, http://americamagazine.org/issue/716/article/visitors-guide.

16. Anne Marie Mongoven, OP, "We Did What the Church Asked Us to Do," *National Catholic Reporter*, August 7, 2009, http://ncronline.org/print/14350.

17. Letter by Jane Burke, SSND, "LCWR Letter to Members," January 30, 2009.

18. Letter by Jane Burke, SSND, "LCWR Letter to Members," February 9, 2009.

19. Letter by Leadership Conference of Women Religious Board, "Letter to Members," February 22, 2009.

20. Memorandum by International Union of Superiors General, Board of Directors, "Statement of the Board of Directors, International Union of Superiors General concerning the Apostolic Visitation of Women Religious in the United States," April 23, 2009, http://www.apostolicvisitation.org/en/materials/iusg.pdf.

21. Conference of Leaders of Religious Institutes in New South Wales, Australia (Barbara Bolster, RSM, president) to Marlene Weisenbeck, FSPA, October 9, 2009.

22. Leadership Conference of Consecrated Life in South Africa (Patrick Rakeketsi, CSS, president; Fiona Vallance, SP, vice-president; Marie-Luise Faupel OP, secretary general) to Leadership Conference of Women Religious, November 2, 2009.

23. Thomas C. Fox, "Asia, Oceania Women Religious Offer Support to Beleaguered U.S. Sisters," *National Catholic Reporter*, October 20, 2009, http://ncronline.org/news/asia-oceania-women-religious-offer-support-beleaguered-us-sisters.

24. Thomas C. Fox, "Louise Akers elevates Women's Issues at CTA Meeting," *National Catholic Reporter*, November 9, 2009, http://ncronline.org/news/louise-akers-elevates-womens-issues-cta-meeting.

25. Provincial Ministers of the Order of Friars Minor in the United States to Sisters of Charity, BVM, February 6, 2010, http://members.bvmcong.org/SistersBVM/Members/leadership/AV_Provincial Ministers.htm.

26. Thomas R. von Behren, CSV to Jane Burke, SSND, October 30, 2009.

27. Thomas C. Fox, "Two Heartfelt Support Letters Regarding U.S. Women Religious," *National Catholic Reporter*, February 5, 2010, http://ncronline.org/blogs/ncr-today/two-heart-felt-support-letters-regarding-us-women-religious.

28. ibid.

29. Lawrence Jurcak, JCL to Marlene Weisenback, FSPA, October 19, 2009.

30. Joseph Tobin, CsSR quoted in John L. Allen, Jr., "Vatican Must Hear 'Anger and Hurt' of American Nuns, Official Says" *National Catholic Reporter*, December 7, 2010, http://ncron-line.org/blogs/ncr-today/vatican-must-hear-anger-and-hurt-american-nuns-official-says.

31. Letter by superior general of an international community with sisters in the United States to Marcia Allen, CSJ, July 21, 2013.

32. Patrick McCormick, "Culture in Context: Mothers Superior," *U.S. Catholic*, January 2010, 40–41.

33. Diana Knolla, Susan Mann, and Angie Urenda to Editor, *Wichita Eagle*, "Sisters Serve," August 16, 2009.

34. Ruth Graham, "What the Nuns Built," *The Boston Globe*, February 24, 2013, sec. K, 1–4, http://www.bostonglobe.com/ideas/2013/02/24/what-american-nuns-built-what-american-nuns-built/IvaMKcoK8a4jDb9lqiVOrI/story.html.

35. Carol Marin, "Nun Investigations about Stifling Dissent," *Chicago Sun-Times*, July 3, 2012.

36. Brad Lowell, "Our Thanks to the Sisters of St. Joseph," *Concordia Blade-Empire*, June 29, 2012.

37. Moises Sandoval to Ginger Downy, OLVM, July 10, 2013.

38. Bishop William J. Dendinger, "Bishop's Corner," *Southwestern Nebraska Catholic Register*, November 20, 2009.

39. McCarthy, "Apostolic Visitation Survey Analysis."

40. Honoring the Historical Contributions of Catholic Sisters in the United States, H.R. Res. 441, 111th Cong. (2009). https://www.govtrack.us/congress/bills/111/hres441.

41. ibid.

Chapter Seven

Theological Reflection on the Apostolic Visitation

"Were not our hearts burning within us?"

Addie Lorraine Walker

THEOLOGICAL REFLECTION:
A WAY OF MAKING SENSE OF OUR EXPERIENCE

Theological reflection is one way of making sense of our personal and collective experiences in light of our faith and God's revealing presence in our lives. It is a way to put our experiences into dialogue with the wisdom and insight of Scripture and our religious heritage: our personal and collective ponderings of our spiritual pathways of following Jesus, the Christ; our trusting the Spirit at work in and among us; our shining the light of the charisms of our founders and foundresses on current events and our collective response. The experience of the Apostolic Visitation is one occasion that begs our attentive theological reflection to help us sort through the layers of meaning and questions for further dialogue and action.

Because the Apostolic Visitation was experienced broadly and was not an experience that any one congregation chose or had control over, it had the indirect effect of drawing religious congregations together into multiple groupings of collaborators and pilgrims on a journey without a map, without a clear vision of where God is in this. The unintended consequence of this forced journey is a common experience with potential for collective reflection and meaning making. That is to say, this forged or forced journey offers us the opportunity to reflect together and draw new meaning from our lives as women religious in the U.S., embracing the significance of this moment in our collective history. This Visitation becomes for us, then, a way or an occasion through which we can process and come to understand how women religious today make sense of our lives in adverse and confusing times, bringing into bold relief a gospel witness of women of faith and courage in this new millennium that mirrors the trailblazing of founders and foundresses in a previous time. [1]

Responses to the Apostolic Visitation Survey (survey) describe the thoughts and feelings of the respondents when they learned of the Apostolic Visitation and as they moved into a process of making their response. The collective expressions indicate the collective tail-spin the project caused. This was true not only for women religious but for friends, colleagues, employees, and associates, as well. Because none of the leaders or sisters was directly involved in the call for, or the design of, such an intervention, it left all with questions and emotions demanding personal and collective pondering: What is this? Why? What does this mean? What is the point? Why us? Why now? How can this be? What must we do?

The accompanying emotions—shock, anger, fear, dismay, apprehension, betrayal, incredulity, confusion, disbelief, etc.—confirmed our need for immediate and ongoing reflection to manage a response and to access what God might be saying in the whirlwind as we moved forward into the future, our future in mission here in the U.S. "[W]e were surprised and wondered what it was all about and why it was being done." "We were surprised by the announcement of the Apostolic Visitation, confused about why such a Visitation was taking place, resentful that our lifestyles and ministries were under scrutiny, and anxious about how the information collected would be used." "We were angry, confused, disappointed, and surprised because we were neither given an advanced notice nor a reason." [2]

Wittingly or unwittingly we were forced to take up the painstaking work of reading the social reality of our situation and bringing it into dialogue with the Scripture and the traditions of our congregations, and religious life and culture in the U.S. This is the essence of what it means to do theological reflection. Recognizing and naming, as accurately as possible, one's feelings aroused by the experience is an important first step in beginning the process of theological reflection. [3]

The task was big, because it was not just about any single congregation alone. But, what affected one of us, affected all of us. These are skills we have acquired and practiced over the years to develop vision or directional statements or to come to consensus on some issue facing our province or congregations. But, this event called religious leaders across congregational lines to study together; to work together; to ponder together; to examine the issues raised by the Apostolic Visitation from various perspectives, together; to look together at options for responding; and to support each other in the process, no matter the diversity of responses.

Responses to the survey indicate that the respondents were aware of walking by faith, not by sight, and had a clear awareness of the power of the Spirit at work among us. "We women religious place our faith in God's providence on a daily basis. I found peace in that." We had the "awareness that the Spirit works through processes even when we don't understand or agree with them initially." On another level there was "excitement at being involved in something meaningful, challenged, peaceful, led by the Spirit, united with many of my sisters in leadership as we were led together by the Spirit and as we listened and responded." "There was a great movement of the Holy Spirit between the time the *Questionnaire* arrived and the deadline for answering. A great solidarity of leaders developed."

Though some feelings of apprehension and caution remained constant, some indicated that some of their feelings shifted because of the openness of interactions with Mother Mary Clare, the visitors who were non-threatening, and the positive experience and feedback of other communities. "The experience was better than we thought [it would be]. It gave us a new sense of pride in our identity as consecrated religious women in the U.S. and increased our solidarity with other communities in the U.S. and around the world." "The Visitation strengthened our unity with one another and gave us an opportunity to 'claim our voice' in the Catholic Church."

All of the responses place what we understand as reaction to the experience of the Apostolic Visitation in the realm of theological reflection. They reflect a clear awareness of being accompanied by the presence of the Spirit, of the importance of giving voice to the truth of the great works begun in us and continuing in us, and a consciousness of the lingering challenges that confront us and all Christians in these times. The movements to face the challenge, to be open to the experience, listening to many diverse perspectives and holding all in prayer, personal and communal, was a process that called us all in retrospect to declare, "Were not our hearts burning within us?" (Luke 24:13-35, NAB)[4] And, like many faith-filled women before us, in a time when they were deeply troubled and confused they "pondered all these things" in their hearts (Luke 2:19, 51).

THEOLOGICAL REFLECTION: ATTENDING TO CONNECTIONS

Theological reflection in the first place requires of us a spiritual noticing, or awareness, of being in relationship with God, self, others and the broader universe, especially when the experience suggests or arouses the question of a deeper meaning in terms of these relationships in the present and future. In reality, it also requires a greater self-understanding as an individual, as leaders, and as a congregation. It implies a dynamic movement of being informed, formed, shaped and transformed by the energy and interactions among us and around us, with Jesus, the Spirit, and even with the wisdom of the saints who have gone before us.[5]

The survey highlights that from the earliest moments the respondents acknowledged the dynamic energy of God present with them and within them in this surprising and overwhelming happening. As the Visitation proceeded, they additionally indicate an awareness of the connection to the gospel story and the disciples trying to make sense of their experiences. They also recalled experiences of the founders and foundresses that shed light on the situation and gave them courage to continue. The connecting of "this burning within us" with the gospel and religious heritage is at the heart of what we know as theological reflection and more specifically in this case, gathering "spiritual wisdom."[6]

The survey invited participants to make explicit the connections they were making with Scripture and stories of their congregations. First, to address the Scripture stories: many highlighted themes of faith and trust in God even when God's plan is not clear; at times, we may suffer for our faith . . . following God's plan for us. Others referred to passages calling them to "Fear not, for I am with you" (Isaiah 43:5) and to the knowledge of "my grace is sufficient for you" (2 Corinthians 12:9). Still others suggested scriptural wisdom acknowledging that whatever the "Visitation" was it was somehow connected with what God was doing in the larger scheme of things. "See, I am doing something new! . . . do you not perceive it?" (Isaiah 43:19) "Behold, I am sending you like sheep in the midst of wolves; so be shrewd as serpents and gentle as doves" (Matthew 10:16). "I am the way, and the truth and the life" (John 14:6). "For I know well the plans I have in mind for you—oracle of the Lord—plans for your welfare and not for woe, so as to give you a future of hope" (Jeremiah 29:11). ". . . if this endeavor or activity is of human origin, it will destroy itself. But if it comes from God, you will not be able to destroy them . . . " (Acts 5:38-39). "With God all things are possible" ". . . for nothing will be impossible for God" (Luke 1:37). "God is faithful, and [God] will not let you be tried beyond your strength, but with the trial [God] will also provide a way out, so that you may be able to bear it" (I Corinthians 10:13).

The ability to recognize the connection between the personal/collective experience and the sacred texts of our faith witnesses to the capacity to identify God's self-disclosure or self-revelation in the midst of the journey. This is another important step in theological reflection and in coming to a deeper understanding of the ultimate meaning of the overall encounter. Another Scripture that respondents noted they used for prayer and contemplation during the time of the Apostolic Visitation, because of its obvious connection, is that of the visitation of Mary to Elizabeth in Chapter 1 of the Gospel of Luke. One respondent indicated that for her this was "the prototypic visitation." As the story comes to us in the Lucan tradition our attention is called to the theological intent in how the story is presented. The two women come together recognizing and affirming the presence of God active in their lives. The elder affirms the younger for her trust in God, her trust that God's word would be fulfilled in her. "When Elizabeth heard Mary's greeting, the infant leaped in her womb, and Elizabeth . . . cried out in a loud voice and said, 'Most blessed are you among women. . . . Blessed are you who believed that what was spoken to you by the Lord would be fulfilled'" (Luke 1:39-45). The use of story and ritual, praying with this ancient text, seemed to mirror this encounter in that some experienced a movement of the Holy Spirit within and the development of great solidarity with other leaders going through the same process. "Mary journeying to greet Elizabeth to acknowledge the life in her womb—to be present to one another. This is what we did for and with one another these past years. It has been a rich journey!"[7]

Other respondents stated "The grace of the Holy Spirit was so present in our congregation both individually and collectively that we experienced great peace amidst the chaos." And, another: "There was a growing appreciation of the solidarity that had grown among women religious all over the world." "The warm personal contacts among women religious of various congregations have definitely been the most effective influence in strengthening our commitment to continue working toward greater authenticity and collaboration. . . ."

THE APOSTOLIC VISITATION
THROUGH THE LENS OF THE EMMAUS STORY

The most often mentioned Scripture was Luke 24: 13-35, the Emmaus story. The themes highlighted in this story parallel central themes for women religious in the U.S. experiencing the Apostolic Visitation—the themes of journey, faith as seeing, and hospitality.[8] In the Gospel of Luke the theme of journey is presented as an image of discipleship, following Jesus on his way. The experience of the Apostolic Visitation, though a journey in itself, was held and seen within the context of the larger mission and journey with Jesus Christ: "Our mission is the mission of Jesus." "Sisters have gone about their ministry and engaged in the community life and prayer life that they always have." "The whole experience was immersed in prayer from day one . . . our sisters joined in prayer for everyone involved. As the time went on the solidarity strengthened and we also became even more rooted. . . ." "We continued to live our apostolic, consecrated way of life as before." "[We continued] our lives of service and prayer, devotion to the church as the people of God." Important for the process of theological reflection is seeing the experience or encounter in relationship to the unfolding story of our life with Jesus as is clearly evident in the overall responses of the respondents.

Following the storyline of the Emmaus story, within the context of our journey of dealing with the 2009–2011 Apostolic Visitation, we could say that as we were going on our way, following Jesus, a radical interruption happened. A stranger appeared, we disciples were confounded, we shared our story, our eyes were restrained from seeing (a spiritual blindness). We were distressed, disappointed by happenings, and unable to believe that this event which was happening to us was not known, understood, and felt by all like we felt it. As we made our way, the Scriptures were interpreted and our hearts were burning within us. We continued to walk with the stranger/ strangeness and welcomed the stranger into our space, our hearth place. In this intimate space, our homes, our giving thanks and breaking bread together revealed the Christ. The stranger or strangeness disappeared and the Christ remained with us, within us. And, what we learned along the way as we reflected on our stories now makes some sort of God sense: *"Were not our hearts burning within us?"*

Making these theological connections and so stepping back from the immediacy of the event, we could see the event with the eyes of faith: "Ultimately a certain sense of trust in the Spirit emerged." "We were strengthened in a common resolve to remain authentic to our own identity as apostolic women and to support others in their charisms." "Gatherings renewed our hope in the church as the people of God who were in solidarity with each other." "These gatherings were a blessing and sacred. We experienced solidarity, unity, and purpose. They helped us to stay the course." The gatherings with and support from other leaders, as well as positive reports from other groups aided respondents and sisters in seeing a shift in and among themselves and how they welcomed the visitors. Hospitality of heart allows for the possibility of transformed lives and situations.

The theme of hospitality in the Emmaus story is first revealed as the two disciples allowed the stranger to draw near and travel on with them. They made space in their hearts, conversation, and in their journey to include him, to share their own story with him, and to listen to him. Hospitality, according to Henri Nouwen, is an attitude of heart that opens us to others and receives them on their own terms, a move from hostility to friendship, creating a free space where the stranger can enter and become friend.[9] Hospitality, then, becomes a virtue that does not focus on changing people but it is a habit of heart that offers them space where change can take place.[10] The virtue of hospitality of the hosting congregations seemed to transform the actual experience for some, creating a space within persons and within a hostile situation where grace could be experienced.

> When we received word that we would be visited onsite, our sisters painstakingly considered the option to meet with the visitors and [some] chose to do so. At the end of our onsite visit, the congregation joined together over video-

conference and teleconference and celebrated our ability to speak clearly and passionately about who we are as women of the church, committed to God. Even though our sisters would still say that this Apostolic Visitation is wrong, we recognize as an unintended outcome of this process, a deepening in our relationships and in our commitment to religious life. In the end, we were proud and unified.

Were not our hearts burning within us?

"The grace of the Holy Spirit was so present in our congregation both individually and collectively that we experienced great peace amidst the chaos." "After personal experience in our own visits, [and] among the sisters who served as visitors, our positive perspective was confirmed." "Some sisters, having heard stories from friends about how 'nice' the visitors were when onsite, have begun to forget the fact that it is still an official visitation to correct perceived abuses and not just a friendly visit by a few other religious." "The positive experience of the visit was very significant for us. When I first talked with our visit coordinator I asked us to make a pact to make this a positive experience for our sisters. Our visiting team was delightful and affirming. Our sisters didn't want them to leave. We had a special blessing for them at the beginning and end of their time with us." "Our apprehension changed to curiosity and finally to appreciation for the professional way the onsite visit was conducted."

The change in leadership at CICLSAL and multiple favorable reports, along with positive personal experiences helped many to ponder more deeply the events and to ask even further questions about what this experience might mean in the future and to acclaim: *Were not our hearts burning within us,* as we welcomed the stranger into our lives?

Still another aspect of the Emmaus story merits our attention. That is, to probe further the correlation between the unresolved questions and interpretation of the two disciples on the road. The disciples raised questions regarding the events surrounding the crucifixion of Jesus. In this setting, the questions raised by respondents regarding events surrounding the Apostolic Visitation have a somewhat parallel correlation. The disciples' incredulity and extreme disappointment about the events that had taken place in Jerusalem concerning Jesus sound so familiar to us: "Are you the only visitor to Jerusalem who does not know of the things that have taken place there in these days? . . . Jesus the Nazarene . . . how our chief priests and rulers both handed him over to a sentence of death and crucified him . . . we were hoping . . ." (Luke 24: 18-21). Looking at parallels in our own story with the gospel story helps us raise similar questions of incredulity in our own pursuit of making faith-sense in the theological reflection process.

For the respondents, these questions and sentiments surfaced in the following ways: "We wondered what it was all about; what were the reasons;

what would be the outcome. We felt angry and confused." "Why us?" "Why now?" "I was startled and surprised and wondered really why this was occurring. I could not imagine the rationale behind the Visitation." "Given the issues in the church at the time I could not believe that they were focusing on women religious." "I was angry that they would use their and our time, energy and resources to 'investigate' us and our lifestyle and work." One respondent expressed "rage, then anger and a sadness that will not go away. We have been faithful to our calling and continue to actively discern our fidelity. I still feel oppressed by my own church." It seems that there were no answers to these questions and no explanation given that assuage the deep feelings of hurt and anger.

It is also clear that there exists among these women respondents a sense of being marginalized by the church. This sense of marginalization co-exists with a sense of being rooted in the ministry of Jesus and connected to the ongoing presence of the Spirit in their lives and ministries. Their responses also point to the recognition of the great work they do for the mission of Jesus Christ and the church. In the stories highlighted about founders and foundresses, it appears that this is a longstanding tension for women in the church. However, in the midst of the tension, the focus of these heritage stories is "inspirational . . . primarily focused on struggle, challenge, discouragement, and tremendous difficulty; but, with hope and deep faith in God, perseverance and ultimately success." The following examples are illustrative of the responses given:

"[During] all that our sisters went through at the time of the French Revolution and the expulsion of religious in the early 1900s, God took care of them and they came out stronger. God never gives us more than we can bear." "Our congregation has a long tradition of praying, 'Providence can provide; Providence did provide; Providence will provide.' We continue that prayer in the context of the Visitation and in the context of our numerical diminishment. Reflecting on the challenges that faced our foundresses, including misunderstandings with bishops, the legacy of trust in Providence strengthened us."

"In the darkest of times, our foundress never lost hope. She is quoted as saying, 'I have placed all my hope in God and I will not be confounded.' Also, 'One must, in this stormy time, have one's eyes raised continually to the Star of the Sea and go often to the source of living waters so as not to be shaken and to keep the middle of the road.'" "The memory of the great-hearted women in our history inspired us and enkindled courage within us. The re-foundation of our order after the French Revolution served as a reminder to us that chaos often accompanies new life and it requires letting go, speaking difficult truths, and standing in one's own integrity. Our foundress stood up in the middle of a liturgy to protest the presider's actions, knowing this would result in her imprisonment and the guillotining of some of her sisters." "The foundress of our order began in France. Her life was one of struggling with bishops and cardinals who resented her as a woman and didn't believe that a woman could be knowledgeable in theology, spirituality or Scripture. Yet she founded an order that extends itself into today . . . on six continents."

These stories and stories like them inspired and gave courage to leaders and sisters as they faced the challenges of responding to the Apostolic Visitation: "Our founders also faced the challenges of living within and loving a church that sometimes focused more on structures and investigation than on vitality and growth/life. Their lived experiences supported us." "Our support and inspiration came from the following: . . . our pride in the story of our own history and charism. . . ." "We drew strength from our patrons and our foundress."

THEOLOGICAL REFLECTION:
RECOGNITION OF MARGINALIZATION

Questions raised by women religious throughout the survey also reflect their feminist critique of the current mixed read on the relationship of what is termed "the church," or otherwise called "the hierarchy" or "the institutional church," and U.S. women religious' congregations.[11] The concerns of these women religious respondents echo the concerns of many Catholic women in the church today. As indicated in the heritage stories above, there is a long history of women struggling against discrimination on the basis of their gender. Despite the great contributions of women to the building of the church in America, women continue to experience being marginalized: no seat at the table, no voice in the shaping of the report or follow-up decisions that impact the oversight of religious life, and no participation in the overall governance of the church. The "genius,"[12] talents, and the collective giftedness of U.S. women religious' leadership, for the most part, is experienced as absent from the overall process of the Apostolic Visitation: the identification of the need for such an investigation, the consultation with congregational leadership about the concerns calling for such a formal visitation of the majority of congregations in the U.S., the announcement to the congregations and the public, the design and implementation of the process.

Responses from the survey expressed this sense of struggle in the following ways: "As [a group/order] who has served the church and the people of God faithfully for [many] years, I deeply resented any attempt to silence or control the Spirit speaking in and through us." "We were deeply offended that the church we love and serve so faithfully initiated such a humiliating public process." Other leaders expressed "dismay, anger, shock, suspicion, apprehension, betrayal, incredulity, confusion, lack of understanding, disbelief, uncertainty as to purpose and outcome, wondering what it would require of us as leadership." "Why us? Why now?" "It seemed that the initiative for the investigation had come from the Stonehill College Symposium as well as complaints by some bishops and cardinals in Rome, as well as some others who had expectations of what religious life should look like." Some voiced anger because it was done in a secretive way with no transparent communication during or after the on-site visit. Others expressed concern that some would feel guilt, sensing that the investigation meant we were doing something wrong and our wrongful actions prompted the need for the Visitation. Some felt that "the report was already written and that the entire process was a waste of time and money."

"Our first thought was WHY and then suspicions and almost paranoia grew. As rumors flew and others tried to second guess what was really behind the Visitation, we found ourselves questioning our own loyalties to a church that seems to betray and belittle women religious at every turn." "We felt disrespected because of the manner in which the Visitation was announced publicly via press conference, at least ten days prior to our receiving a Xeroxed copy of the official announcement."

Further concerns identified anxiety about what would be demanded of religious as a result of the final report: "Concerns that there may be some repercussions for some congregations."

> We fear that the Vatican will want us to return to a form of religious life that was never part of our tradition and will therefore not be authentic for us. As women religious, we came to believe through this Apostolic Visitation, that we can stand up for ourselves and indeed, we must. Therefore, we worry that any refusal on our part will not be understood and may become a source of scandal in the church.

"We are concerned that mandates might come from CICLSAL that are not acceptable to us."

> Our fear is that this process will not really change the lack of understanding of our life as women religious in the U.S. today. We fear that decisions will be made about us without dialog and understanding of our lived experience of religious life. We fear that ultimatums for reform will be handed down causing us to reconsider our canonical status.

"[We fear] that the gap between the Vatican interpretation of American religious life and our own will be widened as a result of this investigation." "We are also concerned about a lingering cloud of suspicion that hangs over women religious in the U.S. because the Visitation implies an offense on our part…one more failure to treat women as equals, to respect persons, to inspire rather than to exert power over." And the litany could go on and on.

This critical consciousness of the condition of their role and relationship in the church uncovered and exposed the Visitation as a devaluation or marginalization of women's voice, perspective, gifts, and contributions.[13] Accordingly, this reflection was set within the framework of what can be called a feminist style of theological reflection and an interpretation that could lead to a critique of the Christian tradition in its current expression. The lasting take away from the final reflection on the experience is a reinterpretation of the experience in light of faith and tradition, a reinterpretation that offers clues and insights to a pathway forward for renewed and sustained wholeness.

A WAY FORWARD: A WOMANIST INSIGHT

The Apostolic Visitation was a communal experience for women religious in the U.S. and its impact has been transformative. This communal transformative experience has changed us and even who we include when we say "us." As an African American women religious and practical theologian who was in leadership during the Apostolic Visitation and who now is reflecting on the results of the survey, I recognize immediately common themes in the story of the experience of the Apostolic Visitation story and my own story of struggle, marginalization, liberation, and hope. Opening up those common themes may perhaps give some hints of how we walk by faith together now and into the future.

Reading through the lens of my own experience, several themes come to the fore: the importance of community and collaboration (reading identity); marginality (reading power); struggle/suffering and liberation (exposing violence, championing freedom, dignity, and justice); faith and hope (disciplined God talk). These categories reflect anew women religious' thinking and seeing with new mind and eyes, as well as naming and claiming in a collective voice, the Good News of Jesus Christ. Perhaps we can even say this is an experience of U.S. women religious doing contextual theology or spirituality flowing from the reality of their lives. Four themes surfaced, during the experience of the Apostolic Visitation, that suggest a now and future way for apostolic women religious to live in fidelity to their vocation and to the people of God.

The Apostolic Visitation, though viewed by most respondents and their colleagues and friends as an unwarranted, unwanted, and unnecessary project, in the end, uncovered a new or renewed strength among U.S. women religious: identity as apostolic women religious, affirmed in community and beyond in collaboration. I name it here the strength of a communal, collaborative orientation. Nearly half of the respondents identified the development and strengthening of solidarity and unity among and within diverse institutes of women religious as a positive result of the experience of the Apostolic Visitation.

This experience described by leaders of women's congregations is one based on recognition of personal power mutually shared among leaders of various groups, sisters within the same group, and collaboration with others who could share resources and gifts for the facing of this hour of Visitation. In very concrete ways, the respondents indicated that they sensed and claimed a divine power and dynamic energy that enabled them to witness to and engage the Spirit power within themselves and receive Spirit power from others whom God had provided as companions on the journey. This somewhat latent power of community called to the fore creative energy from the heart of the various charisms and evoked courageous fidelity to the very mission of apostolic religious life itself, not just for a particular congregation, but for all congregations together—truly a collective vocational moment for women religious in the U.S. Who are we, together? Whose are we? And, what must we be, together, for God's sake, for the sake of the people of the world? What is our work, together, now and into the future, for the sake of the mission of Jesus Christ? *Were not our hearts burning*? Did we not recognize God with us, Jesus among us, as we shared our gifts and resources?

As we race back to the other disciples to tell our story, we recognize and claim anew for ourselves a way forward that includes a communal-collaborative style as our way of life, as our way to work together, to journey together, as our way to solve problems or deal with challenges, together. The way forward for us women religious includes collaboration and dialogue, finding strength in telling our faith stories, sharing our gifts and resources, more intentionally engaging our noble selves in cooperation, compassion, and in generous efforts in ministries across congregational lines. Finding our way forward to address issues with the institutional church means standing together, respecting and valuing who we are and why we have been called and sent as gift to the church in these times.

Additionally, support from and collaboration with laity and clergy were also indicated as two important strategies to nurture and maintain as we journey in faith and live the mission of Jesus Christ in these challenging times. Unwittingly, the Apostolic Visitation strengthened the relationship among religious within groups and across congregations. As expressed in many of the responses throughout the survey, mutual support and collaboration has become the way forward: "The unity of women religious throughout the world is important for the future of our church as the people of God." "We grew in an understanding of our role in the church and the world. Affirmed by our brothers and sisters, lay, religious, and clergy, we stand on our integrity and fidelity to the gospel and to the teachings of Vatican II."

"Important elements are the . . . communication and solidarity among congregations of women religious, clarity of vision and purpose of very well educated and professionally competent women religious." "We were united in concern and daily prayer for those communities being visited." *Were not our hearts burning within us?* "As a community we have grown in trust of one another and gained an understanding of the solidarity of women religious around the country and the world." "We were strengthened in a common resolve to remain authentic to our own identity as apostolic women and to support others in their charisms." "We experienced an American sisterhood emerging instead of individual congregations and from that solidarity we derived the courage to speak up for the integrity of our lives."

The survey makes it very explicit that leaders found strength, creativity, resourcefulness, and very strong support in members of their communities, in gatherings and sharing among leaders of various groups, as well as among friends and colleagues. These communal ways of working together, praying together, learning together, and sharing resources left leaders feeling empowered and strengthened for facing the complex dilemma of the Apostolic Visitation in all its phases. The sense of a successful outcome to the Visitation appears to be connected to the deep and strong bonds affirmed among members, leaders of various congregations, and other collaborators who gave advice, affirmation, and encouragement.

This communal framework affirmed the value of collaboration, dialogue, mutuality, and subsidiarity. Collaboration and dialogue are described as essential and normative, especially if any change is to happen going forward. Respondents expressed a desire for a "roundtable church" where all are invited to share and no one is muzzled. Others expressed it in the following ways. "[We] recognize the need for communality and collaboration with other religious congregations; networking with and honoring the U.S. sisterhood are essentials as we face choices and decisions before us. [We are called to] deepen bonds between religious institutes so that we can even more effectively witness to the gift that religious life is in the church and in the world today."

Still others expressed, "I think more broadly now. The relationships created by the collaboration during the Apostolic Visitation have helped me to think of religious all over the world when I am making decisions." "It is no longer possible to function as the leadership team of a single congregation; it is imperative that we work together and challenge one another." "The experience has strengthened our belief that we cannot lead in isolation. It encourages us to continue to bond and to see the unity among us as leaders of congregations of women . . . and men . . . religious." "I have been convinced of the power of women religious when we act as one." "We've come to a greater appreciation of the complementarity of the charisms and are open to exploring new ways of collaborating with one another and connecting in diverse ways. We are not alone as leaders of religious institutes. We are truly sisters." *Were not our hearts burning within us?*

Based on the survey results, Catholic women religious sense the Apostolic Visitation was, at the extreme, an act of oppression and, at minimum, an act of disrespect of women religious, an action imposed by the hierarchy without consultation or dialogue. This sense of marginality flows from the experience of persistent exclusion and disregard of the voice and participation of women in all levels of governance in the church. Some identified the source of their frustration to be linked with what they described as an Apostolic Visitation process that was "paternalistic and un-pastoral." Others expressed that "officials of the church" do not respect women in the church as equals nor engage with them in dialogue and conversation around issues of our life as religious in the U.S. Some feel "so misunderstood and judged by the hierarchical church such that we have growing concern that the Apostolic Visitation has increased a sense of alienation from the church."

However, it was in the midst of this sense of marginality or within a context of subjugation that women religious found a unique sense of liberating power along with the meaning and purpose of their prophetic voice. As "sisters became more educated about the nature and purpose of the Visitation, they moved from initial anxiety, to freedom in claiming their religious identity." "We claimed more of our own truth and power. We became more grounded in our . . . evangelical life. We gained more understanding of the prophetic role of religious life." "As women religious, we came to believe through this Visitation that we can stand up for ourselves and indeed we must."

The Apostolic Visitation seemed to force women religious to come to grips with their situation of subordination: finding voice, claiming and affirming identity, critiquing the situation in light of their vocational call. So from the experience of being marginalized, an *anawim*, they found themselves journeying with their God who sees their plight, who knows well their struggles, who has heard their cry for help, and who has come into their midst to do something liberating.[14] And this God empowers them to stand and to speak for themselves. Just like Moses did. Just like Judith in the Hebrew Text.[15] Marginality puts women religious in a position of solidarity with many marginalized and oppressed peoples in the world. And, it is from this privileged position that their prophetic voice is heard. *Were not our hearts burning within us?*

The experience of the Apostolic Visitation when viewed through the lens of women religious' struggle, pain, and suffering of going through what was clearly an ordeal, heightened collective self-awareness of what it means to be a woman in the church today. On the one hand the survey indicates the strengthening of community and identity, as well as the affirmation of that identity within the church, by priests, bishops, and laity. However, it was the very context of "suffering through the struggle" to deal with the reality and implications of the Apostolic Visitation that produced the affirmation of identity and a collective recognition of marginality or experience of being *anawim*.

It was in the crucible of this event that women religious "stood" as if at the foot of the cross. The struggle seemed to produce a tenacious identification with the suffering Christ and a re-affirmation of their commitment to witness to the ways of Christ, recognizing the cost of discipleship. This collective struggle and suffering confirmed for many the purpose and meaning of the mission of Jesus Christ and the work of God Spirit among them doing infinitely more than asked or imagined. In the time of struggle God was experienced as an ever present help, a liberating energy, giving faith, courage, and hope. The experience of suffering together bonded women religious in a way that no other single event had; and they were transformed, forming a *new* sisterhood.

> We are afflicted in every way, but not constrained; perplexed, but not driven to despair; persecuted, but not abandoned; struck down, but not destroyed; always carrying about in the body the dying of Jesus, so that the life of Jesus may also be manifested in our body. (2 Cor. 4: 8-10)

Were not our hearts burning within us? Emmanuel, God is with us.

Faith and trust in God who accompanies were clearly the prevailing virtues accessed throughout the process. They provided the foundation of much of what the sister respondents experienced in the Visitation and expressed in the survey. Seemingly the biggest unintended and unexpected consequence of the collective experience of women religious in the U.S. was enduring hope.

Hope is the virtue that allows us to be open to the now and future involvement of God acting in humans' lives. It is that virtue that for liberation theologian Major Jones meets at the intersection of faith and social-political action focusing on the betterment of humanity through non-violent means. [16] This experience of hope highlighted in the survey of women religious leaders includes a communal expression of affirming the humanity, dignity, and integrity of women and their role in God's vision of creation. It is a role of being caught up in God's mission, of affirming the human agency and power of women religious and, thus, of opening up to communal transformative experiences in the lives and witness of the various congregations. [17]

The respondents expressed hope in these ways: "[We hope] that through open, two-way communication, CICLSAL will come to understand that U.S. women religious are faithful women of the church and love religious life; that the bishops will come to a greater knowledge of, and appreciation for, the essential role that U.S. women religious have played and continue to play in the U.S. church." "We hope that the hierarchy will recognize the diversity of charisms and the variety of ways in which we answer the gospel call, returned to our charism and studied the signs of the times." "The greatest hope is recognition by the hierarchy of the Catholic Church regarding the ongoing struggle of religious women to live their mission in community in a manner faithful to their traditions despite diminished resources and an aging population." "[We hope] that the life and mission of U.S. religious women will be affirmed."

"My hope is that this experience will have encouraged us to recognize who we have become since Vatican II. I hope that we can strengthen the identity that we have been shaping over all these years and that we can celebrate the power that we have when we know who we are and work together." "[We hope] that the support and care we have experienced and the ability to come together for each other will continue and be strengthened." "[We hope] that the solidarity among women religious that resulted from these processes will endure. . . ." "My hope is that the prophetic role of religious women will be acknowledged."

An expression commonly attributed to St. Augustine states that hope has two beautiful daughters: anger and courage—anger over what could be and is not and courage to make things different. The dance of hope, anger, and courage through the entire experience of the Apostolic Visitation is evident throughout the survey: anger at the status of relationships between U.S. women religious and the church, and anger at the imposition of an Apostolic Visitation; courage to come together, to access resources to understand more fully what was happening in the Apostolic Visitation; and courage to stand with integrity. Hope, with her two daughters, continues to carry the leadership to collect lessons learned during the Visitation and live these lessons, day to day. This courage to act on the lessons and insights learned brings our theological reflection to its full and final phase.

The movement in theological reflection is always toward insight and insight always toward action. The four themes collected here provide a framework for collecting our insights and for shaping deliberative actions as women religious. U.S. apostolic women religious have been changed into a new sisterhood who have already begun to walk together in faith and hope on a new path of collaboration and dialogue, clear affirmation of identity, renewed understanding of God's mission for them as women religious, with strength to stand together in times of adversity. Telling the story of the journey will continue to yield insight that will lead to other action and further proclamations of *"Were not our hearts burning within us?"*

NOTES

1. "Relief," defined as the state of being clearly visible or obvious due to being accentuated in some way; (special usage): a method of molding carving or stamping in which the design

stands out from the surface, to a greater (high relief) or lesser (bas-relief). *The New Oxford American Dictionary* (New York: Oxford University Press, 2005).

2. Margaret Cain McCarthy, "Apostolic Visitation Survey Analysis: The Apostolic Visitation as Experienced by Women Religious in the United States" (report, October 15, 2011). This chapter includes numerous quotations from survey respondents. Unless otherwise noted, responses to the Apostolic Visitation Survey are the source of quoted material.

3. Robert L. Kinast, *What Are They Saying About Theological Reflection?* (New York: Paulist Press, 2000), 21.

4. Scriptural references cited by the author are taken from *The New American Bible* (Nashville: Thomas Nelson Publishers, 1987).

5. Kinast, *What Are They Saying*, 15-26.

6. ibid.

7. McCarthy, "Apostolic Visitation Survey Analysis."

8. Common Lucan themes that appear in the gospel again and again, especially in this story. See Raymond E. Brown, SS, Joseph A. Fitzmyer, SJ, and Roland E. Murphy, Carm., eds., *The New Jerome Biblical Commentary* (Englewood Cliffs, NJ: Prentice Hall, 1990), 720, no. 196.

9. Henri Nouwen, *Reaching Out: The Three Movements of the Spiritual Life* (New York: Image Books, 1986), 50-51.

10. Gerald M. Fagin, SJ and Joseph A. Tetlow, SJ, *Putting on the Heart of Christ* (Chicago: Loyola Press, 2010), 115-128.

11. "The church" used here and in the quotes from respondents usually refers to the institutional Roman Catholic Church: bishops, cardinals, the Congregation for Institutes of Consecrated Life and Societies of Apostolic Life or other dicasteries or departments with oversight or authority. In other cases the expression refers to "the church" as the people of God.

12. "Genius" refers to the phrase "the feminine genius," expressed by the Pontifical Council for Justice and Peace, Compendium of the Social Doctrine of the Church, 295, and quoted in the *Evangelii Gaudium, The Joy of the Gospel*, Apostolic Exhortation of the Holy Father Francis, 2013, para. 103. From *The Joy of the Gospel*:

> The church acknowledges the indispensable contribution which women make to society through the sensitivity, intuition and other distinctive skill sets which they, more than men, tend to possess. I think, for example, of the special concern which women show to others, which finds a particular, even if not exclusive, expression in motherhood. I readily acknowledge that many women share pastoral responsibilities with priests, helping to guide people, families and groups and offering new contributions to theological reflection. But we need to create still broader opportunities for a more incisive female presence in the church. Because "the feminine genius is needed in all expressions in the life of society, the presence of women must also be guaranteed in the workplace" and in the various other settings where important decisions are made, both in the church and in social structures.

13. Kinast, *What Are They Saying*, 28.

14. *Anawim* is Hebrew for "the poor who depend on the Lord for deliverance."

15. Hebrew Text or Hebrew Scriptures is used in preference to Old Testament.

16. Elaine Brown Crawford, *Hope in the Holler: A Womanist Theology* (Louisville, KY: Westminster John Knox Press, 2002), 5.

17. See Elizabeth A. Johnson, CSJ, on hope in feminist theology, *Quest for the Living God: Mapping Frontiers in the Theology of God* (New York: Continuum International Publishing Group, 2007) and *She Who Is: The Mystery of God in Feminine Theological Discourse* (New York: Crossroad Publishing Company, 1992); and Crawford on hope in womanist theology, *Hope in the Holler*.

Chapter Eight

Balanced on Thin Ice

The Most Important Part of the Story

Donna Day and Cathy Mueller

THIN ICE AS METAPHOR FOR THE EXPERIENCE
OF THE APOSTOLIC VISITATION

Many images, many diverse experiences, many emotions ripple out from the lives of the faithful women who participated in the Apostolic Visitation and shared their story. Within the multi-layered and multi-textured contours of that story, there rests a key question: "Assume for a moment that the U.S. women religious will be able to write and share the story of the Visitation in our own words. From your experience of it, what is the most important part of this story to convey?" The focus of this chapter derives its inspiration and content from responses to that question in the Apostolic Visitation Survey (survey), *The Apostolic Visitation as Experienced by Women Religious in the United States.*[1]

Throughout these chapters you have been hearing a variety of elements included in the story of the Apostolic Visitation. Stories have a beginning, middle, and end; yet how they are put together depends on the storyteller, the audience, and the purpose of the story. How is the story of the Visitation told? The overall theme is the transformation of what was a difficult situation into one that was life-giving. However, a single theme does not tell the whole story.

While women religious know deep in our hearts that God promises us a better future as described in the gospels, we also realize the fulfillment of this hope is not easy to attain. Our vision unfolds in complex situations. Sometimes we receive it as God doing something new and at other times we are challenged by this time in history. We skate on "thin ice."

Thin Ice on Mary's Lake, February 2011

The silver semicircles swoop
in diamond swaths across the lake
intervalled by greying starshapes
left perhaps by skating wraiths
or a skittering of winter birds.
Wildly dangerous beauty
in this month of somber days.

Thin ice the surface shared by all of us.

Those TV images from Cairo's square,
a friend who waits for mortal word,
curbside-piled belongings of eviction,
spiritual biographies so vulnerable,
news of trafficking for sex or sweat,
unanswered notes a puzzlement,
wayside bombs and robot drones,
and—no symbol now—the waning polar ice.

Holding hands, we risk our way across
to cheer and weep, protest and mourn
as, wary of each revelation of the heart,
we balance on the thin tensility of hope. [2]

THE MOVES WE MAKE ON THE ICE

Telling the Story

A story is always more than words. A good story makes the words speak, fills them with light and life and conveys a message that is worth remembering. Good stories are often richly textured narratives about how events touch people's lives and remind us of our own experiences and the lessons we have learned. When J.R.R. Tolkien talked about stories, he used the image of the cauldron. [3] The cauldron has been boiling since the beginning of time. Into it are put all the tastiest bits of life: images of the terrible, the comic, the awesome, the littlest, the biggest, the high and the mighty, the low and the humble and so on and so on. . . . And so it is with our story.

As women religious reflecting on the experience of the Apostolic Visitation, we put all the pieces together to see which elements rise into a metaphor with meaning and possibly even magic. What is the story we choose to tell? Each of us has a unique perspective and might emphasize a certain detail. We are challenged to think about the elements of our story: the characters (the archetypes and stereotypes); the images that rise from our emotions and attitudes; the problem as named by all who are involved; the action and turning points; the conclusions which may include surprise and new ways of working it out.

Questions emerged out of our frustration, defensiveness, and anger. Early on, however, we began to welcome deeper contemplative moments. After more insights, reflection, conversations, and long silences, we asked: What common truths did we share? Could we risk our religious commitment being examined? We have come through challenging times before; could we do it again? What happens if we don't comply with the investigation? We pondered many questions in our hearts. We let each other into our sacred spaces as we focused on how to answer questions and shape responses. These challenging conversations led us inward as well as outward often taking us to the place of understanding what the next steps might turn out to be. We lived the questions as a mystery unfolding far beyond ourselves.

Responding with Integrity

The Visitation challenged women religious in the U.S. to explore the interplay between what we knew to be the truth of our lives, which included collaboration and solidarity, and the heavy-handedness of the Visitation format. The hidden agenda of the process was not readily understandable. It was not an easy journey; stories from many communities began with feelings of disappointment, self-doubt, invasive questioning, and a lack of trust.

The difficult questions came from our communities to those of us in leadership: "What did we do wrong? Why these misunderstandings about our life? Who wants to know about our finances? What business is it of a Vatican office? Where does the information go?" The canonical *Questionnaire* did not tell us. Obviously, we had more questions than answers. The poet says it well: "Thin ice the surface shared by all of us."

What were the expectations of the Vatican as it embarked on the Apostolic Visitation with U.S. women's congregations? Did they think it would straighten us out? Scare us? Did they feel they were losing control and did not know how to get it back? We no longer fit their image of us. Quickly we realized that part of the church we love did not understand the integrity reflected in the lives of women religious.

We felt a little like the early Christians. Pope Francis, in his homily of April 23, 2013, talked about these Christians who had apostolic fervor in their hearts; and so the faith spread!

> Some Christians came to Antioch and began to speak also to the Greeks. This is yet another step. And so the church moves forward. Who took this initiative of speaking to the Greeks, something unheard of, since they were preaching only to Jews? It was the Holy Spirit, the one who was pushing them on, on and on, unceasingly. But back in Jerusalem, when somebody heard about this, he got a little nervous and they sent an *Apostolic Visitation*: they sent Barnabas.

> Perhaps, with a touch of humor, we can say that this was the theological origin of the Congregation for the Doctrine of the Faith: this *Apostolic Visitation* of Barnabas. He took a look and saw that things were going well. [4]

How would those early preachers of the Word in Antioch tell the story of Barnabas' visit? Probably there would be a variety of responses with a great deal more detail about why they stepped out of bounds; however, we can only imagine what the stories were since they were not recorded.

As we tell our story, we come back to the "why" and the "what" of the Visitation. Have sisters stepped out of line by proclaiming the gospel to all people, especially those who are economically poor? Had the church marginalized women religious when our ministry evolved from running Catholic institutions to directing soup kitchens? Did the church expect traditional ministries when we knew there were many new ministries evolving? Were communities so prophetic that the church could not tolerate their expansion into new works? Had the church officials never read the documents from Vatican II that we all read? What is the work of the Spirit? How does it move us out of the structures created by humans? How do we recognize the work of the Spirit, since the Spirit resides in everyone?

> The Apostolic Visitation has led to a cooling of relationships between women religious and the hierarchy and clergy and there is a shedding of illusions about religious in the church. We are no longer the work force of the church. Even before the Apostolic Visitation, women religious had become focused on ministry to the needs of the wider society. We were/are pushing the boundaries of ministry in response to these needs which those in positions of authority in the church may not see as important. [5]

Collaborating

The Visitation investigation quickly became, not just about one community, but about all our communities. We were disheartened when all we had done for renewal, in obedience to Vatican Council II documents, was being questioned. Archbishop Oscar Romero's words written in 1979, as he was surrounded by violence and destruction in El Salvador were still relevant.

> Let it be quite clear that if we are being asked to collaborate with a pseudo peace, a false order, based on repression and fear, we must recall that the only order and the only peace that God wants is one based on truth and justice. Before these alternatives, our choice is clear: We will follow God's order, not men's. [6]

Women religious try to operate out of gospel priorities, renewal mandated by the Second Vatican Council and our charisms—not hierarchical priorities.

How could we articulate that reality to the church through a process like the Apostolic Visitation? Many sisters mused, "If they only knew us."

Congregations joined with each other in solidarity, strength, and unity. We were awakening the power within us and received gifts for a lifetime. "We are proud of the fact that throughout the process we chose to respond out of our charism. We might have been angry, but we did not respond in anger."[7]

The Benedictines overflowed with hospitality as their leadership shared their vision of welcome to all. The Sisters of St. Joseph spoke about reaching out to the "dear neighbor." The Franciscan Sisters of Mary taught us about the compassionate healing of Jesus. The Sisters of Charity of the Blessed Virgin Mary told us about "being freed in God's steadfast love." The sharing of these charisms and those of many other congregations created mutual relationships of care, trust, and solidarity as we shared the struggle of how to respond to a "senseless investigation." Hospitality, service, healing, freedom, and Loretto's charism of "standing at the foot of the cross" were some of the watchwords we needed to support each other and to welcome the presence of Christ among us and through us to those we served. We had an authentic community of communities and we were united. The congregations found a place of deep connection to each other during the Visitation process; we were part of something bigger than just our individual congregations. This was a transformational experience, led by the Spirit who sustains all life leading us to a hope-filled future.

We felt the Visitation called us to mutuality, vulnerability, and accountability. Was it a labor of love? Only in so far as it steeped us in our constitutions and strengthened us in our resolve to be women of the gospel. Even with the apparent tensions among us, we knew we could not rush the investigation, but we could live into the mystery of it and help each other be strong in its tension. Women religious in the United States have always known that community is for mission. It remains a challenge to us as we face complex situations in the church and world today.

As intelligent, loving women we made conscious choices to act with restraint, not retaliation, against what felt like an external threat to our integrity and mission. "We could not act out of self-protection; we had to take risks on behalf of all women who labor in the church but do not have the safety net women religious have."[8]

Within our individual congregations we created time for contemplative silence, personal responses, and many communal conversations. We welcomed the visitators to our motherhouses and provincial houses. They too were our sisters, who came with a task to do. We invited them into our lives and spoke of what was most important to us. Their questions mirrored those in the official canonical *Questionnaire* yet gave us the opportunity to personally speak of the community we each loved so much. We expanded the boundaries of the original Visitation printed *Questionnaire* and told the visitors of our charism, of our prayer life, and about our mission work. For example, Loretto proudly explained to them their core statement: "We work for justice and act for peace because the gospel urges us." Every congregation visited shared their story. While the motives of the Apostolic Visitation were vague, our responses were not.

> While the action of the church in this matter was a devastating blow to the religious of the U.S., we faced this challenge with integrity, openness, non-violence, and hope and did not compromise what we felt to be the truth of our life and lifestyle. This is not new; it has been the way we have conducted ourselves over the years as we faced the truth of our reality. [9]

As women open to transformation—embracing strengths and weaknesses, confident in what is possible—we chose to forge ahead. We remember when Barbara Marx-Hubbard told the Leadership Conference of Women Religious (LCWR) 2012 assembly, that crises precede transformation. The future is the God ahead. We kept being reminded that God is seldom in our plans, rather always in the unexpected. Congregations did the inner-work they needed, without fear, being true to their charism and their life in community. "We took the Apostolic Visitation seriously. We responded with integrity after input, reflection, and prayer." [10]

Any responses we made to the Visitation documents flowed from community and the soul-searching we did together. We would say to each other, "Tell me more—why does that matter?" Each community became a container of gospel living and from the containers of our life flowed the hopes of religious life in our time.

FINDING OUR FORM ON THE ICE: EMERGING THEMES

The responses were many, falling into several themes each one capable of being *the* story of the Apostolic Visitation. Themes included the relationship with the institutional church, support from the laity, living our charism, and the gift of solidarity.

Relationship with the Institutional Church

The relationship with the institutional church continues to be a source of tension. Elements of this story will include the distance, the disconnection with the institutional church, the feeling of being de-valued. We were apprehensive at what might be lost or stifled and wondered what would be gained. "Of utmost importance is that the Vatican Office is disconnected from the women religious in the U.S." [11]

The church we hope for is the one centered on Jesus and his vision. His story, in gospel tradition, told to us from the communities of his followers, was the vision of a church as peaceful not violent, compassionate not self-righteous, and loving not judgmental. As we made connections between the Apostolic Visitation and the gospels, we recognized ever more clearly that our church, in the stress of its institutional form of holiness, is reverting to the very forms of violence that Jesus rejected. Some congregational leaders felt the Visitation was a form of institutional violence and their members were the victims. We tried to respond thoughtfully and honestly. We never wanted to be the violence we deplored.

We have been challenged through the years to serve a prophetic role in church and society. This challenge includes critiquing societal and church structures by calling for systemic change and being transformed by those we serve. Communities of all species are formed from the need for self-determination and the need for community. Neither reality can be ignored to satisfy a doctrine or for conformity to a cause. The gospel choice is choosing freedom. In the face of these challenges, we held the Visitation experience in deep contemplation. We knew we had to speak truth to power. Our story was a powerful and holy journey, which respected the courage of our congregations to act on their Christian convictions in their search for what was just. The Spirit of God was not bound; it revealed itself in the lives of everyone.

Another important aspect of the Visitation was the struggle to maintain our integrity and dedication to service for the people of God, as we face an oppressive hierarchical structure.

> We had the courage and integrity to claim our own authority as women of the church; that there is solidarity within congregations, that this might serve as a model for the laity to claim their authority as the people of God who have a voice in all those issues that pertain to their lives. [12]

Because our love of the church and the people of God is so deep, the process was never easy. The metaphor of "thin ice," used so profoundly in Cecily's poem, quickly became for us cracked ice on which we never wanted to walk, much less skate. We could use this poem as a link to any of society's crises; however, in terms of the Visitation event, the focus of that process shook our balance and escalated the experiences of protest and mourning. "We would want to convey that the church IS the people of God and as part of that church, women everywhere have much more that they can contribute." [13]

Support from the Laity

We were and are sisters to each other, a reality important for the American and universal church. Countless friends—lay, religious, and clergy—affirmed our stance of a non-violent response to the investigation always knowing we would not compromise the truth of our life and the ways we live. Years ago, women religious liberated themselves from power, prestige, and security. We knew we could risk again, speaking our truth about what we uphold and not just about what we oppose. We knew that we must follow our dedication wherever it takes us. We have a commitment to the gospel.

As leaders from around the country responded to the question of what to include in their story, words used to describe our stance included: open, gracious, prayerful, non-violent, contemplative, and hopeful. We saw even more clearly how God's Spirit works through women religious for the life of the world, being faithful to the transformation of religious life during a period of social upheaval. We experienced a partnership with the laity, knowing that we are together in the struggle to live the gospel in a difficult time when there is little support or nourishment from the institutional church.

The support that flowed from laity around the U.S. and the world was an unexpected consequence of the Apostolic Visitation. People began to publicly express appreciation for the work of the sisters, their stance for justice and peace, and their work as advocates and direct service providers for the economically poor and people on the margins. They offered recognition, support, and encouragement. We knew that our actions were not just for ourselves. We were stepping onto thin ice to balance hierarchical authority and inner authority. We did not act alone and were not divided through the process. The laity stood in solidarity with us and offered us courage to be faithful. We realized our response was giving hope to those who yearned for a church of service, not power. At the 2012 LCWR national assembly, notes and letters from thousands of supporters were distributed among the tables and profoundly demonstrated the sincere and holy trust the laity bestowed on us.

Living our Charism

A key part of some of the stories would be our resilience as women religious. We witnessed our faithfulness to our charisms, our mission, and our ways of living the gospel and ultimately to a church where some members of the hierarchy do not seem to value us. We know that we have important contributions to make to our church and our world. We modeled dialogue, inclusivity, collaboration, discernment, prayer, and contemplation in the midst of many hardships and found it difficult to not be able to enter into honest dialogue with those who stand in judgment of us. "We are women faithful to the gospel, reading and responding to the signs of the times. We are serious about living the gospel and our community charism. Religious life does not look like it did in 1200 or 1800 or 1950. Still we are true to the values and vision."[14]

Cecily Jones' poetic words do not leave us with a totally negative image. We must always have hope. In a regional meeting a member of a community remarked that self-examination is not always a bad thing. There was grace in the struggle. In Loretto there was renewed energy for their charism during the preparation for the Visitation. It was a gift indeed. That, in itself, is an important part of the story to tell. Every religious community could say, as the Sisters of Loretto do in their constitutions:

> The same Spirit who inspired and guided our founders gathers us in community today. We walk with all those "Friends of Mary" who for two centuries have lived a vowed life of praise, prayer, and service. Their courage, concern, and energy, nourished by the gospel and communal love are with us as a lasting endowment of hope. [15]

The Adorers of the Blood of Christ, the Congregation of the Humility of Mary, the Dominicans, School Sisters of Notre Dame, Servants of Mary, Sisters of Divine Providence, Ursulines, Sisters of Mercy, the Franciscans, and the list goes on and on—thousands of women, all blessings to the people of God, faithful to the transformation called for by Vatican II now await the next work of the Spirit of God in their midst.

> It is important for the story to convey that . . . the Apostolic Visitation provided a moment for women religious to model ways to respond respectfully in times of ecclesial tension, claiming our rights—staying with the dialogue and being true to collaboration and consultation among ourselves . . . we tried to be present to the Spirit and speak our truth with integrity. Our voice was heard. [16]

Another important aspect of the Visitation was the intensification among us regarding our commitment to live the gospel fully. Renewal is a common word within religious congregations of women. Responding to the challenge of Vatican Council II, we returned to our founders, renewed ourselves in our charisms, and listened to the signs of the times as we searched for ways to live our commitment in our fractured world.

> Thus the council rightly insists on the obligation of religious to be faithful to the spirit of their founders, to their evangelical intentions and to the example of their sanctity. In this it finds one of the principles for the present renewal and one of the most secure criteria for judging what each institute should undertake. In reality, the charism of the religious life, far from being an impulse born of flesh and blood or one derived from a mentality which conforms itself to the modern world is the fruit of the Holy Spirit, who is always at work within the church. [17]

"We rose to the challenge of self-examination; we did so graciously and openly . . . we were non-violent and even contemplative in the process." [18]

Because we lived into the renewal mandated by Vatican Council II to return to our roots, to renew ourselves in our charisms, we could look at our reality and not compromise the truth of our lives. We realized that our response to the Visitation as women of integrity gave hope to those who yearned for a church of service not power.

We took seriously the challenge presented in the Vatican II document, *Perfectae Caritatis, Decree on the Appropriate Renewal of the Religious Life,* "The appropriate renewal of religious life involves two simultaneous processes: (1) a continuous return to the sources of all Christian life and to the original inspiration behind a given community and (2) an adjustment of the community to the changed conditions of the times."[19] Respondents to the survey were clear about the importance of noting the fidelity of our implementation of Vatican II:

> Include in the story: That U.S. women religious have been faithful to living and spreading the gospel in the church and in our world. That we have been faithful to the challenges and calls of Vatican II to refound our congregations; to deepen our understanding of the vows; to live out the values called forth by our charisms and constitutions.[20]

The Gift of Solidarity

For many who experienced the Visitation, solidarity is the kernel of the story. "Happily it engendered unprecedented bonds of solidarity and support among and within religious institutes in the U.S. and many heartfelt and strong expressions of support from women religious . . . around the world."[21] The poet reminds us:

> Holding hands, we risk our way across
> to cheer and weep, protest and mourn
> as, wary of each revelation of the heart,
> we balance on the thin tensility of hope.[22]

Our solidarity enabled us to move beyond the negative parts, transforming them and us in ways we could not plan. We were invited into each other's lives; we found it amazing how easily people opened themselves to new levels of sharing when they felt safe and understood. It was empowering to know that we were all in the Visitation experience together. In the *Questionnaire,* sisters shared parts of the experience that touched us to the depths of who we are as women and as women religious. Our persevering participation took us to risk, to joy, to fear, and to wholeness. We were one with the story of everyone's courage, grieving, and tenderness.

We responded in a manner true to our lives. We talked with one another, shared emotions, possible scenarios, and strategies. The value of conversations both within congregations and among congregations helped us to look at the Vatican's request, to remember who we are, and to move to a response that could be constructive. This was a turning point. We encouraged one another to follow our own charism and to rely on the wisdom in our communities. As individual congregations made different responses, the other congregations treated each congregation's response with respect. We could honor the diversity among us; we experienced the solidarity.

THE MOST IMPORTANT PART OF THE STORY: THE ESSENCE OF OUR STRENGTH ON THIN ICE

We emerged stronger, aware of our call, committed to live the gospel with each other and with all those in need in the world. The sense of most communities in responding to the survey is that the Visitation experience led to a significant change, due to our reflection, prayer, and the reclaiming of our constitutions. The partnership and support of the laity and some clergy around the world was especially encouraging. Our own desire was to navigate the shift and not be reactionary because we do belong within this church. Some of our ecclesiology clashed in language and practice. For instance, the apparent dichotomy between the church as the people of God and the church as a hierarchical structure has long been a difficult paradigm. As with all the baptized, women religious have a universal call to holiness and a relationship to the pope.

We experienced solidarity with the laity of many faiths around the world. We claimed our own authority as mature women in the church today with an appropriate sense of freedom and self-direction. We took comfort in knowing that each of us has a piece of the truth that does not rely on our position in the church or in society. We believed and continue to believe that it is in honest dialogue that common ground is found, which propels us forward in living the gospel. "We hope that our collective story will reflect the way God's Spirit is alive and working through women religious today 'for the life of the world.'"[23]

The Apostolic Visitation was an all-consuming venture. At what we thought was the conclusion of the process, we received yet another letter for more information. Many congregations responded: not one more minute of time, not one more dime, not one more use of energy which is taking us away from our responsibilities. And then we were asked to pay for something that we did not choose to do! It would be absurd to pay for our own investigation. We were asked to look at ourselves, and we did—intentionally, carefully, and passionately.

We continue to hope for mutuality in our interactions with the Vatican. We are human and in the absence of information, which happened regularly throughout the Visitation, many believed the Visitation was disrespectful, punitive, and expressed a misunderstanding of women religious in the U.S. We have worked to find the Spirit of God in the Visitation. Our experience is the story of transformation: from darkness, misunderstanding, and mistrust to the light of truth, revealing the beauty and goodness of American women religious. It has been, and will continue to be, a journey of trust in the Spirit and in each other. "We are all very human and in the absence of information, we are often quick to assume the negative. However, given time of prayer, reflection, and dialogue, we come to realize that God can be found even in something like an Apostolic Visitation."[24]

The stories of the Visitation lead us, as good stories can do, to a place where American women religious have never been before. This story has its place in our time, in this age, in the history of congregations of women religious in America. We have no insights about how the story will end, however we do know that the most important part of the story is the solidarity that women religious all across our country and world created from the experience. LCWR member congregations became aware of how the institutional church, while praising us for some of our traditional ministries, did not understand the reality of our lives as women of the gospel today. All the stages of renewal that motivated us after Vatican Council II seemed unimportant or even misunderstood in the eyes of the Vatican officials.

As the American educator and consultant Margaret Wheatley writes, "Reality doesn't change itself. We need to act." She offers these principles:

> We acknowledge one another as equals; we try to stay curious about each other; we recognize that we need each other's help to become better listeners; we slow down, so we have time to think and reflect; we remember that conversation is the natural way humans think together; and we expect it to be messy at times.[25]

As congregational members dialogued, we unknowingly followed Wheatley's principles for a deeper conversation, although it was primarily with ourselves.

We wanted all our community members who prayed so hard for a successful Visitation outcome to know that this event was surely a Paschal Mystery moment—a dying and rising to new life. We turned a negative into a positive experience and wanted to lift each other up in the experience of being connected to something larger than us. God called us to attend to the Spirit in each other.

As we kept what was true before us, we were changed by grace. Where did we get the strength? From our openness to the grace of God and from the courage of our founders, women like Mary Frances Clarke, Mary Rhodes, Catherine McAuley, Mary Mackillop, Caroline Gerhardinger, Nano Nagle, Mother Xavier Termehr, and hundreds more. Courage came from our ongoing works of mission, from the freedom promised us as we proclaimed our vows, and from the experience of being together. We found commonalities in our feelings and attitudes that we never knew existed as we sought truth. The Spirit of God opened a new threshold and shoved us all across.

A major benefit of the Apostolic Visitation was that it called us to pay attention to a deeper conversation with each other because the stories of each person matter. Individuals were heard to say: "I am proud to say . . . I was one of us. . . . I was there. I was listening to the Spirit in our congregational discussions; I was listening in our LCWR regional meetings; I was listening during the annual LCWR Assemblies. I learned from others. I wept with them. I prayed with them. I was as angry as they were. I called for solidarity among us and always, always I had hope. I had to trust myself and my sisters."

When people or groups are confronted by a challenge that they did not choose to engage in, often barriers are quickly put in place, attitudes sharpen, and negative emotions rise to the surface. We asked ourselves: what can we, many of us educators, teach the world about this experience? Surely it is not just about power from a Vatican office. Surely it is not just about control. How will we keep what is true before us? We believe God created women and men equal in God's sight. We believe baptism is the door to a discipleship of equals—in work, and in decision-making and leadership.

THE STORY CONTINUES—ON THIN ICE

No matter where one starts the story of the Apostolic Visitation, we will never look at religious life in America in quite the same way. We will remember, laugh, and cry. We will tell stories and each one will lead to another story. For the women who lived through the Visitation, the journey along the road was filled with twists and turns. New maps and new signs were needed. We were going places we had never been before. It was a time of graced crossroads. Crossroads we hoped would lead us into a new lens for our lives, into new questions, into a deeper faith that would clarify who we are and the truth of our experiences.

To be in conflict is often a lonely place. For many, this was their experience of the Visitation. On many levels, the solidarity among us pulled us through this time of tension. We were called to patience, to waiting, to perseverance, and to communal contemplation. Each step was like a Lenten journey, each phase entailed trust in whatever insight we had. It was a vulnerable time when many people were watching to see our personal and collective response. Was our vulnerability more than just opening old wounds? Could this vulnerability be part of our transformational path? Could we walk through this vulnerability into the deeper reality that God is doing something new in us? It was important to enter the complex issues and discern our steps based on the values we held dear. Our experience was similar to Margaret Wheatley's notion that, "This is what uncertainty feels like and it's a very healthy place to dwell."[26]

So this is what we know: In the experience of the Visitation many emotions and many stories have taken shape. And along the way . . . turning points, questions of identity, and new consciousness emerged as we tried to analyze communication and understand broken institutional structures. We found each other for support and encouragement. Through it all we had courage, for the sake of the whole church. We took the road to healing and wholeness and began to discern next steps and new definitions. We quickly found out that there was not one story to tell, there were thousands. "Our story is a story of transformation from the darkness of misunderstandings and mistrust to the light of truth, beauty, and the goodness of U.S. women religious."[27]

This chapter has included many of the themes that responders to the survey wanted included in the story, a cauldron of some of the tastiest bits of life: images of the terrible, the comic, the awesome, the littlest, the biggest, the high and the mighty, the low and the humble and so on. . . . Each of us, through our experiences along with our personal and communal reflection, will put the pieces together in our own way.

The Apostolic Visitation is a challenging story about solidarity, integrity, and transformation. No doubt, more chapters, more stories are being told and will one day be written. There is always a risk walking on thin ice and women religious today are willing to walk it together and take that risk for the sake of the people of God and the future of religious life.

Just as dialogue among and between many congregations deepened our solidarity, it is our hope that dialogue between women religious and the hierarchy will result in mutual respect, understanding, and commitment. Thanks to the learnings from the Apostolic Visitation, we move into the future, balanced on *thin ice*, inspired by the story of *Old Turtle and the Broken Truth,* a story that the Apostolic Visitation has made our own:

> The Broken Truth, and life itself, will be mended only when one person meets another—someone from a different place or with a different face or different ways—and sees and hears . . . herself. Only then will the people know that every person, every being, is important and that the world was made for each us.[28]

What all the stories and the experiences of the Apostolic Visitation taught us was simply what Old Turtle knew so well—we need each other. We women religious are the inspiration for each other and for the many lives we touch . . . this is our story.

NOTES

1. Margaret Cain McCarthy, "Apostolic Visitation Survey Analysis: The Apostolic Visitation as Experienced by Women Religious in the United States" (report, October 15, 2011).

2. Reprinted with permission of the Loretto Community. This poem first appeared in Mostly for Promise, Loretto Community, 2013. Cecily Jones, SL, *Mostly for Promise, Poems by Cecily Jones, SL* (Nerinx, KY: Hardin Creek Press, 2013), 9.

3. J.R.R. Tolkien, *On Fairy Stories, Essays Presented to Charles Williams* (London: Oxford University Press, 1947).

4. Francis, "Eucharistic Concelebration with Eminent Cardinals Resident in Rome on the Occasion of the Feast of St. George," homily presented at Pauline Chapel, Vatican City, April 23, 2013, http://w2.vatican.va/content/francesco/en/homilies/2013/documents/papa-francesco_20130423_omelia-san-giorgio.html. For the development of this story in scripture, see the Lucan account in the Acts of the Apostles, Chapter 11:19–26, *The New American Bible* (Nashville: Thomas Nelson Publishers, 1987).

5. McCarthy, "Apostolic Visitation Survey Analysis."

6. Oscar A. Romero, *The Church is All of You: Thoughts of Archbishop Oscar A. Romero*, comp. and trans. James R. Brockman, SJ (Minneapolis, MN: Winston Press, 1984), 88.

7. McCarthy, "Apostolic Visitation Survey Analysis."

8. ibid.

9. ibid.

10. ibid.

11. ibid.

12. ibid.

13. ibid.

14. ibid.

15. Sisters of Loretto at the Foot of the Cross, *I Am the Way, Constitutions of the Sisters of Loretto at the Foot of the Cross* (Nerinx, KY: 1997), Article 6.

16. McCarthy, "Apostolic Visitation Survey Analysis."

17. Paul VI, *Evangelica Testificato, Apostolic Exhortation on the Renewal of Religious Life According to the Teaching of the Second Vatican Council*, June 29, 1971, http://www.vatican.va/holy_father/paul_vi/apost_exhortations/documents/hf_p-vi_exh_19710629_evangelica-testificatio_en.html.

18. McCarthy, "Apostolic Visitation Survey Analysis."

19. Paul VI, *Perfectae Caritatis, Decree on the Appropriate Renewal of the Religious Life*, in *The Documents of Vatican* II, ed. Walter A. Abbott, SJ (Piscataway, NJ: America Press, 1966), 468. The entire decree is found on pages 466–482.

20. McCarthy, "Apostolic Visitation Survey Analysis."

21. ibid.

22. Jones, *Mostly for Promise*, 9.

23. McCarthy, "Apostolic Visitation Survey Analysis."

24. ibid.

25. Margaret Wheatley, *Turning to One Another* (San Francisco: Berrett-Koehler Publishers, 2002), 29, 51.

26. Margaret Wheatley, *Perseverance* (Eugene, OR: Berkana Publications, 2012), 15.

27. McCarthy, "Apostolic Visitation Survey Analysis."

28. Douglas Wood, *Old Turtle and the Broken Truth* (New York: Scholastic Press, 2003).

Chapter Nine

The Experience of the
Apostolic Visitation

Remembered, Revisioned, Reclaimed, Released

Mary Ann Zollmann

FRAGMENTS OF MEMORY
SEEK THE COHERENCE OF NARRATIVE

Five years after its announcement the simple utterance of the words "Apostolic Visitation" evokes thoughts and feelings as vivid and raw as the moment they first occurred. It is as though we carry an embodied archive still so immediately accessible that a single catalyst opens the soft files of mind, heart, and spirit rendering the event once again real and present. Images tumble out, taking us off-guard with the ease of their availability, the thickness of their texture, the persistence of their endurance.

- We recall exactly where we were when we received the letter dated February 2, 2009, from the Congregation for Institutes of Consecrated Life and Societies of Apostolic Life informing us of the Apostolic Visitation "to look into the quality of the life of apostolic congregations of women religious in the United States of America." And, we are stirred anew by the sensation that, in its unsealing, we were opening ourselves to a defining moment.
- We feel the firm grip of the fragile hand of an elderly sister who, on the threshold of death, musters up sufficient breath to speak her fear aloud, "We have done the right thing, haven't we?" We hear the equal firmness of our response, "Yes, we have and when you meet God face to face you will know that for sure." And, we derive assurance even now from the

mutual healing bestowed in her wide smile and the tears that fell between us.

- We see the faces of our sisters from communities in the U.S. and around the world who gave unveiled expression to anger, confusion, and betrayal; who discerned their own faithful response to each phase of the Visitation while honoring the equally faithful choices of others; and who, in the requisite asceticism, have formed a stronger, more expansive sisterhood honed in the communion of our diversity.

- We remember lying awake in the night as our founders broke through the darkness whispering that they, too, had been rendered sleepless by haunting feelings of aloneness, responsibility, and desire to do God's will. We see the circles of women religious they brought with them, women who went before us and who understood what we were going through. And, we hear enduring echoes of their confidence, born of a perspective shaped by eternity, that all will be well.

- We feel in the core of our bodies the wrenching tension as we took legal action to protect our congregations' assets from potential control by Rome, secured canonists to assist us in the delicate process of remaining within the bounds of canon law while preserving our freedom to be true, and undertook these negotiations in disbelief that our relationship with some official authorities in a church we love had come to this.

- We recall how we combed Vatican documents on consecrated life seeking common language to answer questions in the canonical Visitation document, *Instrumentum Laboris,* about identity, governance, formation, spiritual life, community life, and mission. We tap into our sense of validation as historical papal letters and encyclicals mirrored back to us evidence of our fidelity. And, we linger even now with the joy of being returned by those documents to the inspirational beauty and power of our congregational constitutions.

- We rehearse the spoken and written words we in leadership shared with our sisters at every step of the process as we devoted ourselves to transparent truth-telling while communicating unmitigated care and unrelenting hope.

- We recall, with co-mingled pride and tenderness, comments from our sisters after their on-site interview with the visitors: "Sharing who we are and what we do was one of the best experiences of my life; it made me happy all over again to be a member of this community. Yet, to sit before another person, pour out my heart and soul, and receive no response was the hardest thing I have ever done."

- We sit at dinner with the visitors on the last day of their visit, looking them in the eye as an expression of an inaudible plea: "Please just give us a clue about what you see, feel, believe about this community we so love."

And, we surrender into a conversation that politely and politically evades what is on the minds of all of us and matters most.

- We hear voices of the laity who, in focus groups during on-site visits, and in letters, emails, phone calls, and prayer vigils encouraged us to be true for the sake of our own integrity and for their sake as they counted on co-creating with us a more inclusive and compassionate church. And, we attend to some among them who, challenging us with their belief in the necessity of the Visitation, preserved our openness to taking an honest look at our lives.
- We revisit the celebratory relief of our communities as, having negotiated the rigors of the on-site visit, we moved into prayerful rituals, healing de-briefing sessions, and long-anticipated parties. We relive the utter exhaustion that, on the day after it all, kept us staring at walls or out windows, walking purposelessly in warmth of sun or crunch of snow. And, we rest both then and now in the quiet certitude that we are being drawn into a future vulnerable and uncertain, yet full of grace.

From the wellsprings of our consciousness we receive each image as a discrete snippet, a disparate snatch of an experience that, even with the passage of time, invades our minds, tugs at our hearts, churns in our bodies, stirs our souls. Slivers and slices that they are, these fragments of memory arise bearing a necessary question: Are they important; if so, why? They come seeking participation in something that weaves the images together and, at the same time, takes them beyond themselves to connections with something larger. They arrive begging for a context that renders them mean-ingful. They, and we who remember them, rise up in search of a story.

To embark on a narrative of meaning is no lulling, consoling enterprise but, as described by Mary Catherine Hilkert, leads us beyond our comfort zone into a location that is transformative, liberating, and dangerous:

> Narrative does not simply repeat history; it shifts its configuration, thus chang-ing it fundamentally. . . . This shift of narrative is no small exchange: one's human identity at the deepest levels of values, character, and relationships is at stake. . . . Retelling the story becomes a "subversive" way of reinterpreting history, criticizing oppressive power, and empowering the impulse toward liberation. [1]

What story can we tell that gives us a context sufficiently wide and deep to hold our experience and to illumine it anew? What story is familiar enough that we already carry it appreciatively and yet is still strange enough to attract us toward another re-reading, re-telling? What story has the capacity to draw us into its characters, its symbols, its words, pulling us beyond facile custo-mary meanings into its untapped multi-layered potential? What story has proven trustworthy enough that we can willingly follow its lead, letting it beckon us to places we never thought the story, or we, would go?

For us women religious, any story that would offer an adequate interpretive context for our experience needs to be one that reaches back into our Christian tradition, is sourced in the gospels, and has inspired us through centuries of religious life. One such story is the gospel story of the visitation. Through the various phases of the Apostolic Visitation most of us were aware of the lingual resonance between these two "visitations." Some of us attempted to use the Lucan scriptural story to revision our participation in the Apostolic Visitation, while others intentionally evaded any mention of the gospel story so as not to taint its preciousness to us.

Yet, beyond echoes of language, the potential ease of superficial connections, and even concerns about touching its intact sacredness, the gospel story of the Visitation pulls at our consciousness suggesting a radicality resistant to dismissal. In the life of the woman who birthed the Body of Christ and mothered our church into being, the visitation holds priority of location. It is a pivotal event. Something revolutionary happened in the home of Elizabeth. Accordingly there may be no more salutary contextual narrative than the story of Mary as she moves into, through and beyond her own visitation, letting our companionship with her illumine the significance of our Apostolic Visitation. [2]

PRE-VISITATION ANNUNCIATION: AWAKENING TO THE SPIRIT OVERSHADOWING AND DRAWING NEAR

The gospel story in which the visitation occurs as turning point begins with a pre-visitation life-clarifying annunciation: "Rejoice, highly favored one! God is with you" (Luke 1:28 NAB). [3] We first meet Mary of Nazareth in a moment which gathers up the whole of her life thus far and which, pending her assent, impels her toward a future for which the past was necessary preparation and prelude. This event is an illuminative one for Mary. In the ordinary day in and day out of her years, the life of God has been slowly, quietly, unostensibly growing within her. The Annunciation marks the in-breaking of that awareness into Mary's consciousness as she grapples, in awe's co-mingled terror and amazement, with how the Spirit of God has been overshadowing her, drawing near to her, doing something new in her through the whole of her life. Her relationship with God has been a virginal one defined not primarily by biology but by her primary passion: single-hearted desire to let God labor in her, stirring her to imagine or conceive God's will, and so bear and birth, give flesh and blood to the longings of God in her time. In the familiar imagery of pregnancy, Mary has been "growing big" with God.

Similarly for us women religious, our entire individual and collective story has been one of setting our hearts on God. Spanning centuries, decades, and life-times our intentional centering in God has been making space in the womb of our lives for God to do God's work in us. Most often, the labor of God in us moves in the ordinariness of the everyday without our explicit consciousness; yet, all the while we, like Mary, have been "growing big" with God.

We have become steeped in contemplation, a habit of prayer that situates us in silent openness before the wordlessness of Holy Mystery. We listen as we are drawn in a single movement inward and outward where there is only God and the union of all people and creation in God. Everything is one. The God in all and still infinitely beyond all is just that big and inclusive. There is no face or place where we are not looking at God and God is not looking back at us. Contemplation calls us to a great wide whole and holy vision and a generously expansive embrace.

This contemplative relationship with God instills in us a thirst to know God. We seek ongoing theological education, engaging insights from spiritual writers and theologians who open our Christian tradition to meanings applicable for our time. Reflective study of *theo-logos*, the word of God, shapes and re-shapes the way we see ourselves as made in the image of God. We outgrow understandings of God too small to inspire our commitment and heed the invitation to follow the lead of a God previously beyond our imagining. Theological reflection exercises an ethical claim on us, impelling us to live and act in fidelity to the God we have come to know and love, no matter what the cost.

The Spirit of God comes upon us in the spirit of our particular religious communities, a charism given original expression in the life of our founders. From the moment of our beginnings, we have turned to our charism for direction in living our lives. For this we keep company with our founders letting them reveal their spirit and so learning from them how to retrieve that spirit in our times. What we have uncovered are women and men unafraid to move beyond comfortable boundaries of geography, socially defined relationships, or ecclesial law. These were big women and men, pioneers who stretched existing frontiers to broaden the horizons of our consciousness. Imagining definitions of mercy and compassion, justice and peace, freedom and equality that envelop all people and creation, they were bent on living in accord with those meanings. Our communities were founded and are re-founded daily in the charismatic energy of a very big God. This is the spirit that has taken up residence in us, labors in us, and becomes incarnate in us.

Trusting our experience that God is first, foremost and always a God of love, we wrote our constitutions in the conviction of that certitude. Employing poetically open words capable of pulling us to the edges of our potential, our Rule of Life is directed toward a single purpose: to keep us growing into

God our whole lives long. Although the language and style of our articulation reflects the bountiful diversity of each congregation, the statements on every page of every constitution illumine a common inter-congregational experience: We find "ourselves everywhere coming face to face with the appeals of an affectionate tenderness that cannot leave out anyone, a tenderness that is and remains subversive."[4] Awake to the Spirit of God laboring in us, we understand our sisterhood as a relationship of love with all that is.

Grounded in this self-understanding, we live as women in community, aware that each member of the community is a unique incarnation of God's love and worthy of being honored and reverenced for who she is. Recognizing that each member brings experiences and perspectives essential to the well-being of the whole community, we seek to engage the insights of all, discerning together how God's dream seeks fuller realization in the life and mission of our communities. More and more we live into the truth we utter with increasing clarity: The life of each member is our most important asset.

Our understanding of sisterhood in community keeps widening as the boundary lines between communities and between religious life and laity become more porous. The historical competition between and among religious congregations has been giving way to collaboration as women from different communities share life together in apartments and retirement centers, work collaboratively in commonly determined ministry projects, tap each other's wisdom in creating formation and governance processes, and keep each other in mind as we plan for a future that will inevitably transcend the boundaries of any single congregation. Additionally, we are much more conscious of our companionship with associates, former members, co-ministers, alumni, and benefactors. Recognizing the depths of their spiritual and ministerial gifts, we are moved to explore with the laity specific and creative ways to work together as we live our common vocation of building the household of God.

Appreciating our sisterhood with all persons and creation, our understandings of mission and choices for ministry have continued to expand. The embrace of our care is inclusive as we reach out to those at the centers of social, political, economic, ecclesial, and ecological influence and those at the margins. Our ministries extend from centers for legislative advocacy and archdiocesan offices to schools and hospitals, to homeless shelters and prisons, and to those beyond the familiar geography of our own country, culture, and spiritual praxis. Wherever we go and whatever we do, we attempt to bring the conviction of our universal sisterhood and brotherhood, inviting those with whom we interact to awareness of and action for the common good. In our ministry for and with others, the Spirit of God overshadowing and drawing close to us compels us to make God's borderless love transparent.

We live our sisterhood as women in the church. Instilled over time with a passion for the primacy of communion we advocate for a church inclusive of difference and appreciative of diversity. We long for creative theologians to be granted a place in genuine theological dialogue. We long for tables with room for those whose authentic loving broadens our accustomed understandings of love: the divorced and the remarried; the homosexual, bi-sexual and transgendered; the married with family whose care for their children precludes the responsible conception of another child. We long for the full release of the gifts of women and laity into positions of leadership in the church, bringing the whole church to life in new ways. And we long for intentional conversations with women and men of religious traditions different from our own to enhance our common quest for the Divine.

As was true for our sister Mary, the Spirit of God has been coming upon us, drawing near to us. Since the original conception of the Spirit's charism at our founding, the Spirit has been laboring in us to birth the Body of Christ as a body of boundless communion. Like Mary's, the pregnancy that is ours is unconventional, independent of any domesticated arrangements and outside the control of traditional androcentric structures. Underscoring the power of the virgin woman, our fruitful fullness in the Spirit is a threat to existing established systems of patriarchy and hierarchy. Overshadowed by the Spirit of God, we take our place among our Judeo-Christian foremothers: Tamar, Rahab, Ruth, the wife of Uriah, and our sister Mary.

> These women all found themselves at some point outside the patriarchal family structure, and consequently in danger. . . . The link among the women consists in the fact that there is (a) something extraordinary, irregular, even scandalous in their activity, (b) which places them in some peril, (c) in view of which they take initiative, (d) thereby becoming participants in the divine work of redemption.[5]

In this long line of faithful feminine continuity,

> Mary's pregnancy is suspicious; socially and legally within the patriarchal culture there is more than a hint of disrepute. Yet in the midst of this dangerous trouble something holy is going forward. God's Spirit moves amidst the threatening situation to bring about the birth of the Messiah.[6]

Incarnating an unconventional covenantal divine largesse in a patriarchal church we women religious knew that it was just a matter of time before there would come, from out of the future, some kind of summons to a critical moment of demarcation, clarification, and decision-making. We just did not know what form the defining event would take—until February 2, 2009, when the leadership of our congregations received the letter from the Congregation for Consecrated Life and Institutes of Apostolic Life informing us of the Apostolic Visitation "to look into the quality of the life of apostolic Congregations of women religious in the United States."

The announcement sent its searing sanction directly into our hearts sparking an electricity of emotions. For over fifty years we had been faithful to the directives of Vatican II:

> A life consecrated by a profession of the counsels is of surpassing value. Such a life has a necessary role to play in the circumstances of the present age. That this kind of life and its contemporary role may achieve greater good for the church . . . the manner of living, praying and working should be suitably adapted to the physical and psychological conditions of today's religious and also, to the extent required by the nature of each community, to the needs of the apostolate, the requirements of a given culture, the social and economic circumstances.[7]

Taking seriously the church's call for the renewal of religious life had required of us an unparalleled faith, a wrestling with God, with one another, and with our own deep selves as we discerned what God was asking of us. After years of external structure solidified in stable prayer forms, predictable daily schedule regulating community living, participation in a common flourishing ministry, unquestioned acceptance of homogenous images of God, and security vested in compliance with authority, the ground shifted seismically from under us and everything broke wide open. We lost members, groped for new ways of connecting with one another from the inside out, discerned our own gifts for ministry, prepared resumes and applied for positions, and engaged personally and communally in new questions about the meaning of religious life and about the existence and nature of God. We did it first for the sake of the church that called and, once having embarked on the journey, we did it for the sake of the life bubbling up inside of us and bubbling over into our church and world. Implementing the directives of Vatican II, we women religious grew big with God.

Accordingly, the Apostolic Visitation landed in our lives as a judgment on the women we had become in response to the invitation of our church. Having entered into the discipline of being faithful, many of us felt betrayed, devalued, dismissed. We were angry, hurt, confused; throughout the process we remained unclear about its origin and purpose. We were saddened and frustrated by the lack of ecclesial attentiveness to situations in our church, like that of clerical abuse, crying out for healing justice. We were concerned that our own need to focus on the requirements of the Visitation could detract us from our mission. We felt some anxiety as we wondered what the process, touching the very nerve and fiber of our religious life, would evoke within the membership of our communities. We experienced the vulnerability and apprehension of not knowing where our engagement with the dynamics of the Visitation would lead our communities and religious life as a whole. We also felt a sense of relief that the latent tension with some of the ecclesial hierarchy had an identifiable shape and form, and would provide an opportunity for us to tell our story.

The announcement of the Apostolic Visitation served as our moment of annunciation. Significantly its message arrived, not just to one of us women religious nor even to an individual community, but rather to all of us U.S. apostolic women religious simultaneously and together. What God had been doing in the long unfolding history of religious life came to a focus in this moment; and the awareness of its significance and potential implication pierced the collective consciousness of women religious. It was a communal clarifying event that, holding in sum the whole of our past, impelled us toward a future for which everything before it was necessary preparation and prelude.

Compelled by an intuition of the gracefulness of the moment and the sense that a larger purpose was at work and "believing that there would be a fulfillment of what had been spoken to her by God" Mary set out to travel the terrain of a hill country toward a love that drew her from afar (Luke 1:45).[8] Sisters to Mary propelled toward a Visitation of our own, we set out calm in our assurance that the Spirit would continue to overshadow us and alert to the stirrings of the Word becoming flesh in us.

THE VISITATION: MAKING A REVOLUTIONARY JOURNEY THROUGH THE HILL COUNTRY

"Mary set out with haste to a Judean town in the hill country where she entered the house of Zechariah and greeted Elizabeth" (Luke 1:39). Mary's entire time in the hill country is summarized in a single declarative sentence as if she moved from here to there by a smooth and uneventful route. There is nothing about what it must have been like to be a woman, pregnant in an unconventional way and accordingly under suspicion, traveling a rugged terrain. What happened along the way to her, in her, and around her is left to our imagination.

For those of us called to make a similar journey the vacuous silence in Luke's account of Mary's story grants us welcome space to walk with her, letting the path unfold according to the contour and content of our own Apostolic Visitation journey. We came to the moment as post-Vatican II sisters grown "big with God" through the practice of contemplation and commitment to inclusive community. Little could we have anticipated the power of the hill country to revolutionize our experience of contemplation and our capacity for communion.

From the outset we were tossed into God. Individually, on leadership teams, in community meetings, and in regional and national assemblies, we called upon God in familiar prayers learned by heart, in psalms releasing layers of emotion. We searched the daily scriptures for messages bearing the Spirit's word of insight and encouragement. We opened ourselves to the outpouring of grace flowing through the rhythmic melody of song and the physicality of gesture and dance. However, what set our prayer apart at this moment was the way it carried us beyond the boundaries of our own communities. We shared with one another original music created for the Apostolic Visitation, its strains echoing like a mantra across the country. We wrote a common prayer to accompany us in this time and heard that prayer voiced in relay from one congregational chapel to another.

And, perhaps most significantly, we chose a single scriptural passage to hold in the silence of contemplation: "Remember not the former things, nor consider things of old. Behold, I am doing something new; now it springs forth; do you not perceive it?" (Isaiah 43:19) We sat in silence as Holy Mystery spoke these words to us. We did this as individuals, as communities, and inter-congregationally, one passage reverberating in the communal soul of our sisterhood.

As developed by Walter Brueggemann, uttering these words and having them heard in community signals a transformative moment creating "new standing ground . . . upon which new humanness is possible. . . . However that will come only with the recognition that life has not been fully consigned to us, [that] the community receives a newness it cannot generate for itself [and rests in the] godness of God."[9]

"They who wait for the Lord shall renew their strength; they shall run and not be weary; they shall walk and not faint" (Isaiah 40:31). Expanding on the significance of these words of the prophet Isaiah, Brueggemann continues:

> For those who take initiative into their own hands, either in the atheism of pride or in the atheism of despair, the words are weary, faint, and exhausted. The inverse comes with waiting: renewed strength, mounting up, running, and walking. But that is in waiting. It is in receiving and not grasping, in inheriting and not possessing, in praising and not seizing. It is in knowing that initiative has passed from our hands and we are safer for it.[10]

Waiting together upon God, we took every step in our hill country confident that we were being led by God's power working in us and through us, and not Rome's power over us. And, we were safer for it.

Needing a whole host of eyes and ears, hearts and minds to make our way with integrity, we were freshly alert to the imperative of companionship. We turned to one another in our own communities. Whatever responses we made to each phase of the Apostolic Visitation we wanted to make them as a community inclusive of our differences in experience and perspective. We had to do what we did and go where we would go together, excluding no one, leaving no one behind. Our founders came to life among us with unprecedented vividness as we communally probed their choices of courage and risk, their non-bartered commitment to being true to themselves, which is to say to the will of God within them. No longer able to take our fidelity to our constitutions for granted we read and re-read them, letting them scrutinize our hearts and inspire us with authentic direction.

We explored with one another in community the questions of the *Instrumentum Laboris*, the canonical instrument, about our spirituality and prayer, community life and ministry, governance and stewardship of resources. As we worked with the language of the document and its assumptions about our life, many of us came face to face with the undeniable gap between our own self-definition and the official church's expectations of us. We had grown beyond the boundaries of those questions; they simply did not fit us; they were too small for the women we had become. Not just individually or in small affinity groups but as whole congregations we went to the core of our identity: Who are we as women of the church? Figuratively and literally, we took long and deep breaths as we hoped against hope that, in such radical territory, our bonds with one another in community would hold. And, bound with ties forged in the gracefulness of taut elasticity, they did!

Pulled beyond the ease of superficial conversation toward the edge of a precarious precipice where our whole lives were at stake, we tread with great care. A palpable tenderness welled up among us as we regarded each sister more reverently, not wanting to violate the beliefs and convictions of any one among us in our efforts to move forward together. In this process we discovered a spacious place of affection with room for the beauty and the challenge of all our differences. The bonds of affection that had always defined us leapt off the pages of our constitutions and came to fresh life in us.

Accordingly, at critical junctures in the Apostolic Visitation journey, we were all there. When our elected leader communicated with Mother Mary Clare in person or via letter her words were those of all of us. When the community chose its mode of response to the canonical instrument, the direction taken was informed and shaped by all of us. When the visitators held interviews with some in the community, all of us were there in spirit. When community leadership engaged canon lawyers to assist us in creating a pathway that would honor and preserve the charismatic and financial patrimony of the institute, entire communities participated in the dialogue. When difficult decisions were made to legally separate the canonical congregation from the civil corporation, community members had the knowledge they needed to understand the rationale for the action. Walking the journey of our hill country, we could feel surging within us the renewed energy and unmistakable joy that comes from living with integrity as sisters in community.

As soon as the Apostolic Visitation was announced, we were drawn instinctively to seek the companionship of our sisters beyond our own communities. We were pulled toward one another inter-congregationally as never before and utilized all our creativity to be connected. We organized and activated telephone trees; locally, we got together in small circles; we selected central areas of the country to gather in larger numbers. We shed common tears, surfaced common fears, voiced common outcries, charted common through-ways. We recognized that what was happening was not just about a single community, but about all of us as women religious. We had a strong sense that what one of us did affected all of us. It was essential only that we walk together.

And our moving together was not dependent upon but rather eschewed homogeneity of response. Some congregations chose to participate fully in each phase of the Visitation; others chose not to respond at all. Yet, what mattered was not so much the mode of our response as the open and honest way we shared across congregational boundaries the directions we were choosing and why. This kind of communication afforded all of us a rich and wide cross-congregational context for our own decision-making and called us to our own authenticity. We grew in respect and admiration for one another and in appreciation for the value of our differences. In our truthful speaking we moved beneath surface connections to uncover a deep common bond: the desire to be faithful. United in the communion of integrity, we grew into a sisterhood beyond any single charism and inclusive of the charisms of all.

Transcending the distance of geography, our sisters from around the world traveled the hill country side by side with us. They were with us in messages crafted from national conferences of women religious and in letters they sent for publication by U.S. media. They were with us at international assemblies, especially the gathering of 800 members of the International Union of Superiors General in Rome. Speaking their blessings in Chinese, Japanese, and Vietnamese, in Portuguese and Spanish, and in the multiple dialects of Africa, their common language was one of loving support. On our part, we needed these women from around the world, so focused on concerns of economy and ecology, health and trafficking, violence and governmental oppression, to put our challenges of the Apostolic Visitation in a larger perspective, to keep us centered on ministry to others, and to let our learnings from the Visitation pull us more authentically into mission. Although much remained uncertain about the contours of our future, we knew for sure that we could rely on the companionship of a great wide global sisterhood.

And yet, with all the gracious and necessary company of a kindred sisterhood, the Visitation journey brought with it sisters traveling the same road with whom we did not experience such ease of affinity. The visitators, sisters to us in sister communities, joined up with us as visitors among us for a portion of our time in the hill country. Their role as official assessors of the quality of our life created a psychological, emotional, and spiritual divide that was difficult to breach with the welcome of our words, the hospitality of our actions, and the willingness of our investment in the interview processes. We were courteous but cautious, formal rather than familiar; the atmosphere, though cordial, felt strange and strained.

We opened up our homes and, even more, we opened up our hearts. Impassioned by a yearning to tell the truth about the evolution of a community we love, we poured out our narratives. We highlighted critical turning points in our personal lives and the life of our communities. We named strengths born of our challenges, voiced our fears, and described transformative ministerial experiences. Yet, as is the format for visitations such as this, the flow of our speaking was met with the required protocol of silent listening on the part of the visitors. In the end, we did not know what their experience of us had been, what descriptions of us shaped the content of their final report.

During the celebrations that, in most communities, followed upon the visitors' leave-taking, we rejoiced not so much in their "disappearance" from among us but rather in our singular "appearance" as women in community. We had become visible to one another as faithful women, women who had engaged the visitors with integrity and had done so together. In that moment, we knew that what mattered most was not any external assessment but what was happening from the inside out: our own growing appreciation for who we are and who we are still becoming.

At the same time, our visitors never really left us but remained among us as a necessary lingering ache. Everything about our time with them was contrary to the mutuality and transparency that defines our sisterhood. We recognized with sadness and regret that in circumstances unencumbered by a Vatican evaluation we would readily enter into genuine sisterly relationships. The felt absence of that potential bond, the acute pain of the gap between what we experienced and what we desired compels us to seek ways to be true to our sisterhood even under adverse external pressure.

On our journey in the hill country there were also those of our sisters present in silence and shadow. These women were not among us when we gathered locally, regionally, in larger assemblies. They chose not to lend their voices to the survey that underlies and inspires the telling of the story in this book.[11] We miss the inclusion of their experience; we miss hearing what the Apostolic Visitation journey has been like for them. There is a hole in the community of our sisterhood.

These sisters have chosen a different way of living out their vocation in the church. For the most part, they wear an identifiable habit, share community in convents, serve in a common ministry, and keep a specific communal prayer schedule. The form and content of their religious life is more in accord with the expectations suggested by Rome in the language of the Visitation's canonical instrument, the *Instrumentum Laboris* and the *Questionnaire.* This contributes to a perception that these women religious are more faithful to the church than those of us who entered into the requirements of the Vatican II renewal and creates a divisive incision at the very heart of communion, the identifying gospel hallmark of religious life and of our church.

For us women religious whose integrity depends upon working toward relationships of reciprocity and inclusion, the reality of this division between two valid expressions of religious life wells up among us as an enduring sore and, for some, even a scandal. Experiencing the tension between communities affiliated with LCWR (Leadership Conference of Women Religious) and those with membership in CMSWR (Council of Major Superiors of Women Religious), we know as close to home as within our sisterhood the requirements and the cost of communion. Even as we desire more inclusive, collaborative relationships honoring our diversity as gift, we ourselves adhere to dynamics that perpetuate dualism. In an effort to protect forms of religious life we love and believe in, we become fearful that any movements toward mutual understanding may weaken the influence of our form of religious life, that attempts at dialogue may dilute the strength of our hard-won commitment and may even be an abdication of our call to be true. Internally polarized we go our separate ways.

Although it was silence that fell between us as we walked our common Visitation journey, questions shouted out to us loud and clear: How do all of us women religious find ways to maintain fidelity to our distinctive vocational call while expanding the boundaries of our sisterhood? Instead of our differences leading us to irreconcilable dualisms, can we welcome our diversity as essential to the possibility of genuine and ever so much richer community? What steps do we need to take to make that happen for the sake of our own credibility as sisters, our viability among the people of God, and the truthfulness of our voice in church and world? Walking the hill country with sisters who are "other," we felt the labor pains as a bigger God stretched us straining toward birth in us and among us.

Beyond the circles of vowed women religious, we experienced the supportive and challenging companionship of laity and clergy. Strongly connected to us through the contagion of our charism, our lay associates were with us every step of our Visitation journey. Intimately tied into our congregational future, they encouraged us to be true to the spirit that attracted them to us. As they generously participated in our community prayer, reflection, and dialogue generated by the Apostolic Visitation, we witnessed the depth of their spirituality, their passion for justice, the consonance of their lives with our congregational charism. We grew in appreciation for the daily and long-term relationship we share with them and became more committed to the intentional inclusion of their gifts as we collaboratively promote our congregational life and mission into the future.

Our journey would have been very different without the companionship of those in our focus groups who met with the on-site visitators. These lay women and men, clergy persons and bishops spoke on our behalf with no strings attached except the ties that bound them so respectfully to us. Although we were not present to hear their exact words, our conversations with them gave us a sense of what they said and how they said it. We felt the strength of their emotion as they recalled how grace flowing through us changed their lives. They reflected back to us our gospel-based vision for our church and world and noted the risks we have taken to bring that vision to realization. They lifted up aspects of our lives we did not know were visible, much less so deeply valued, and they brought to our awareness facets of our lives we were too close to see. Their words revived our courage and strengthened our hope.

We were companioned by past and present co-workers, those we have served and presently serve in our ministries, donors, men religious, clergy, and bishops. Their presence with us often took the form of small but significant communications. There were notes simply to say thank you, to let us know that our vision of the church is theirs, too, and that they are with us in actively bringing about the realization of our common dream. Sometimes it was a phone call from benefactors to advise us that they were contributing to our development office in lieu of their parish weekly collection or that they were increasing their gift. We opened local and national newspapers and were buoyed by letters from communities and conferences of men religious as well as bishops. Cards and messages from laity and clergy confirmed that we were walking in a good direction, not just for ourselves but for the people of God.

Equally significant were those communications that, expressing a lack of support, gave us pause. Former students and colleagues contacted us in anger and disillusionment; we were no longer the women they had come to know and they could not see how we were being faithful to God and to the church. Donors called to voice their disapproval of us, to withdraw financial support and request removal from our mailing lists. We heard from bishops and clergy who praised us for who we had been as we staffed schools and hospitals, served in parishes and worked among the poor, but who could not commend the mutuality and reciprocity, equality and inclusivity underlying, directing, and clearly evident in our every ministerial action. Taking seriously those who critiqued us, we became clearer about ourselves and the cost, relationally and financially, of being true to our mission. Even these critical, questioning companions in our hill country meant a lot to us; they humbled us, preserved us from arrogance, prevented us from myopic and tunnel vision. They kept us mindful of the need to seek out deliberately those whose experiences, perspectives, and beliefs are contrary to our own.

Walking with laity, clergy and bishops, both in their support and in their challenge, sensitized us to the truth that, in our similarity and difference of theology, spirituality, ecclesiology, and gospel interpretation, our future is bound up together. The experience made firm our commitment to connect more regularly and at greater depth with the broader community of the people of God, even at times beyond seemingly insurmountable divides; and, in so doing, engage more whole-heartedly in the labor of co-creating a universal household in the image of a very big God.

We walked the pathway of the hill country for almost two full years from the time the Apostolic Visitation was announced in early February, 2009, until the last on-site visit in mid-December, 2010. It was a liminal time when, lifted out of the ordinary taken for granted flow of everyday life, our sensibilities were sharpened. We became acutely attuned to the contemporary critical nature of our assent to growing big with God. In the depths of our contemplation, we were being converted, "turned in an attitude of profound friendship toward all others, even those most unlike ourselves." And, in the breadth of our company, we were being tutored "through the power of profound companionship that respects differences and values them equally." [12]

The liminal place of the hill country confirmed us in the mutual, inter-relational inclusive communion we were bent toward living prior to the Apostolic Visitation. Yet, our journey offered us so much more than an affirmation of what was. Renewed investment in our characteristic processes of contemplation and community not only solidified our pre-Visitation bonds within our communities, inter-congregationally, and with the laity, but expanded those relationships, opening us to new possibilities for communion. Realizing the urgency of porous, inclusive, boundless community within our sisterhood, society, world, church, and universe, we claimed the living of community as our identity and its creation as our mission. And, most significantly, we were formed in that mission and identity not just as individual women or individual communities but as women religious together. In the pertinent words of Keri Hulme:

> They were nothing more than people, by themselves. Even paired, any pairing, they would have been nothing more than people by themselves. But all together, they have become the heart and muscles and mind of something perilous and new, something strange and growing and great. Together, all together, they were instruments of change. [13]

The liminal time in the hill country was a rite of passage into our communal adulthood as women religious. We stood on the threshold of something new, something ready to be birthed in us. In the company of Mary we crossed over the threshold, entered the home of Elizabeth, and came face to face with the maturity of our sisterhood.

> When Elizabeth heard Mary's greeting, the child leaped in her womb. And Elizabeth was filled with the Holy Spirit and exclaimed with a loud cry, "Blessed are you among women, and blessed is the fruit of your womb . . . As

soon as I heard the sound of your greeting, the child in my womb leapt for joy . . ." And Mary said, "My soul magnifies the Lord, and my spirit rejoices in God" (Luke 1:41-42, 44, 46-47).

Into the silence of patriarchal androgynous voices absent, as personified by Joseph, or made mute as with Zachary, the feminine voice breaks forth in an embodied greeting of mutuality. The life in one leaps toward the life in the other, recognizing kinship closer than cousinhood. The home of Elizabeth overflows the confines of male-defined female domesticity as Mary and Elizabeth proclaim without restraint that, through their agency as women, God is dismantling prevailing hierarchical and patriarchal domestic order and birthing a new order of relationship in God's own household. Pregnant with the life of God they sing into being the subversion of all oppressive structures and the advent of egalitarian relationships, a right and just order focused on the flourishing of life for all. In speech, nothing less than prophetic, they dare to voice the "divine intent . . . to build up a community of sisters and brothers marked by human dignity and mutual regard."[14] And, if not miraculously, at least unconventionally, this divine desire will be incarnated in them. For Mary and Elizabeth and for all who come after them nothing will ever be the same again. In the imagery of Elizabeth Johnson the visitation is "joy in the revolution of God."[15]

In a home spacious enough for all of us women religious wherever we are in the world, we are together transformed by our time in the hill country. We see in each other's eyes the beauty of the women we have become as, confounding any efforts at diminishment by established Roman powers, the God-life we bear grows ever bigger within us.

Mature adult women, honed by the asceticism of ongoing contemplation, we proclaim our self-authentication with an assurance that it is the God within us who sings:

> My soul magnifies the Lord,
> and my spirit rejoices in God my Savior. . . .
> The One who is mighty has done great things for me,
> and holy is God's name (Luke 1:47, 49).

Mature adult women, honed by the asceticism of life-long commitment to community and trusting that it is the God within us who acts, we claim our mission as communion brought about by the reversal of customary social and ecclesial expectations:

> God scatters the proud in the imagination of their hearts;
> puts down the mighty from their thrones;
> exalts those of low degree;
> fills the hungry with good things;
> sends the rich empty away;
> all in remembrance of God's mercy (Luke 1:51-54).

Mature adult women, strong in unprecedented solidarity and grace-filled confidence, we rely on the Spirit of God to do in us individually and together what the Spirit always does: "Vivify, knit together, and uphold the world in unquenchable love."[16]

POST VISITATION:
LIVING LARGELY FROM A MANGER TO AN UPPER ROOM

Claiming communion as the irrefutable mission of our sisterhood come to full maturity, we go forth from the house of Elizabeth to bear the Body of Christ in the way of our sister Mary: seeking a manger, dwelling in a temple, making a feast, standing by a cross, unlocking an upper room.

We seek a manger, birthing life at the margins (Luke 2: 1-20). The Apostolic Visitation brought to public visibility an amazing number of people, vowed and lay, who believe in a common vision for the universal household of God and who desire to formally engage with us in the realization of that vision. Finding creative and realistic ways to include them in planning for and living our mission, we have all that we need to reach out to those at the margins of our social, political and global systems, church, and earth. Even as the intentional praxis of our expanded communal self-understanding gifts us with resources of personnel and finance to reach all the way to those at the margins, those at the edges reach back to us with essential gifts of their own. Listening to the stories of those without access to food, health care, housing, and education, we access the offices of our politicians to make those stories heard and submit our own acts of injustice to the healing power of those at the margins. Spending time with our sisters and brothers who live daily inundated by sounds of violence, we spend more of our time in peace-making locally, nationally, and internationally; and submit our own violent actions to the healing power of those at the margins. Hearing the call of those excommunicated from our church, we find our voice to speak the justice of inclusive Eucharistic communion; and submit our own exclusionary practices to the healing power of those at the margins. Awakened to earth's plea for survival, we steward the preservation of our environment; and submit our own earth-depleting practices to the healing power of nature at the margins. In the reciprocity of our need for one another, it becomes less clear who is at the center and who at the margins; power differentials dissolve in the mutuality of our transformative influence. Symbolically in our lives right here and now, shepherds and kings, stable animals and angels participate together in the nativity of genuine communion. As for Mary, so for us: there is no room for the big God we are bearing in the small comfortable inns of existing exclusive power structures, including our own. Our birthing seeks a manger place.

We dwell in a temple, letting wisdom emerge (Luke 2: 22-32). The Apostolic Visitation processes confirmed the essence of our mission as commitment to inclusion, mutuality, equality, unqualified compassion, and the dignity of self-authentication. They strengthened our resolve to incarnate those values wherever we are and in whatever way we can. Recognizing that those dynamics are most often not the determinative ones in our socio-political, ecological and ecclesial centers of decision-making, we know that it will take unwavering courage to bear witness to them with our lives in more forthright and unequivocal ways going forward. Accordingly, we sink into God where we remember the origins of all creation in God, where we preserve our mindfulness that all that is belongs to one family sharing a single holy genetic composition and where that recollection makes a non-negotiable ethical claim for the inclusiveness of our care. Like Mary, we are drawn to the temple, drawn to contemplation. There in that sacred space wisdom, not of our own contriving, is revealed in symbolic apparitions of Anna and Simeon. There we hear that our lives will bring healing and wholeness and, at the same time, will be opposed with such force that it will feel like a sword piercing our very soul. There habitual patterns, choices and plans are subject to discernment cutting away what is no longer valid for us and leaving as remnant only what matters. And there, like Mary, who traced her lost son to the temple, we are honed in the difficult understanding that the life we birth and foster does not belong to us at all but belongs to God and goes where God wills. As for Mary, so for us, going to the temple is a purifying event. Attuned to the one whose life we bear, we grow in wisdom of waiting upon God. We grow in age, in maturity of heart, speaking the right words at the right time in the right way. And, we grow in grace assuming responsibility for what we say and do. As we nurture into the future the life of the big God we bear, we are moved, more than ever before, to go to the temple letting wisdom emerge.

We make a feast, speaking out boldly for what is missing (John 2:1-11). Shaped in a covenantal consciousness, we stand with Mary at a wedding, the most vivid celebration of covenantal relationship, where the wine essential to the feast of communion is missing and where she is the one to voice boldly its absence. Her fearlessness catalyzes a gender-inclusive, non-hierarchical partnership between herself and Jesus and releases the gifts of all, including the servants, making it possible for the feast of union to continue. Having become, through our own Visitation, more acutely sensitized to the necessity of genuine communion and its absence within our sisterhood itself, and in our church, world and universe, we are compelled to speak out where there is no wine of diversity, freedom, equality, and justice integral to the feast. We let the ache of the separation among us as sisters living different expressions of religious life work its way in us, naming the division aloud and taking the first steps in initiating dialogue essential to reconciliation. We refuse to dismiss as unredeemable the rift between us and church officials both in Rome and in the U.S., and seek opportunities to invite them to personally experience the reality of our life. We persist in calling attention to the dismissal of laity and women as liturgical presiders in our church and insist on creating alternative rituals that honor their gifts. We toll the bells in our congregational chapels across the country to mark the execution of a death row inmate holding both perpetrator and victim in a single compassionate gesture. We stand year after year in Fort Benning, Georgia at the gates of the School of the Americas and show up on the borders between the U.S. and Mexico advocating for resolutions to international conflict respectful of a global humanity. We pool our resources of finance and personnel to collaborate in projects for education and health care in South Sudan and ride a bus in the U.S. to lobby for those same services closer to home. We claim earth as our mother and attempt to be true to the intimacy of that relationship by installing eco-friendly systems in our buildings and promoting an eco-spirituality. Impelled to break the silence that perpetuates division, we name the lack of communion and practice the covenantal dynamics integral to wholeness, no matter what the personal or communal consequences. We make a feast speaking out boldly for what is missing.

We stand by a cross, facing a costly love (John 19:17-20). Although the cross has always been central to our Christian spirituality, the Apostolic Visitation pulled us experientially into the stark reality of what it means to be and to bear the Body of Christ. Followers of Jesus, we are women in the world for the healing and wholeness, the salvation of our world. In the spirit of the church, we have tended the grief of others as our own and alleviated suffering caused by unjust systems and structures. The Visitation directed at the quality of our lives felt like an accusation of infidelity; and evoked pain and suffering in our communal body as women religious. We felt the anguish of realizing that the vision for our church which had energized us with such liberating hope was being dimmed and, at times, dismissed as heretical. We felt the angst of being stripped of an image of God who would reciprocate our fidelity by bringing our efforts to immediate successful recognized fulfillment. We stand with Mary at the cross facing a costly love. Stretched in an embrace that reaches to the four directions of the universe, Jesus gives unequivocal visibility to the cruciform requirement of bearing inclusive communion in the world. Refusing to be paralyzed or numbed or to walk away in avoidance or denial, Mary stays there letting herself be invaded by the agony of loss. Her own eyes locked with the eyes of suffering Love, Mary remains non-defensive, non-adversarial, steadfast and secure in who she is. In her company, we do the same. We wait in patience, in passion, until the cross itself utters a promise of generativity: behold here mother and son; behold from out of this place of suffering issues ongoing birth. We open our arms to receive the body of Christ bearing it into the future as our own, willing over and over again to stand by a cross facing costly love.

We unlock an upper room, releasing church to the ends of the universe (Acts 1:8-14; 2:1-13). In ways we could not have anticipated at its inception the Apostolic Visitation evolved into an event of Pentecost. Being involved in its processes as our experience of communion gradually expanded from within our own communities, through inter-congregational bonding and global sisterhood, to solidarity with laity, men religious, clergy and bishops, we have become conscious of and awed by the contagion of our lived vision of church. Beyond individual communities with their unique charisms, beyond religious life with its common charism, we have been transformed into a people of God drawn together by the energy of the Spirit. Experiencing the coming together of persons from all parts of the globe representing multiple socio-economic sectors of society and cultural traditions, holding different political perspectives, speaking diverse spiritual languages and yet sharing a common hope has been akin to that of sitting with Mary in the upper room. We see and feel the Body of Christ moving among us dispelling fear that keeps doors locked, windows closed and walls thick, and igniting us with Christic courage to unlock doors, remove barriers, and be love let loose in the world. The feel of it is that of a new Pentecost, a re-birth of our church. In the grace-filled way of the Spirit the potential for our church has been catalyzed from latency into dynamic visibility by the public accessibility and attraction of our vision as women religious during the Visitation. And, in that same grace-filled way of the Spirit we women religious have found our unique place as sisters in a great wide community bigger than we are, begun before us, and undoubtedly enduring beyond us. Taking up residence in that community side by side with our sister Mary, we live our boundless mature sisterhood in companionship with the whole people of God and all of creation. Joyfully, freely, serenely we unlock the upper room releasing church to the ends of the universe.

THE NARRATIVE CONTINUES
IN PROPHETIC COMMUNITY ON THE MOVE IN THE COSMOS

Taking the fragments of memory from our experience of the Apostolic Visitation and placing them in an unfolding narrative intersecting the story of our sister Mary has been a proactive activity. Companioning Mary from, through and beyond her own revolutionary time in the home of Elizabeth, we women religious, in a powerful co-creative act with the Spirit of God, have become the makers of meaning, not just of the Visitation, but of the whole of our lives. In response to authority outside ourselves, we have found our own mature voice as a sisterhood of women and have become the authors of a story we are making with God laboring in us to birth something new.

Because prophecy is engendered not through human aspiration but divine inspiration, it is right that we resist identifying the new emerging in us as prophetic. And, yet, listening to our story in the context of Walter Brueggemann's reflection, we can do nothing less than acknowledge that God has been raising up our sisterhood as prophetic:

> God can "raise up prophets" and authorize prophetic voices and deeds in the fullness of God's own freedom, anywhere, anytime, in any circumstance. However, some social environments are more hospitable than others to prophets and more likely to be the locus of their emergence. . . . Prophets are "naturally" in subcommunities that stand in tension with the dominant community. . . . Such a subcommunity is likely to be one in which there is
>
> - a long and available memory that sinks the present generation deep into an identifiable past that is available in song and story;
> - an available, expressed sense of pain that is owned and recited as a real social fact, that is visibly acknowledged in a public way, and that is understood as unbearable for the long term;
> - an active practice of hope, a community that knows about promises yet to be kept, promises that stand in judgment on the present;
> - an effective mode of discourse that is cherished across the generations, that is taken as distinctive, and that is richly coded in ways that only insiders can know.
>
> Such a subcommunity knows itself to be positioned for the long-term in tension with the dominant community that responds to the subcommunity at best as an inconvenience, at worst as an unbearable interruption. [17]

True to Brueggemann's description of the genesis of a prophetic subcommunity, we have, in the telling of our story, reached deep into our traditional memory to retrieve the song and symbols of Mary's visitation letting it illumine our own Apostolic Visitation. We have made public the pain of our tension with hierarchical ecclesial structures and, similarly with all dominating political, social, economic, and ecological systems. We have relied on a mode of discourse distinctive to us women religious, a richly coded language that, passed and thickened with nuance from one generation to another, reveals us to ourselves and others, offers inspiration and necessary self-critique, and preserves our authentic evolution as women in community. And we have felt the promise of hope breathing through every word we have uttered. The story not only narrates how the Spirit overshadowing us and drawing near has been forming us into a prophetic subcommunity but, in the act of telling it, we are becoming the prophets we are.

Putting words to our experience of the Apostolic Visitation we have remembered, revisioned, and reclaimed the critical meaning and significance of the defining activity of our lives that got us to the Visitation in the first place: contemplation and communion. We know whose we are, who we are, and why we are. Now it remains for us, in "boundless happiness, absolute fearlessness, and constant difficulty," to release the story in lives faithful to what we have seen and spoken.[18] In a narrative as borderless as its content, we trust that "unbearable, unstoppable energy at the heart of the cosmos" will continue to reinvent us, our world, our church, and our universe in love.[19]

NOTES

1. Mary Catherine Hilkert, *Naming Grace, Preaching and the Sacramental Imagination* (New York: Continuum, 2006), 96–97.

2. Entering into the scriptural accounts of the Annunciation and Visitation, the author acknowledges the significant work of Elizabeth A. Johnson, *Truly Our Sister: A Theology of Mary in the Communion of Saints* (New York: Continuum, 2003). The connection between the various events in Mary's life and the foundational Christian experience of community is a significant one in general and has been both formative and inspirational for the author of this chapter. Johnson has catalyzed the chapter author to ever deepening reflections on Mary and the meaning of her sisterhood to all of us and, in the context of this book, the particular significance of her sisterhood to women religious in these times. Accordingly, the author acknowledges Elizabeth, herself a Sister of St. Joseph, with great gratitude. Like the woman of whom she writes, Elizabeth is "truly our sister."

3. For the complete scriptural account of the Annunciation, see Luke 1:26-38, *The New American Bible* (Nashville: Thomas Nelson Publishers, 1987).

4. Dorothee Soelle, *The Silent Cry, Mysticism and Resistance,* trans. by Barbara Rumscheidt and Martin Rumscheidt (Minneapolis, MN: Fortress Press, 2001), 292.

5. Johnson, *Truly Our Sister: A Theology,* 223–224.

6. ibid., 227.

7. Paul VI, *Perfectae Caritatis, Decree on the Appropriate Renewal of the Religious Life,* in *The Documents of Vatican II,* ed. Walter A. Abbott, SJ (Piscataway, NJ: America Press, 1966), 467, 469.

8. For the complete scriptural account of the Visitation, see Luke 1:39-56, *The New American Bible.*

9. Walter Brueggemann, *The Prophetic Imagination,* 2nd ed. (Minneapolis, MN: Augsburg Fortress Press, 2001), 77.

10. ibid., 78.

11. See information regarding participation in the Apostolic Visitation Survey presented in the "Prologue" to this book.

12. Elizabeth A. Johnson, *She Who Is, the Mystery of God in Feminist Theological Discourse* (New York: Crossroad, 1992), 218, 219.

13. Keri Hulme, *The Bone People* (New York: Penguin Books, 1983), 4.

14. Johnson, *Truly Our Sister: A Theology,* 270.

15. ibid., 258.

16. Johnson, *She Who Is: The Mystery,* 135.

17. Brueggemann, *The Prophetic Imagination,* xvi.

18. Soelle, *The Silent Cry, Mysticism,* 298.

19. Ilia Delio, *The Unbearable Wholeness of Being, God, Evolution, and the Power of Love* (Maryknoll, New York: Orbis, 2013), 202.

Epilogue

The Power of Silence

Mary Ann Zollmann

As we prepare to submit the text for this book to the publisher, it is more than five years since the Apostolic Visitation was announced on December 22, 2008, by Cardinal Rodé, then Prefect of the Congregation for Institutes of Consecrated Life and Societies of Apostolic Life. In the years between then and now, as the story of this book tells, we women religious engaged in personal visits with and letters to Mother Mary Clare Millea, ASCJ, the Vatican appointed Apostolic Visitator. We responded to questions in a comprehensive canonical instrument. We were visited on-site in our respective communities by a team of visitators. That three-part process concluded in December 2010 with the last on-site visit when Mother Mary Clare began the fourth and final phase of the Visitation: the preparation of the general summary report as well as a report on each of the institutes that were part of the Visitation. Just a little over a year later, on January 9, 2012, the following media release was posted on the Apostolic Visitation website:

> Mother Mary Clare Millea, ASCJ, Apostolic Visitator for Institutes of Women Religious in the United States, recently presented an overall summary of her findings to Archbishop Joseph Tobin, CSsR, Secretary for Institutes of Consecrated Life and Societies of Apostolic Life (CICLSAL). In addition to the comprehensive report, which fulfills the mandate's original decree, she has submitted most of the individual reports for each of the nearly 400 religious institutes that were part of the Apostolic Visitation. The target date for completion of the remaining institute reports is spring 2012 . . . CICLSAL has not yet specified when it will announce its conclusions pertaining to the Apostolic Visitation. [1]

It is now more than two years since the release of the above statement and there has been no communication from CICLSAL, either in a general report or in the form of a report to individual institutes, about the Visitation and its results. However, that is not to say that nothing has been occurring in the absence of official word.

Notably, all of the significant persons in Roman offices directly connected with the Apostolic Visitation have chosen to retire, have resigned, or have been reassigned. On January 4, 2011, Cardinal Franc Rodé retired from the position of Prefect for the Congregation of Consecrated Life and Societies of Apostolic Life and, on that same day, Cardinal João Braz de Aviz became the new prefect. Additionally pertinent to CICLSAL, an American Redemptorist, Joseph Tobin, CSsR, was assigned to that office as secretary on August 2, 2010, a little less than two years into the Visitation process. It was to Joseph Tobin that Mother Mary Clare submitted her final reports. Interestingly, Tobin proposed that Rome initiate a "strategy of reconciliation" with women religious and acknowledged the "depth of anger and hurt" provoked by the Visitation.[2] On October 18, 2012, Pope Benedict reassigned Tobin from his Curia post to be archbishop of Indianapolis. On February 2, 2013, Pope Benedict announced his resignation effective February 28, 2013. And, on March 13, Pope Francis was elected and assumed the papacy. Although the publically perceived tone of leadership in the papacy and within CICLSAL seems to be one that is more personable and relational, there has been no communication with women religious about the findings from the Apostolic Visitation.

However, even more significant than the changes in Rome is what has been happening in us women religious transformed by the experience of the Visitation. During this sustained period of silence on the part of Rome, we have been actively dwelling in that silence turning it into gift. Had we had a more immediate official presentation of results we would have undoubtedly spent the past few years engaging our own response to Rome's assessment of us as women religious and as individual congregations. Instead, the silence has offered us clear and uncluttered space to sink into the experience of the Visitation and to let its learnings seep into our lives. Non-reactive to a potential Rome assessment we have been pro-active in claiming our own outcomes to the experience of the Visitation.

The text for this book has originated in and emerged from words formed and claimed in that fertile place of silence:

- *Our love for our vocation, our congregation and its mission has been deepened through this event.*
- *We U.S. women religious have been faithful to living and spreading the gospel in church and world. We have been faithful to the challenges and calls of Vatican II to refound our congregations, to deepen our under-*

standing of the vows, to live out the values called forth by our charisms and constitutions.

- *We have grown in our understanding of our role in the church and in the world affirmed by our brothers and sisters: religious, lay, and clergy. We have a vitality nourished by a new solidarity among us.*
- *We have been inspired to unite our gifts and skills with those of the laity so that together we may serve the greatest needs and contribute to the growth of faith, of compassion, and of community in our world and church.*
- *We have modeled and learned better how to respond respectfully in times of ecclesial tension, staying with the dialogue, and speaking our truth with integrity.*
- *Our ongoing story needs to be one of dialogue between the hierarchy and religious based in what both groups have learned so that living the Visitation into the future can be life-giving and not dominating.*
- *We have gained strength from our increased solidarity that will fortify our ability to stand together as we take the next steps in the evolution of religious life. We will continue to preach the truth as we are called by the gospel to do, and to do that respectfully, without hesitancy, without fear of censure.*
- *The Apostolic Visitation has increased our awareness of the public nature of religious leadership at this time in our church and society. It calls us to greater transparency and courage in our leadership.* [3]

In this time of Vatican silence, we women religious have found our true voice and pierced the silence by our firm and courageous word and action. What we are saying and doing speaks, without compromise or equivocation, to our understanding of the identity and mission of religious life in our times, testifies to our joy-filled awareness that community is ever more expansive than what we had imagined it to be, and tells a story of redemption from fear evoked by external authority for freedom to live with courageous integrity. As one woman wrote, "We are freer for having understood so clearly." [4] In an ironic and paradoxical way, the lack of a Vatican evaluation has given us the opportunity to cull out our own meanings and learnings from the event, liberating us to break through and beyond the confines of Rome's assessment of us.

Yet, in the midst of this generative silence, we still wonder what words about us are sitting somewhere in the office of the Congregation for Consecrated Life and Societies of Apostolic Life. We wonder if the original reports are stacked on shelves, if anyone is reading them, and what the intention is about their disposition. As the months and years have moved along since the last official word on the Visitation, we have been asked if there will ever come a time when it will not matter if we hear from Rome or not. Some have suggested that the best response we might hope to receive may be that of perpetual silence from Rome. However, for many among us, the enduring realization that it is the heart of our life that rests somewhere in a Vatican office stirs and disturbs us. We care what happens next. We put our whole selves and our fullest energies into this process and the lack of response feels like one more dismissal, one more injustice. We are women of the church, a church that admittedly is much larger than Rome, but which does include our brothers in Rome. As women whose defining essence is to live in community for community, the lack of dialogue with Rome is yet another affront to who we are; and, with more passage of time, feels like yet another stinging betrayal.

However, what is not happening on the part of Rome is not keeping us from moving forward with commitment and conviction, with consecration made new and fresh by what has opened up in us in these past five years. Again, in the words of the women who carry this experience now into the future:

- *We are intelligent, loving women who will continue to respond with passion, all-inclusive love.*
- *The vowed life we are living holds the threads needed to create a future unknown to us at the present time. The process of creating this future will be transformative and needs to be based on these key values: solidarity with the poor, community, prayer and discernment, responsiveness to the signs of the times. There will be a cost to living the gospel radically, a kind of living which will bring us to a new awareness of who we are and who we are called to be.*
- *Of course we don't know the end of the story yet, but here is my preferred outcome: this peaceful, non-violent stand against the institutional violence of the church was a turning point in the relationship of the church and women. In this process we were seen as real persons with courage and integrity, intelligence and rights. It would be wonderful to write in the history books that this was the beginning of true equity in the church, true inclusion of women as equal partners.*[5]

Without reserve, with no holding back, we hand all of who we are over to Holy Mystery that never stops doing something new in us for the sake of our world, our church, and the universe. Even as we give the lives given to us to the future, it is right and fitting that we pause in this powerful place of generative silence to remember with thanksgiving the story we hold, to acknowledge with awe how full of grace it is, and then to let it go by going with it, letting it fall as blessing wherever the Spirit wills.

NOTES

1. This statement can be accessed at www.apostolicvisitation.org/en/materials/close.

2. When Tobin arrived at CICLSAL, it was already conducting a visitation—a critical inspection of ministries and organization—of women religious in the U.S. In December, 2010, Tobin said that Rome needed to acknowledge the "depth of anger and hurt" provoked by a visitation, saying it illustrated the need for a "strategy of reconciliation" with women religious. See John L. Allen, Jr., "Vatican Must Hear 'Anger and Hurt' of American Nuns, Official Says," *National Catholic Reporter*, December 7, 2010, http://ncronline.org/blogs/ncr-today/vatican-must-hear-anger-and-hurt-american-nuns-official-says. In August, he publicly criticized the way his predecessor had managed the visitation from the start: "I believe a visitation has to have a dialogical aspect, but the way this was structured at the beginning didn't really favour that." See Cindy Wooden, "Vatican Aims to Regain Trust of U.S. Religious Women, Official Says," Catholic News Service, last modified August 10, 2011, http://www.catholic news.com/data/stories/cns/1103169.htm.

3. Margaret Cain McCarthy, "Apostolic Visitation Survey Analysis: The Apostolic Visitation as Experienced by Women Religious in the United States" (report, October 15, 2011).

4. ibid.

5. ibid.

Bibliography

Ackerman, Eva-Maria, FSGM. "Remarks of Sister Eva-Maria Ackerman." News release. January 30, 2009. http://www.apostolicvisitation.org/en/news/resources/conference_remarks130 2009.pdf.

Alesandro, John A. "General Introduction." In *The Code of Canon Law: A Text and Commentary*, edited by James A. Coriden, Thomas J. Green, and Donald E. Heintschel, 1–22. New York/Mahwah, NJ: Paulist Press, 1985.

———. "The Internal Ordering of Particular Churches." In *The Code of Canon Law: A Text and Commentary*, edited by James A. Coriden, Thomas J. Green, and Donald E. Heintschel, 378–415. New York/Mahwah, NJ: Paulist Press, 1985.

Allen, John L., Jr. "Vatican Must Hear 'Anger and Hurt' of American Nuns, Official Says." *National Catholic Reporter*, December 7, 2010. http://ncronline.org/blogs/ncr-today /vatican-must-hear-anger-and-hurt-american-nuns-official-says.

"Apostolic Visitation Begins Phase 3." Apostolic Visitation of Women Religious in the United States. http://www.apostolicvisitation.org/en/materials/av_phase_begins.pdf.

Apostolic Visitation of Institutes of Women Religious in the United States. "Apostolic Visitation Closes with Final Report Submission." News release. January 9, 2012. http:// www.apostolicvisitation.org/en/materials/close.pdf.

———. "Apostolic Visitation Gathers Religious in Preparation for On-Site Visits." News release. March 1, 2010. http://www.apostolicvisitation.org/en/materials/AV_news_release _03-01-10.pdf.

———. "Apostolic Visitation Gathers Religious in Review of On-Site Visits." News release. March 8, 2011. http://www.apostolicvisitation.org/en/materials/av_news_releases_03-07-11.pdf.

———. Letter, "Questionnaire for Major Superiors, Part A," n.d. http://www.apostolic visitation.org/en/materials/ques_A.pdf.

———. Letter, "Questionnaire for Major Superiors, Parts B and C," n.d. http://www.apostolic visitation.org/en/materials/ques_BC.pdf.

———. "Vatican Initiates Study of Catholic Sisters' Institutes in the United States." News release. January 30, 2009. http://www.apostolicvisitation.org/en/news/resources/news _release_1302009.pdf.

Beal, John P. "The Apostolic Visitation of a Diocese: A Canonico-Historical Investigation." *The Jurist* 49 (1989): 347–98.

Benedict XVI. "Address of His Holiness Benedict XVI to the Roman Curia Offering Them his Christmas Greetings." Address, December 22, 2005. http://www.vatican.va/holy_father/ benedict_xvi/speeches/2005/december/documents/hf_ben_xvi_spe_20051222_roman -curia_en.html.

Brown, Raymond E., SS, Joseph A. Fitzmyer, SJ, and Roland E. Murphy, Carm., eds. *The New Jerome Biblical Commentary*. Englewood Cliffs, NJ: Prentice Hall, 1990.

Brueggemann, Walter. *The Prophetic Imagination*. 2nd ed. Minneapolis, MN: Augsburg Fortress Press, 2001.

Burke, Jane, SSND. Letter, "LCWR Letter to Members," January 30, 2009.

———. Letter, "LCWR Letter to Members," February 9, 2009.

Butler, Sara, MSBT. "Apostolic Religious Life: A Public, Eccesial Vocation." Speech presented at Stonehill College Symposium on Apostolic Religious Life Since Vatican II . . . Reclaiming the Treasure: Bishops, Theologians, and Religious in Conversation, North Easton, MA, September 27, 2012. Zenit. Last modified October 13, 2012. http://www.zenit.org/en/articles/sister-butler-at-symposium-on-consecrated-life.

Caspary, Anita M. *Witness to Integrity: The Crisis of the Immaculate Heart Community of California*. Collegeville, MN: Liturgical Press, 2003.

Chittister, Joan, OSB. "The Past is a Very Living Thing: Try Not to Forget It." *National Catholic Reporter*, April 24, 2009. http://ncronline.org/blogs/where-i-stand/past-very-living-thing-try-not-forget-it.

———. "Vatican Could Learn a Thing or Two about Renewal from Women Religious." *National Catholic Reporter*, March 6, 2013. http://ncronline.org/blogs/where-i-stand/vatican-could-learn-thing-or-two-about-renewal-women-religious.

Conference of Leaders of Religious Institutes in New South Wales, Australia. Conference of Leaders of Religious Institutes in New South Wales, Australia to Marlene Weisenbeck, FSPA, October 9, 2009.

Congregation for Institutes of Consecrated Life and Societies of Apostolic Life. *Instrumentum Laboris for Apostolic Visitation of the General Houses, Provincial Houses and Centers of Initial Formation of the Principal Religious Institutes of Women in the United States of America*. Prot. N. 16805/2008. Vatican City: Congregation for Institutes of Consecrated Life and Societies of Apostolic Life, 2008. http://www.apostolicvisitation.org/en/news/resources/InstrumentumLaboris.pdf.

Congregation for Institutes of Consecrated Life and Societies of Apostolic Life. *Fraternal Life in Community*. Vatican City: Congregation for Institutes of Consecrated Life and Societies of Apostolic Life, 1994. http://www.vatican.va/roman_curia/congregations/ccscrlife/documents/rc_con_ccscrlife_doc_02021994_fraternal-life-in-community_en.html.

Coriden, James A., Thomas J. Green, and Donald E. Heintschel, eds. *The Code of Canon Law: A Text and Commentary*. New York: Paulist Press, 1985.

Crawford, Elaine Brown. *Hope in the Holler: A Womanist Theology*. Louisville, KY: Westminster John Knox Press, 2002.

Delio, Ilia. *The Unbearable Wholeness of Being, God, Evolution, and the Power of Love*. Maryknoll, NY: Orbis, 2013.

Dendinger, William J. "Bishop's Corner." *Southwestern Nebraska Catholic Register*, November 20, 2009.

Dulles, Avery, SJ. *Models of the Church*. New York: Image Books, Doubleday, 2002.

Fagin, Gerald M., SJ, and Joseph A. Tetlow, SJ. *Putting on the Heart of Christ*. Chicago: Loyola Press, 2010.

Foley, Nadine, OP. "Negotiation with Rome: A Reflection on Possibility." *LCWR Occassional Papers*, Spring 2001, 21–28.

Fox, Thomas C. "Asia, Oceania Women Religious Offer Support to Beleaguered U.S. Sisters." *National Catholic Reporter*, October 20, 2009. http://ncronline.org/news/asia-oceania-women-religious-offer-support-beleaguered-us-sisters.

———. "Louise Akers elevates Women's Issues at CTA Meeting." *National Catholic Reporter*, November 9, 2009. http://ncronline.org/news/louise-akers-elevates-womens-issues-cta-meeting.

———. "Mercy Sister Theresa Kane Criticizes Church Hierarchy." *National Catholic Reporter*, September 30, 2009. http://ncronline.org/news/mercy-sister-theresa-kane-criticizes-church-hierarchy.

———. "Two Heartfelt Support Letters Regarding U.S. Women Religious." *National Catholic Reporter*, February 5, 2010. http://ncronline.org/blogs/ncr-today/two-heartfelt-support

-letters-regarding-us-women-religious.

Francis. *Evangelii Gaudium (Joy of the Gospel), Apostolic Exhortation to the Bishops, Clergy, Consecrated Persons, and the Lay Faithful on the Proclamation of the Gospel in Today's World*, November 24, 2013. http://www.vatican.va/evangelii-gaudium/en/#1/z.

_____."Eucharistic Concelebration with Eminent Cardinals Resident in Rome on the Occasion of the Feast of St. George." Homily presented at Pauline Chapel, Vatican City, April 23, 2013. http://w2.vatican.va/content/francesco/en/homilies/2013/documents/papafrancesco_20130423_omelia-san-giorgio.html.

Gottemoeller, Doris, RSM. "A Visitor's Guide: How the Vatican Investigation Could Prove Beneficial." *America*, November 23, 2009. http://americamagazine.org/issue/716/article/visitors-guide.

Graham, Ruth. "What the Nuns Built." *The Boston Globe*, February 24, 2013, sec. K, 1–4. http://www.bostonglobe.com/ideas/2013/02/24/what-american-nuns-built-what-american-nuns-built/IvaMKcoK8a4jDb9lqiVOrI/story.html.

Green, Thomas J. "Particular Churches and Their Groupings; Title I: Particular Churches and the Authority Established in Them." In *The Code of Canon Law: A Text and Commentary*, edited by James A. Coriden, Thomas J. Green, and Donald E. Heintschel, 311–49. New York/Mahwah, NJ: Paulist Press, 1985.

Hilkert, Mary Catherine. *Naming Grace, Preaching and the Sacramental Imagination.* New York: Continuum, 2006.

Hite, Jordan F., TOR. "Institutes of Consecrated Life and Societies of Apostolic Life." In *The Code of Canon Law: A Text and Commentary*, edited by James A. Coriden, Thomas J. Green, and Donald E. Heintschel, 450–52. New York/Mahwah, NJ: Paulist Press, 1985.

Holland, Sharon L., IHM. "Section I: Institutes of Consecrated Life; Title I: Norms Common to All Institutes of Consecrated Life." In *The Code of Canon Law: A Text and Commentary*, edited by James A. Coriden, Thomas J. Green, and Donald E. Heintschel, 453–69. New York/Mahwah, NJ: Paulist Press, 1985.

Honoring the Historical Contributions of Catholic Sisters in the United States, H.R. Res. 441, 111th Cong. (2009). https://www.govtrack.us/congress/bills/111/hres441.

Hulme, Keri. *The Bone People.* New York: Penguin Books, 1983.

International Union of Superiors General, Board of Directors. Memorandum, "Statement of the Board of Directors, International Union of Superiors General concerning the Apostolic Visitation of Women Religious in the United States," April 23, 2009. http://www.apostolicvisitation.org/en/materials/iusg.pdf.

John Paul II. *Redemptionis Donum, Apostolic Exhortation to Men and Women Religious on their Consecration in Light of the Mystery of the Redemption*, March 25, 1984. http://www.vatican.va/holy_father/john_paul_ii/apost_exhortations/documents/hf_jp-ii_exh_25031984_redemptionis-donum_en.html.

_____. *Vita Consecrata, Apostolic Exhortation to the Bishops and Clergy, Religious Orders and Congregations, Societies of Apostolic Life, Secular Institutes, and all the Faithful on the Consecrated Life and its Mission in the Church and in the World*, March 25, 1996. http://www.vatican.va/holy_father/john_paul_ii/apost_exhortations/documents/hf_jp-ii_exh_25031996_vita-consecrata_en.html.

_____. *Apostolic Constitution Sacrae Disciplinae Leges.* In *The Code of Canon Law: A Text and Commentary*, edited by James A. Coriden, Thomas J. Green, and Donald E. Heintschel, xxiv–xxvi. New York/Mahwah, NJ: Paulist Press, 1985.

———. John Paul II to Bishops of the United States, April 3, 1983. http://www.vatican.va/holy_father/john_paul_ii/letters/documents/hf_jp-ii_let_03041983_us-bishops_en.html.

———. John Paul II to Bishops of the United States, February 22, 1989. http://www.vatican.va/holy_father/john_paul_ii/letters/1989/documents/hf_jp-ii_let_19890222_vescovi-usa_en.html.

Johnson, Elizabeth A., CSJ. *Quest for the Living God: Mapping Frontiers in the Theology of God.* New York: Continuum International Publishing Group, 2007.

———. *She Who Is: The Mystery of God in Feminine Theological Discourse.* New York: Crossroad Publishing Company, 1992.

————. *Truly Our Sister: A Theology of Mary in the Communion of Saints*. New York: Continuum, 2003.

Jones, Cecily, SL. *Mostly for Promise, Poems by Cecily Jones, SL*. Nerinx, KY: Hardin Creek Press, 2013.

Jurcak, Lawrence, JCL. Lawrence Jurcak, JCL to Marlene Weisenback, FSPA, October 19, 2009.

Kinast, Robert L. *What Are They Saying About Theological Reflection?* New York: Paulist Press, 2000.

Knolla, Diana, Susan Mann, and Angie Urenda. Diana Knolla, Susan Mann, and Angie Urenda to Editor, *Wichita Eagle*, "Sisters Serve," August 16, 2009.

Kuhn, Thomas S. *The Structure of Scientific Revolutions*. 2nd ed. Vol. 2, no. 2. International Encyclopedia of Unified Science. Chicago: University of Chicago Press, 1970.

Leadership Conference of Consecrated Life in South Africa. Leadership Conference of Consecrated Life in South Africa to Leadership Conference of Women Religious, November 2, 2009.

Leadership Conference of Women Religious. "LCWR Officers Meet with Vatican Officials in Rome." *Update*, May 2008.

————. "Leadership Conference of Women Religious Explores Critical Issues Against Backdrop of Vatican Studies." News release. August 17, 2009.

————. Memorandum, "Statement by the National Board of the Leadership Conference of Women Religious on the Apostolic Visitation," February 20, 2009. http://www.apostolicvisitation.org/en/materials/lcwr.pdf.

————. "Sandra Schneiders, IHM to Receive Outstanding Leadership Award." *Update*, May 2012.

Leadership Conference of Women Religious Board. Letter, "Letter to Members," February 22, 2009.

Lowell, Brad. "Our Thanks to the Sisters of St. Joseph." *Concordia Blade-Empire*, June 29, 2012.

Margaret Cain McCarthy. "Apostolic Visitation Survey Analysis: The Apostolic Visitation as Experienced by Women Religious in the United States." Report, October 15, 2011.

Marin, Carol. "Nun Investigations about Stifling Dissent." *Chicago Sun-Times*, July 3, 2012.

McCormick, Patrick. "Culture in Context: Mothers Superior." *U.S. Catholic*, January 2010, 40–41.

Metz, Johannes B. *Followers of Christ: The Religious Life and the Church*. Translated by Thomas Linton. New York: Burns & Oates/Paulist Press, 1978.

Metzger, Bruce M., and Roland Murphy, eds. *The New Oxford Annotated Bible*. New York: Oxford University Press, 1991.

Millea, Mother Mary Clare, ASCJ. Letter, January 12, 2010. http://www.apostolicvisitation.org/iw-cc/command/en/materials/letter_1-12.pdf.

————. Letter, November 5, 2009. http://www.apostolicvisitation.org/en/materials/MajorSupLtr-11052009.pdf.

————. Letter, "*Instrumentum Laboris* Message," July 28, 2009. http://www.apostolicvisitation.org/en/news/InstrumentumLaborisLetter.html.

————. Letter, "Phase 3: On-Site Visit to Religious Institutes, Responsibilities of Major Superior," May 15, 2010.

————. Letter, "Questionnaire Letter to Major Superiors," September 18, 2009. http://www.apostolicvisitation.org/en/materials/ques_ltr.pdf.

————. Memorandum, "Update on the Progress of Phase 1," n.d. http://www.apostolicvisitation.org/en/news/phase1juneupdate.html.

————. Mother Mary Clare Millea, ASCJ, to Superiors General, May 19, 2009. http://www.apostolicvisitation.org/en/materials/letter_superiors.pdf.

Mongoven, Anne Marie, OP. "We Did What the Church Asked Us to Do." *National Catholic Reporter*, August 7, 2009. http://ncronline.org/print/14350.

The New American Bible. Nashville, TN: Thomas Nelson Publishers, 1987.

Nouwen, Henri. *Reaching Out: The Three Movements of the Spiritual Life*. New York: Image Books, 1986.

"Our Approach." Apostolic Visitation of Women Religious in the United States. http://www.apostolicvisitation.org/en/approach/index.html.

Paul VI. *Evangelica Testificato, Apostolic Exhortation on the Renewal of Religious Life According to the Teaching of the Second Vatican Council*, June 29, 1971. http://www.vatican.va/holy_father/paul_vi/apost_exhortations/documents/hf_p-vi_exh_19710629_evangelica-testificatio_en.html.

_____. Letter, *Ecclesiae Sanctae, Implementing Four Council Decrees*, August 6, 1966. http://www.papalencyclicals.net/Paul06/p6ecclss.htm.

———. Letter, *Ecclesiam Suam, Encyclical on the Church*, August 6, 1964.

———. *Lumen Gentium, Dogmatic Constitution on the Church*. In *The Documents of Vatican II*, edited by Walter A. Abbott, SJ, 14–96. Piscataway, NJ: America Press, 1966.

———. *Perfectae Caritatis, Decree on the Appropriate Renewal of the Religious Life*. In *The Documents of Vatican II*, edited by Walter A. Abbott, SJ, 466–82. Piscataway, NJ: America Press, 1966.

———. *Sacrosanctum Concilium, Constitution on the Sacred Liturgy*. In *The Documents of Vatican II*, edited by Walter A. Abbott, SJ, 137–82. Piscataway, NJ: America Press, 1966.

Pius XII. Letter, *Fidei Donum, Encyclical of Pope Pius XII on the Present Condition of the Catholic Missions, Especially in Africa*, April 21, 1957. http://www.vatican.va/holy_father/pius_xii/encyclicals/documents/hf_p-xii_enc_21041957_fidei-donum_en.html.

Provincial Ministers of the Order of Friars Minor in the United States. Provincial Ministers of the Order of Friars Minor in the United States to Sisters of Charity BVM, February 6, 2010. http://members.bvmcong.org/SistersBVM/Members/leadership/AV_ProvincialMinisters.htm.

Quinn, John R., Thomas C. Kelly, OP, and Raymond W. Lessard. "A Report to the Bishops of the United States on the Work of the Pontifical Commission on Religious Life." *Origins* 16, no. 25 (December 4, 1986): 467–70.

Resource Center for Religious Institutes. "The Apostolic Visitation of Women Religious in the United States: A Canonical Reflection," March 9, 2009.

Rodé, Franc Cardinal, CM, and Gianfranco A. Gardin, OMF. Conv. "Decree," Prot. N. 16805/2008. December 22, 2008. http://www.apostolicvisitation.org/en/materials/decree.pdf.

Rodé, Franc Cardinal, CM. Franc Cardinal Rodé, CM to U.S. Bishops, "Donation to the Apostolic Visitation of Institutes of Women Religious in the United States," July 14, 2009.

———. Letter, February 2, 2009. http://www.apostolicvisitation.org/en/materials/cardinal_rode.pdf.

———. Memorandum, "Statement of the Prefect of the Congregation of Institutes of Consecrated Life and Societies of Apostolic Life, Card. Franc Rodé, C.M., on the Apostolic Visitation of Institutes of Women Religious in the U.S.A," November 3, 2009. http://www.apostolicvisitation.org/en/news/CardRodeMsg.html.

———. "Reforming Religious Life with the Right Hermeneutic." Speech presented at Stonehill College Symposium on Apostolic Religious Life since Vatican II . . . Reclaiming the Treasure: Bishops, Theologians, and Religious in Conversation, Stonehill College, North Easton, Massachusetts, U.S.A., September 27, 2008. Zenit. Last modified October 13, 2008. http://www.zenit.org/en/articles/cardinal-rode-at-symposium-on-consecrated-life.

Rogers, Everett M. *Diffusion of Innovations*. Glencoe, IL: Free Press, 1962.

Romero, Oscar A. *The Church is All of You: Thoughts of Archbishop Oscar A. Romero*. Compiled and translated by James R. Brockman, SJ. Minneapolis, MN: Winston Press, 1984.

Sacred Congregation for Religious and for Secular Institutes. *Essential Elements in the Church's Teaching on Religious Life as Applied to Institutes Dedicated to Works of the Apostolate*, May 31, 1983.

_____. *Religious and Human Promotion*, promulgated August 12, 1980. http://www.vatican.va/roman_curia/congregations/ccscrlife/documents/rc_con_ccscrlife_doc_12081980_religious-and-human-promotion_en.html.

Sacred Congregation for Religious and for Secular Institutes, and Sacred Congregation for Bishops. *Mutuae Relationes, Directives for Mutual Relations Between Bishops and Relig-*

ious in the Church, May 14, 1978. http://www.vatican.va/roman_curia/congregations/ccscrlife/documents/rc_con_ccscrlife_doc_14051978_mutuae-relationes_en.html.

Sadowski, Dennis. "Three-Year Study of Women Religious Completed; Vatican Reviews Results." Catholic News Service. Last modified January 11, 2012. http://www.catholicnews.com/data/stories/cns/1200112.htm.

Sandoval, Moises. Moises Sandoval to Ginger Downy, OLVM, July 10, 2013.

Schneiders, Mary L. "American Sisters and the Roots of Change." *U.S. Catholic Historian* 7 (Winter 1988): 55–72.

———. "The Transformation of American Women Religious." Working paper, Cushwa Center for the Study of American Catholicism, University of Notre Dame, Notre Dame, IN, 1986.

Schneiders, Sandra M., IHM. *Finding the Treasure: Locating Catholic Religious Life in a New Ecclesial and Cultural Context.* Vol. 1 of *Religious Life in a New Millennium.* New York/Mahwah, NJ: Paulist Press, 2000.

———. *Prophets in Their Own Country: Women Religious Bearing Witness to the Gospel in a Troubled Church.* Maryknoll, NY: Orbis Books, 2011.

Sheridan, Mother Mary Quentin, RSM. Memorandum, "Statement of the Congregation of Major Superiors of Women Religious concerning the Apostolic Visitation of Women Religious in the United States," n.d. http://www.apostolicvisitation.org/en/materials/cmswr.pdf.

Sisters of Loretto at the Foot of the Cross. *I Am the Way, Constitutions of the Sisters of Loretto at the Foot of the Cross.* Nerinx, KY: 1997.

Soelle, Dorothee. *The Silent Cry, Mysticism and Resistance.* Translated by Barbara Rumscheidt and Martin Rumscheidt. Minneapolis, MN: Fortress Press, 2001.

Synod of Bishops. "Justice in the World," 1971. http://www.cctwincities.org/document.doc?id=69.

"Testimonials." Apostolic Visitation of Institutes of Women Religious in the United States. http://www.apostolicvisitation.org/en/testimonials/index.html.

Tolkien, J.R.R. *On Fairy Stories, Essays Presented to Charles Williams.* London: Oxford University Press, 1947.

U.S. Federation of Sisters of St. Joseph Ongoing Formation Committee. U.S. Federation of Sisters of St. Joseph Ongoing Formation Committee to Member Congregations, Sisters of St. Joseph, August 2009.

von Behren, Thomas R., CSV. Thomas R. von Behren, CSV to Jane Burke, SSND, October 30, 2009.

Weisenbeck, Marlene, FSPA, J. Lora Dambroski, OSF, and Jane Burke, SSND. Marlene Weisenbeck, FSPA, J. Lora Dambroski, OSF, and Jane Burke, SSND to LCWR Membership, April 28, 2010.

Wheatley, Margaret. *Perseverance.* Eugene, OR: Berkana Publications, 2012.

———. *Turning to One Another.* San Francisco: Berrett-Koehler Publishers, 2002.

Wood, Douglas. *Old Turtle and the Broken Truth.* New York: Scholastic Press, 2003.

Wooden, Cindy. "Cardinal Rodé Defends Apostolic Visitation of U.S. Nuns." Catholic News Service. Last modified November 5, 2009. http://www.catholicnews.com/data/stories/cns/0904882.htm.

———. "Officials Say Final Report on Visitation of U.S. Nuns Expected Soon." Catholic News Service. Last modified January 31, 2014. http://www.catholicnews.com/data/stories/cns/1400434.htm.

———. "Vatican Aims to Regain Trust of U.S. Religious Women, Official Says." Catholic News Service. Last modified August 10, 2011. http://www.catholicnews.com/data/stories/cns/1103169.htm.

List of Contributors

Marcia Allen, CSJ, DMin., is a Sister of St. Joseph of Concordia, Kansas. She has a bachelor's degree in French and history, a master's degree in administration, and a doctorate in ministry with an emphasis in spirituality. Over the past thirty years she has facilitated meetings for religious communities and various other organizations. She co-founded the Bearers of the Tradition Institute, a 30-day international program of intense study of the charism and mission of the Sisters of St. Joseph. She edited the manual of orientation for her community's second form of membership. She has written many articles for various religious publications. Marcia was in leadership for her community from 1979–1995. She is a member of the staff of Manna House of Prayer and facilitates retreats and conferences. At present she is president of the Sisters of St. Joseph of Concordia.

Donna Day, SL, MA, has been a member of the Sisters of Loretto at the Foot of the Cross for fifty-two years. She has a bachelor's degree in history from Webster University in St. Louis and a master's degree in religious studies from Mundelein College/Loyola University Chicago. She has contributed to publications for the Diocese of Pueblo in Colorado, to LCWR's Occasional Papers, and Loretto Magazine. Donna's ministry has included education and liturgy work, primarily in Colorado and Wyoming, and social service work as executive director of low-income housing for the homeless in St. Louis. She served as coordinator and vice chair of the Leadership Conference of Women Religious, Region X. For the past nine years, Donna has been vice president of the Sisters of Loretto and is currently co-coordinator of Health Care/Life Planning. She has a great love for baseball, dogs, and all things Irish.

Margaret Cain McCarthy, PhD, earned her doctorate from the University at Buffalo. She is a professor in the Department of Graduate Education and Leadership at Canisius College in Buffalo, New York. Currently the associate vice president for academic affairs, she has served as the dean of the School of Education and Human Services and in a variety of other administrative positions during her long tenure in higher education. The author of the *History of American Higher Education*, a book in the Peter Lang Primer Series, Margaret is grateful to the many sisters who built and taught at Catholic schools and colleges throughout the United States, especially the Sisters of St. Francis of Stella Niagara who provided her elementary education. She is the proud mother of five, a graduate of the Ignatian Colleagues Program, and an associate member of the Sisters of St. Joseph of the Diocese of Buffalo.

Cathy Mueller, SL, MA, is a Sister of Loretto at the Foot of the Cross. She received her bachelor's degree from Loretto Heights College in mathematics and secondary education and a master's degree in psychology and counseling from the University of Northern Colorado. She has done graduate work in scripture and theology at Catholic Theological Union, Chicago, and Graduate Theological Union, Berkeley. She has been a teacher; pastoral minister in multicultural parishes in Colorado; presenter and facilitator of retreats for women and chapters for women religious; co-founder of the non-profit EarthLinks which serves homeless and economically poor persons in Denver, and president of the Sisters of Loretto/Loretto Community. She lives in Colorado and continues to contribute to Loretto, other religious groups, and her local community. Her publications include: "Linking People at Risk with Earth at Risk," *Human Development*, 2012, and "Reflections on the Apostolic Visitation," in *Century of Change 1912–2012, Loretto's Second Century,* 2012.

Nancy Reynolds, SP, MA, JCL, is a member of the Sisters of Providence of Saint Mary-of-the-Woods, Indiana. She taught high school and college math until 1978, when she began working in a diocesan tribunal in Evansville, Indiana. From 1981–1984, she studied canon law at The Catholic University of America receiving her JCL in 1984. She has served on the governing board of the Canon Law Society of America. She was regional chairperson and served on the board of the Leadership Conference of Women Religious for six years. She taught canon law as an adjunct faculty member in several seminaries and universities, among them St. Patrick's Seminary in Menlo Park, California, and The Jesuit School of Theology, Berkeley. Nancy spent ten years as a general councilor and twelve years as general treasurer of her congregation. She is now serving as a canonical consultant for several religious congregations.

Addie Lorraine Walker, SSND, PhD, a School Sister of Notre Dame for over thirty years, is the former provincial of the Dallas Province (2002–2011). Currently, she is an associate professor of pastoral theology and founder and director of the Sankofa Institute for African American Pastoral Leadership at the Oblate School of Theology in San Antonio, Texas. Following the completion of a doctorate in religion and education from Boston College in 1996, Addie Lorraine has continued to minister as a pastoral and practical theologian in university, high school, and parish settings, as well as in seminary formation and ongoing formation programs and retreats for religious congregations across the country. Her current research and writing interests include spirituality and culture, SSND spirituality and formation for contemporary living of religious life, Christian education in the nineteenth and twentieth centuries, reading and reflecting on Catholic social teaching from a Black perspective, and dialogue as a strategy for transformative education.

Patricia Walter, OP, PhD, is a member of the Dominican Sisters of Adrian, Michigan. She served as prioress of her congregation between 1992 and 1998. While prioress, she was a regional councilor for the International Union of Superiors General and a founding member of Dominican Sisters International. Currently associate professor and chair of the Department of Religious Studies at Siena Heights University, Patricia has taught at Aquinas Institute of Theology, St. Mary Seminary in Cleveland, and the Pontifical University of St. Thomas in Rome. She delivered the Mary Ward Lecture at Cambridge University and has given presentations on religious life and Dominican spirituality throughout the United States, in Eastern Europe, and the Philippines. She holds a master's degree in Scripture and systematics from Aquinas Institute, a licentiate in theology from the Jesuit School of Theology in Berkeley and a doctorate in philosophical and systematic theology from the Graduate Theological Union.

Jean Wincek, CSJ, EdD, is a member of the 2009–2014 and 2014–2017 St. Paul Province Leadership Team of the Sisters of St. Joseph of Carondelet. Her previous ministries include teaching and administering in Catholic schools in the Twin Cities and co-teaching graduate courses on effective teaching, brain-based learning, instructional planning, school culture, and educational change. She and her colleague also developed planning processes for school mergers, designed and led strategic planning processes for non-profit organizations and K–12 schools, facilitated large group meetings and provided staff development for school faculties and business groups. Her publications include books and articles on the influence of metaphor in shaping school culture, educational change, strategic planning and development, and celebrating ritual as a faith community. She has served on and chaired several CSJ committees and boards and currently is vice-chair of the board of trustees of St. Catherine University in St. Paul, Minnesota.

Mary Ann Zollmann, BVM, PhD, has been a Sister of Charity of the Blessed Virgin Mary for fifty-five years. She holds master's degrees in French from Purdue University and in religious education from the University of San Francisco. She earned a master's degree and a doctorate in spirituality from Duquesne University. Mary Ann has ministered as a high school and university teacher and has served in leadership in her BVM congregation and as president, from 2001 to 2004, of the Leadership Conference of Women Religious. Currently, she enjoys writing, creating presentations and engaging others on themes of spirituality and leadership, and serving on the boards of Clarke University, Dubuque, Iowa, and Loyola University Chicago. For personal global awareness and as bearer of justice and peace, Mary Ann has traveled to El Salvador, Ecuador, Israel and Palestine, Swaziland and Ghana, and Vatican offices in Rome. Her publications include her PhD dissertation, *Exploring a Spirituality of Higher Education,* and her LCWR presidential address, *Claiming the Power of our Sisterhood.*